Baedeker

MOSCOW

Imprint

85 illustrations, 18 maps and plans, 1 large map at end of the book

Original German text: Birgit Borowski, Bernhard Pollman

Editorial work (German edition): Baedeker (Birgit Borowski)
(English edition): Margaret Court, Crispin Warren

General direction (German edition): Dr Peter Baumgarten, Baedeker Stuttgart
(English edition): Alec Court

Cartography: Christoph Gallus, Hohberg-Niederschopfheim: Gert Oberländer, Munich; Falk
Verlag GmbH Hamburg (large plan/map)

Source of Illustrations: Roland Bader (31); Bildagentur Schuster (1); Birgit Borowski (21);
Fotoagentur Helga Lade (3); Marianne Götz (1); Historia-Photo (3); Leonid P. Lavrov (5);
Eva Missler (11); Bernhard Pollmann (1); Anja Schliebitz (12)

English translation: Brenda Ferris, James Hogarth, Julie Waller

In the present book Russian names and terminology have been rendered in an English
transliteration. For technical reasons it has not been possible to include English transliteration
of place names on the large map at the end of the book or on the plan of the Moscow Metro.

Following the tradition established by Karl Baedeker in 1844, sights of particular interest and
hotels and restaurants of particular quality are distinguished by either one or two asterisks.

To make it easier to locate the various places listed in the "A to Z" section of the Guide, their
co-ordinates on the large city plan are shown at the head of each entry.

Only a selection of hotels, restaurants and shops can be given; no reflection is implied
therefore on establishments not included.

In a time of rapid change it is difficult to ensure that all the information given is entirely accurate
and up-to-date, and the possibility of error can never be entirely eliminated. Although the
publishers can accept no responsibility for inaccuracies and omissions, they are always
grateful for corrections and suggestions for improvement.

3rd English edition 1995

© Baedeker Stuttgart 1994
Original German edition

© 1995 Jarrold and Sons Limited
English language edition worldwide

© 1995 The Automobile Association
United Kingdom and Ireland

Distributed in the United Kingdom by the Publishing Division of the Automobile Association,
Fanum House, Basingstoke, Hampshire RG21 2EA

Licensed user:
Mairs Geographischer Verlag GmbH & Co., Ostfildern-Kemnat bei Stuttgart

The name *Baedeker* is a registered trade mark
A CIP catalogue record of this book is available from the British Library

Printed in Italy by G. Canale & C.S.p.A – Borgaro T.se –Turin

Published in the United States by:
Macmillan Travel
A Prentice Hall Macmillan Company
15 Columbus Circle
New York, NY 10023

Macmillan is a registered trademark of Macmillan, Inc.

ISBN US and Canada 0–671–89684–9
        UK 0 7495 1101 X

Contents

The Principal Sights at a Glance

Preface

This pocket guide to **Moscow** is one of the new generation of Baedeker guides.

Baedeker pocket guides, illustrated throughout in colour, are designed to meet the needs of the modern traveller. They are quick and easy to consult, with the principal features of interest described in alphabetical order and practical details about location, opening times, etc., shown in the marigin.

This city guide is divided into three parts. The first part gives a general account of the city, its population, religion, economy, transport, culture, famous people, history and architecture; A brief selection of quotations leads into the second part in which the principal places of interest in and around Moscow are described; the third part contains a variety of practical information designed to help visitors to find their way about and to make the most of their stay. Both the A to Z and Practical Information sections are given in alphabetical order.

Baedeker pocket guides, which are regularly updated, are noted for their concentration on essentials and their convenience of use. They contain many coloured illustrations and specially drawn plans, and at the back of the book will be found a large plan of the city. Each main entry in the A to Z section gives the co-ordinates of the square on the plan in which the particular feature can be located. Users of this guide, therefore, should have no difficulty in finding what they want to see.

Facts and Figures

Historic arms
of Moscow

General

Moscow (in Russian Moskva) is capital of the Russian Federation – Russia and the Moscow region. The largest city in the country it is also its administrative, economic and cultural centre. Culturally Moscow is still in competition with St Petersburg which superseded Moscow as capital from 1712 to 1918.

Importance

Apart from the Kremlin and the buildings around Red Square Moscow does not have an enclosed historical town centre. For the visitor this may create the initial impression of a busy metropolis which consists of an endlessly overflowing sea of modern houses. It takes time to discover the architectural sights which are spread out over the city. But Moscow has more to offer than impressive buildings. In contrast with St Petersburg, which is more European, Moscow is the heart of Russia, fascinating and full of contrasts, especially at this time of political change.

Moscow is situated in latitude 55° 44′ N (roughly the same as Copenhagen) and longitude 38° E, at an average altitude of 120 m (395 ft), on the River Moskva, a 502 km (312 mile) long tributary of the Oka which rises in the Smolensk-Moscow hills and is navigable downstream from Moscow.

Geographical situation

Moscow lies in the European part of Russia, which extends eastward into Asia. (In modern times the Urals have been regarded as the boundary between Europe and Asia; in antiquity the line between the two continents was drawn on the River Tanais: i.e. the lower course of the Don.) Geographically considered, Moscow lies in the Eastern European Lowlands. The geographical boundary between Western and Eastern Europe is usually taken as the River Vistula. From the political point of view the line between Western and Central Europe on the one hand and Eastern Europe on the other runs along the Elbe.

Within the Eastern European Lowlands Moscow lies between the Smolensk hills in the north and the Central Russian plain in the south.

Thus Moscow is in the temperate continental climatic zone; the average temperatures in January are −10.3° C, in May 11.7° C and rise in July to an average of 17.8° C. The annual precipitation of 575 mm (22 in.) is spread over the whole year, but mostly in the summer months. (For monthly details see entry under Practical Information – Climate.)

Climate

As regards area and population, Moscow is by far the largest city in Russia. Since 1960 the 109 km (68 mile) motorway ring, enclosing an area of 900 sq. km (347 sq. miles), has marked its boundary. In 1986, when all reserves of

Area and population

◀ *The Kremlin; in the foreground the Water Tower*

The exterior of the City Hall with a statue of Dolgorukij

building land had been used up, the area of the city was enlarged by 100 sq. km (39 sq. miles) and Moscow's population increased from 8.5 million to 9.0 million, at present 9.2 million people live in the Russian capital.

Administration

Moscow is governed by Soviets and their Executive Committees. Soviets are state and social bodies of varying levels and fields of competence. Each Soviet consists of representatives elected by the people. Moscow's Town Hall (City Soviet or Mos Soviet) is situated in Tverskaya Street.

The different parts of the city

Moscow can be seen as a series of concentric rings with the Kremlin – an area of 28 hectares (69 acres) in the form of an irregular rectangle above the left bank of the River Moskva – as its focal point.

The Kremlin is the geometric centre of a built-up zone some 4 km (2½ miles) wide which has grown up round it, is bounded by the Sadovaya (Garden) ring of boulevards and forms the centre of Moscow. Within this central area were the old settlements known by the names of Kitay-Gorod, Belgorod and Zemlyanoy Gorod.

Kitay-Gorod, which extends north-east of the Kremlin, beginning at Red Square, is the oldest part of Moscow's central area. Originally a trading settlement, it is still the main business and commercial district, with banks, department stores and other shops, Government and other public offices, etc.
The boundaries of Kitay-Gorod follow the course of the defensive walls which were built between 1534 and 1538 (so-called Chinese Wall) in order to bring the trading quarter within the Kremlin defensive system. The walls were demolished in 1930.

Belgorod, the "White City", takes its name from the limestone walls built in 1586–93, following the Tatar raid of 1571; they encircled the whole of the

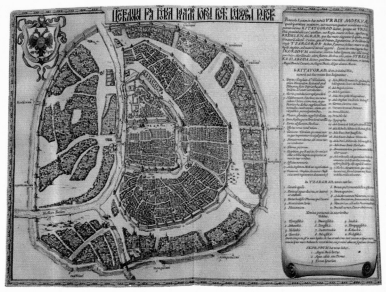

Historic plan of Moscow (late 16th c.)

built-up area north of the Moskva (the Kremlin, Kitay-Gorod, etc.). The walls, which had a total length of 9 km (5½ miles), were pulled down in 1775; their line is marked by the present ring of boulevards (Bulvarnoe Koltso). The name of the White City also bore reference to the fact that the inhabitants were "white" in the sense of being exempt from the payment of feudal-type dues. A settlement of this kind was known as a *sloboda* (liberty). The settlement of Belgorod was occupied by craftsmen, servants, etc., working for the Tsar, the high aristocracy and the Church.

In this area of present-day Moscow are the city's main shopping streets, the Bolshoi Theatre, the Lenin Library, the Puskin Museum of Fine Art, etc.

In 1591–92 an earthern rampart 14 km (9 miles) long topped by a palisade and defended by fifty seven towers was constructed round the area which came to be known as the *zemlyanoy gorod* or "earth town". The area south of the Moskva was now incorporated in the defensive system for the first time. This wall, which was pulled down in 1775 at the same time as the wall round Belgorod, corresponded to the Sadovaya (Garden) ring of boulevards which surrounds the whole of Moscow's central area.

Between the Garden ring and the motorway ring which encircles the city is a zone some 13 km (8 miles) wide, now mainly built up, in which the fortified monasteries lay (many of them are still preserved) built to protect Moscow from Tatar and other attacks (Simonov, Novospassky, Andronikov, Novodevichy, Don, etc.). In this belt are to be found various satellite towns, villages, recreation centres and parks.

Air Pollution in Moscow far exceeds acceptable levels – in the summer the city is nearly always capped by smog. Water pollution and sidespread ground contamination detract from the quality of life in and around Moscow.

Ecological situation

11

Population

Population
development

With a population of 9.2 million, Moscow is by far the largest city in Russia (followed by St Petersburg in second place with "only" 5 million inhabitants). Over the last two centuries the city's population has undergone rapid growth; in 1812 the population of Moscow was 250,000, by 1882 it had already reached 750,000 and by 1917 it was 2 million. This figure remained constant until 1926 when it rose dramatically. In 1939 4 million people lived in the Russian capital and by 1959 the number had risen to 6 million. Strict conditions of immigration were imposed to prevent further expansion of the population. In fact the population of Moscow only increased by 20% between 1959 and 1971 (during the same period the population of all other medium-sized cities in the USSR increased by 44% on average, cities up to 1 million by 38% and cities up to 2 million by around 35%). The immigration restrictions slowed down population growth but did not stop it; in 1979 Moscow had 8 million inhabitants, in 1985 8.5 million and by 1989 9 million people were living in the Russian metropolis. (This development is not due to a natural increase in population, the majority of families living in Moscow have only one child, two children are the exception.)

Composition of
the population

About 90% of Moscow's population are Russian. The second largest group are the Ukrainians (250,000), followed by Jews (175,000) and Tartars (160,000).
Of Moscow's 9.2 million inhabitants about 4.2 million are employed and 2.5 million are pensioners. This high proportion of older people is an increasing social problem in the Russian capital (see Economy).

Living
accommodation

According to official sources during the last years of the Soviet Union every Moscow citizen had 15.5 sq. m/167 sq. ft gross living space. This figure was probably considerably exaggerated. At least 1 million people are still living in communal flats where the bathroom and kitchen are shared with other families. The living conditions in the huge satellite towns which have grown up around the city centre are also unsatisfactory. Many blocks of flats are already dilapidated not long after completion. However, with the serious housing situation many families consider themselves fortunate to get such a flat and have two rooms they can call their own.

Religion

New religiousness

Since the new law on religious freedom in Russia was passed on 1st October 1990 the Russian Orthodox Church has experienced an enormous rise in popularity. According to the most recent estimates only 10% of the population are still atheist with increasing numbers of people being baptised into the Orthodox faith. The churches are full of not only elderly and needy people but more young people, entire families even. As in the rest of the country many sacral buildings under state ownership were and are being returned to the church which is attempting to restore them to their former function. Since 1985 the number of Orthodox churches in Moscow has increased sixfold to 276 with a further 400 churches still to be returned (prior to the October Revolution there were about 800 Orthodox churches in Moscow).
The general trend towards religion is not restricted to the Russian Orthodox Church. Other denominations and religious sects are enjoying increased popularity.

Russian Orthodox Church

Byzantium

Unlike the Russian Catholic Church with Rome as its undisputed centre, the Eastern Orthodox Church never had a unifying central point. Different theologies grew up in different centres, all making claims to universality. We must think, therefore, of Eastern Churches in the plural rather than of a single Eastern Church. Thanks to its political power, however, Constantinople was able to establish its preponderant authority as the "Second Rome".

Prince Vladimir I of Kiev was baptised in 988 as a preliminary to marrying the Byzantine Princess Anne. According to the Christian chroniclers the acceptance of Christianity was followed by a compulsory mass baptism in the Dnieper.

Introduction of Christianity in Russia

As the Church Slavonic language (see Practical Information – Language) introduced to Moravia in the 9th c. by Cyril and Methodius, the "Apostles of the Slavs", could be used in Kiev since it was understood by the Eastern Slavs, it was not necessary to make new translations of the sacred texts. The Christian missionaries (mostly Greeks and Bulgarians) were selective in the texts they made available to the Christians of Kiev, which in addition to the Scriptures themselves were confined to the legends of saints, sermons and treatises on Church law. Anything connected with the "Latins" was shunned, and the literature and philosophy of ancient Greece were also taboo.

Thus the new church in Kiev grew up in the image of Byzantine orthodoxy. The dogma, liturgy, law and constitution of the Byzantine Church were taken over, and the distinction between the ecclesiastical hierarchy and ascetic monasticism was maintained. The Kievan Church, however, was probably headed by a Greek missionary archbishop and totally independent of Constantinople.

This independence was established at an early date, but it was not until 1590 that the Oecumenical Patriarch of Constantinople recognised the Metropolitan of Moscow and All Russia as Patriarch of the Russian Orthodox Church, which thus became "autocephalic". Moscow now took over from Constantinople, which had fallen into the hands of the Ottomans in 1453, and became the "Third Rome".

Autocephaly

The Church Slavonic translations of the Old and New Testaments and the Psalms showed divergences from the Greek originals. The conflicts to which this gave rise within the Russian Church – should a procession go in the direction of the sun or against it? should the sign of the cross be made with two fingers or three? – were settled at a Synod of 1653 in favour of Patriarch Nikon, who had been pressing for reform. Those priests who held to the old texts and liturgical forms became known as Starovery (Old Believers) or Raskolniki (Dissenters), and the resultant schism within Russian Orthodoxy has continued to this day. Perhaps the most popular defender of the old forms was Protopope (Archpriest) Avvakum (1621–82), who died at the stake for his faith.

Conflict

In the reign of Peter the Great the Russian Church became a mere handmaiden of the State. From 1700 Peter left the Patriarchal throne vacant, replacing the Patriarch in 1721 by the "Most Holy Ruling Synod", an ecclesiastical college which was largely dependent on the Tsar. Later in the century Catherine the Great confiscated all Church property, and the Orthodox clergy became salaried employees of the State.

Modern times

After the October Revolution the Synod was dissolved and the Patriarchal constitution of the Church re-established. In 1918 the Church was separated from the State: a separation now enshrined in the 1977 constitution: "In the Soviet Union the churches are separate from the State and the schools are separate from the church" (Article 52).

The Russian Church took over from Byzantium the distinction between the secular clergy (the priests or "popes") who were strongly Russian in outlook, and the monks, who looked towards Greece. The priests, who must

Church structure

Icons

"**T**hou shalt not make unto thee any graven image, or any likeness of any thing that is in heaven above, or that is in the earth beneath, or that is in the water under the earth. Thou shalt not bow down thyself to them, nor serve them . . ." (Exodus 20, 4–5).

The splendid array of icons to be seen in Moscow's churches, cathedrals, monasteries and museums seem in flagrant contradiction of this Second Commandment, an injunction which formed the basis of the Old Testament ban on images and gave rise in Byzantine times to the iconoclastic conflict, the results of which are basic to the understanding of Russian icons.

The word "icon" comes from the Greek *eikon*, "image, likeness", and the earliest icons, which probably originated in the Eastern Roman Empire, were portraits of Christ, the Virgin, saints and martyrs. A model was provided by Antique portraits of tragedians and philosophers, painted likenesses of emperors and the portraits which bishops caused to be hung in churches when they took office.

Christianity came into a world (Greece, Rome, Egypt) which, with the exception of the Jews, thought well of portrait likenesses, and in the long run could not entirely reject images. However, matters developed differently in the Eastern and Western Empires, a major factor being no doubt the proximity of Egypt (mummy portraits) and Syria (where the image was seen as part of the person represented). While Rome laid stress on the symbolic quality of images, with religious painting consequently able to develop unhindered in the West, in the East there was a violent conflict which led to the systematic destruction of images between 726 and 842.

In considering the iconoclastic conflict and the present form of icons it is important to note the distinction between adoration and veneration. Only God may be adored; images may only be venerated. Veneration is expressed by *proskynesis* or bowing down before an icon, kissing it, burning incense or lighting candles, or icons may be publicly displayed or carried in procession. According to Basil the Great, one of the great 4th c. Fathers of the Eastern Church, what was venerated was not the image itself but the person or object represented in the image. The object of veneration was not the icon but the power immanent in the sacred person or object; conversely it was this immanent power that was transmitted to the venerator.

The controversy began in the 4th c. The supporters of images – SS Basil the Great, Gregory of Nazianzus and John Chrysostom among others – could cite in favour of their view the Epistle to the Colossians (1.15) in which Christ is called "the image (eikon/imago) of the invisible God", seeing in this reference a first theological justification of the image. The opponents of images – a leading role among them being taken by Eusebius of Caeserea – relied mainly on the Second Commandment.

The Emperor Leo III's Edict of 730 prohibiting the veneration of images arose – leaving aside political motives – from the fear that the venerators of images (*iconodules*) would show honour to the image but not to the reality immanent in the image. Then in 754 a Synod called by Constantine V decided that the images should be destroyed – the policy that became known as "iconoclasm". The iconodules were persecuted, tortured and even executed, and almost all Byzantine icons before this period were destroyed and are lost to us.

The present Orthodox doctrine on icons was resolved at the Second Council of Nicaea (787), during the reign of the Empress Irene, on the basis of the teachings of John of Damascus ("The image is a likeness which expresses the original image in such a way that there still remains a difference".)

Nevertheless iconoclasm flared up again in the reigns of the Emperors Leo V (813–820), Michael II (820–829) and Theophilus (829–842). Finally, however, in 842/843 the Empress Theodora reasserted the doctrine laid down by the 787 Council, an event still commemorated in the Church's calendar as the Festival of Orthodoxy.

Under the doctrine laid down by the Second Council of Nicaea the icon must, ideally, represent an authentic "copy" of a historical or assumed prototype. This effort to achieve identity explains the stereotyped character of icons, for ideally an icon can be in accord with the aspect of the prototype it represents only in a single version. There are only a few basic types of Christ – the best-known being the Pantocreator – but of the Mother of God there are some 200. An icon is never, however, an act of free artistic creation; if it were it would merely be an idol or graven image. The composition, the general aspect and the colours are for the most part firmly prescribed in special books.

Another representation of the Virgin, with three hands, is associated with a legend about John of Damascus and the iconoclastic controversy. It is said that the Emperor Leo III struck off one of John's hands, whereupon John prayed to the Mother of God, who restored his hand. John then presented a silver hand to the icon, and this third hand also appears in later representations.

Representations of the Virgin occupy a central position in the repertoire of the icon painters. This followed the recognition, at the Council of Ephesus in 431, of the Virgin's status as the Panhagia Theotokos (All Holy Mother of God). The Virgin is still commonly referred to in the Orthodox Church by this title (in Russian Bogmater). Most icons are painted in tempera on panels of non-resinous wood. The panel is covered with a layer of gesso and linen soaked in gesso in order to smooth out unevennesses in the wood, and this is followed by

Andrej Rublyov: "Christ as Pantocreator"

thin coats of chalk or alabaster boiled up with gesso. This *levcas* (from Greek *leukos*, "white") is then smoothed down to form the painting surface.

On this ground the design is sketched, either by incision or in red chalk or charcoal. After gilding of those parts of the image that call for it (e.g. a saint's halo) the ground colours are applied, followed by glazes in successive coats to achieve different shades and tones. The whole picture is then covered with a linseed oil varnish.

Every icon bears an inscription labelling the subject, a requirement introduced by the Second Council of Nicaea in order that icons should no longer be regarded from a purely aesthetic point of view. The use of the word in conjunction with the image referred back directly to the authentic prototype.

From the 12th c. onwards first the frames and later the background and parts of the figures began to be given metal (usually silver) covers. In the 19th c. the practice grew up in Russia of painting only those parts that were not covered by clothing (the face, the hands) and concealing the rest under a metal cover, the clothing, etc. being depicted by embossing. The covers – which were originally votive offerings – served to protect the surface of the icons from incense, soot from candles, dust and the kisses of worshippers.

be married, do no pastoral work but confine themselves to celebrating Mass and dispensing the Sacraments. The monks, who are vowed to celibacy, fill the higher posts in the Church (the Patriarch, metropolitans, bishops, abbots, priors, etc.).

Liturgy

Since pastoral work plays no part in the Russian Orthodox Church, religious life centres on the liturgy, the celebration of the Eucharist and other services with prayers, singing and an elaborate ceremonial which is sometimes reminiscent of the pomp of a princely court. An important part is also played by the veneration of icons (see Practical Information – Icons).

The Church year

The central event in the Russian Orthodox year is Easter, to which the whole Church calendar is related. Certain festivals diverge from those of the "Latin" Church – the Descent into Hell (or Limbo), the Transfiguration and Mid-Lent, the mid-point of the Fast (the twelve-year-old Jesus in the Temple). The Virgin plays a central part in many festivals, her status as the Mother of God being recognised as a dogma.

Transport

Roads

Thirteen trunk roads from all parts of the Soviet Union run into the 109 km (68 mile) long motorway ring, which since 1960 has marked the municipal boundary of Moscow. The ring was completed in 1962.

City transport

The main form of public transport within Moscow is the modern underground railway system (Metro; see Baedeker Special, p. 104/5), with almost 140 stations and a total network of some 200 km (125 miles). The city's buses, trolleybuses and (in peripheral districts only) trams are hopelessly overcrowded at peak times. Other forms of transport available are taxis and group or communal taxis.

Rail services

Eleven electrified lines from all parts of the Soviet Union run into Moscow's nine termini, all situated in the outer zone between the Garden Ring and the Motorway Ring (see Practical Information – Railway Stations).

Airports

Moscow is the focal point of all air traffic within the Soviet Union and an important centre of international traffic. It has four international airports. Almost all Western visitors arrive at Sheremetyevo 1 International Airport, 30 km (19 miles) north-west of the city centre (see Practical Information – Airports).
Other airports are Domodedovo (for the Urals, Far East, Central Asia and Siberia), Vnukovo 1 (to the cities on the Black and Caspian Seas), Sheremetyevo (flights to St Petersburg, Murmansk, Kaliningrad and Riga) and Bykovo (shorter domestic flights) and Vnukovo 2 (State visits).

Shipping

Moscow has three large ports – the North Harbour on the Moskva Canal, and the West and South Harbours on the Moskva itself.
The 128 km (80 mile) long Moskva Canal, constructed between 1932 and 1937, links Moscow with the Upper Volga, making Moscow the Soviet Union's most important river-port. Since the canal thus provides a link with the Black Sea, the Caspian, the Baltic, the White Sea and the Arctic Ocean, Moscow is entitled to call itself the "port on five seas". Inland navigation is hindered, however, by long periods when the waterways are blocked by ice.
The canal was originally known as the Moskva–Volga Canal. It was given its present name of Moskva Canal (Moscow Canal) in 1947, on the 800th anniversary of the foundation of Moscow.
In spring and summer motor-launches and hydrofoils ply on the Moskva, both as a regular form of public transport ("Moscow trams") and for the benefit of visitors (cruises, sightseeing trips).

Entrance to Kropotkinskya Metro station

Culture

Of the 528 state universities and higher education institutions in Russia 76 are based in Moscow. The largest universities are the Lomonosov University founded in 1755 and the Patrice Lumumba University founded in 1960. Moscow is also the seat of the Academy of Sciences, the Academy of Art and the Academies of Medicine, Agriculture and Educational Science. Nearly all students matriculated at state institutions of higher education receive grants, the lowest amount being 80% of the minimum income. Since 1992 the state universities have been joined by private institutions where tuition fees are payable. Examples include the International Independent University of Ecology and Politics sponsored by various Russian and Western companies and the Jewish and Islamic universities which are based in the Old University buildings on Managen Square. There are fears that in future there will be a two-tier system consisting of free second-rate state institutions and elitist private schools.

Universities and academies

Moscow has more than 4000 libraries with some 300 million books. The largest is the Russian State Library (formerly the Lenin Library) with over 36 million volumes in 247 languages.

Libraries

There are about eighty museums in Moscow covering a very wide range of interests: history, the history of the Revolution, art, literature, the theatre, music, science and technology. The leading museums of art are the Tretyakov Gallery and the Pushkin Museum of Fine Art. Numerous private galleries have been opened in recent years providing an insight into the contemporary art scene.

Museums

Moscow has more than 30 theatres including the internationally renowned Bolshoi Theatre. Numerous smaller studio theatres have prospered from the mood of cultural freedom in Russia.

Theatres, music

The famous Bolshoi Theatre

The focal point of Moscow's musical life is the Conservatory opened in 1866. An evening at a concert in the Great Hall of the Conservatory with its fantastic acoustics is always an experience although the institution suffered considerably from the effects of Soviet cultural policy. It was often not qualifications or personality which decided a musical career but party membership.

Economy

General

Moscow is the largest industrial city in Russia. It forms part of the region known as the "Industrial Centre", which covers an area with a radius of some 1000 km (620 miles). The district around Moscow with a radius of about 350 km (220 miles) forms the heart of the Industrial Centre. The armaments industry is concentrated on the region around Moscow.

Branches of Industry

The most important branches of industry are metal-working and construction of machinery, the manufacture of cars and lorries, together with textiles, publishing and book-printing, foodstuffs and electronics.

Transition to the market economy

In contrast with Gorbachov's reform programme President Yeltsin is striving for a radical transition to the free market economy. In October 1991 freedom of trade was introduced, in December 1991 Boris Yeltsin ordered the land of the sovkhozes and kolkhoses to be distributed among those who worked on them together with the privatisation of state industries. In January 1992 prices in the Russian Federation were given free rein.
In reality, however, the market economy made little headway in Russia in 1993. The promised economic revival failed to materialise. In 1992 produc-

Fruit and vegetables: beyond the means of most Russians

tion and investment fell and this was repeated in 1993 (industrial production fell by 20% from the previous year). Galloping inflation (at the end of 1992 it was 2600% higher than the previous year) drove most of the population into poverty. Although pensions and incomes were raised several times they still lag far behind the drastic price increases.

The devasting economic situation has its causes in the continual break up of the planning and steering system, in the destruction of the existing economic relations (e.g. shortage of deliveries of raw materials from the other former Soviet republics), but also in general demoralisation, financial irregularities and flight of capital.

So far there has not been a wave of rationalisation in Russia, only a few armaments firms have closed down. However, Western economic experts are of the opinion that more rational production methods will make mass unemployment unavoidable. At the end of 1992 the unemployment level was still less than 1%.

Everything can be bought in Moscow, the numerous currency shops in the capital have an extensive range of Western goods, at the markets best quality fruit and vegetables are for sale – but at prices which are unaffordable for the average family. A kilo of sausage costs a week's wages, luxury goods such as bananas cost a third of an average month's salary. To avoid hunger riots prices for basic food items are still fixed by the state. It is not clear who is responsible for the difference between retail price and production costs. So many of the goods disappear on to the black market.

Supply situation

The relatively homogenous social structure in the former Soviet Union has broken up in recent months. There are people on the streets again who have to beg a living as well as "nouveau riche" who are almost provocative in their display of wealth. There is a growing strata of successful young capitalists, bankers and stockbrokers together with many speculators and black marketeers operating on the fringes of legality as well as criminals. Those who are employed by the state and are excluded from the black

Social situation

19

market are badly off at present. Teachers and doctors, bus drivers, railway workers, policemen and postal workers are living close to the poverty line with their salaries. Old people have to get by with less than the subsistence minimum; if their families cannot help then they have to resort to begging (according to official figures 30% of all Russia's citizens are living below subsistence level, unofficially it is 70%). Those who can try to adjust to the new situation, housewives and workers from all social classes can be seen selling all kind of goods by the side of the road or at Moscow's markets. By selling homegrown vegetables more can be earned in a few hours than an office or factory worker can earn in a month. In many cases, however, selling is not a lucrative sideline, but absolute necessity; the poor sell everything that they can survive without.

Foreign investment

A way out of the inexorable collapse of the economy with its vicious circle of hyperinflation and shortage of money is inconceivable for many without large-scale foreign investment. Joint-venture undertakings with a minority Western share have been possible since January 1987 in the Soviet Union. This resulted in communal projects with mainly German and Scandinavian partners primarily of a gastronomic nature. From October 1990 foreign companies have been allowed to have a capital share of 100%. This has made it more rewarding for many firms to invest in the present day CIS, but this is not happening to the extent it was hoped for. The political instability and lack of a market for high-value (and expensive) products combined with unclear conditions with regard to taxations and transfer of profits has caused foreign companies to shy away from high investments.

Tourism

Tourism in the former Soviet Union has collapsed in recent years, the number of visitors has fallen by almost 40%. An official committee was established in mid-1993 to put a stop to this.

Today there is still a shortage of hotel beds in Moscow in the medium price range. On the other hand foreign investment has however brought 3000 new hotel beds in the luxury sector. Further luxury hotels are under construction or being planned.

Famous People

Boris Godunov was a relative and favourite of Ivan the Terrible, though not belonging to the high aristocracy, and a member of the much-feared private army (dissolved 1572) of Ivan's personal domain, the Oprichnina. When Ivan was succeeded in 1584 by the feeble-minded Fyodor, his son by his first marriage with a Romanov, Boris Godunov became *de facto* ruler of the country. After eliminating all claimants to the throne and establishing his undisputed authority he had himself proclaimed Tsar after Fyodor's death in 1598 – the first Tsar not of the Rurikid dynasty. The kingdom he inherited was politically weak and economically ruined; and although Boris achieved great successes in external policy – both Russian and non-Russian observers praised his political and intellectual capacity – he had only partial success in restoring internal social peace. His greatest domestic achievement was perhaps the creation of the independent Patriarchate of Moscow in 1589.

During his reign Boris was the target of numerous intrigues directed against him as a usurper, particularly by the Romanov family. The mysterious death in 1591 of Dmitry, Ivan the Terrible's youngest son, cleared the way for Boris's accession to the throne, and in 1601 he eliminated the Romanovs after a trial for witchcraft; but rumours continued to circulate that Dmitry had survived the attempt on his life, which inevitably was ascribed to Boris Godunov.

The supposed murder of Dmitry, the heir to the throne, and the appearance of a "False Dmitry" provided the theme for Pushkin's "Dramatic Chronicle of the Muscovite Kingdom, Tsar Boris and the False Demetrius" (1825). This tragedy and the "History of the Russian Empire" by N. M. Karamzin (1816–29) were followed by Mussorgsky's opera "Boris Godunov" (first performance in St Petersburg, 1874; now usually performed in Rimsky-Korsakov's arrangements of 1896 and 1908), which made the name of Boris Godunov internationally known.

Boris Godunov (c. 1550/51–1605) Tsar 1598–1605

Ivan I fully merited his nickname of Kalita (Money-Bags). Skilful courting of the Khan of the Golden Horde earned him the commission to collect the tribute due to the Khan from the principality of Vladimir and the city of Novgorod. Of the money collected he was able to divert considerable sums into his own purse, enabling him to purchase extensive territories, from small villages and towns to whole principalities. Favourable opportunities for these acquisitions were provided by the splitting up of principalities as a result of the laws of succession. His purchases of land were consolidated by a shrewd marriage policy. He is accordingly known as the "first collector of Russian soil".

In 1325–26 Feognost (Theognostes), Metropolitan of Kiev and All Russia, chose Moscow as his seat as Ivan's policy of good relations with the Tatars seemed to him to make Moscow a safer place than the neighbouring city of Tver, and the Tatars had shown tolerance towards the Church. In the same year Ivan laid down the foundation-stone of the Cathedral of the Dormition, later to become the place of coronation of all Grand Princes and Tsars.

In 1327, by means of skilful political manoeuvering, Ivan used an uprising by the people of Tver in protest against the Mongol poll-tax to strike a decisive blow against that principality which, apart from Moscow, was the only serious contender for the title of Grand Prince; the punitive action taken by the Mongols, in which Ivan himself took part, meant the political and economic ruin of Tver. Thus Ivan disposed of Moscow's last rival. In 1328 the Khan of the Golden Horde made him Grand Prince, confirming Moscow's predominance; the highest secular and religious powers were combined within Moscow.

Ivan I Kalita (1304–40) Prince of Moscow 1325–28 Grand Prince of Vladimir and Moscow 1328–40

Thereafter Ivan acted as a kind of agent for the Khan (collecting tribute, etc.), and the *baskaks* who had been the permanent representatives or envoys of the Khan were gradually withdrawn. The Khan also presented Ivan with the "Cap of Monomakh" which remained the symbol of royal authority until Peter the Great's coronation as Tsar in 1724.

Ivan died in Moscow at the age of thirty-six and was buried in the Cathedral of the Archangel Michael in the Kremlin. He divided up his kingdom between his sons and his wife, and was succeeded as Grand Prince by his son Semyon.

Ivan III, the Great (1440–1505) Grand Prince of Moscow 1462–1505

Ivan the Great, son of Grand Prince Vasily II (1425–62), laid the foundation of the autocracy later practised by the Tsars, and made Moscow the strongest political force in Eastern Europe. During his reign almost all the Russian petty principalities were incorporated in the hereditary domains of Moscow. If Ivan Kalita is famed as the "first collector of Russian soil", Ivan III is the "collector of the Russian lands".

In 1472 Ivan took as his second wife Zoe (Sophia), niece of the last Byzantine Emperor. Sophia had been brought up as a Catholic during her exile in Rome, and her marriage with Ivan was engineered by the Roman Curia; but the Pope's hopes of gaining influence in Russia were disappointed when Sophia went over to the Russian Orthodox faith after her marriage. (Ivan's aim had been not only to "collect Russian lands" but also to free Christians in the conquered territories from the "scourge of the Latins", i.e. of the Roman Catholics.) It has been suggested that Ivan had seen this marriage as giving him a claim to the succession of the Byzantine Emperors; it is true that Byzantine Court ceremonial procedure was introduced at the Moscow Court and that the double-headed eagle became a royal emblem. But in fact Sophia had no claim to the Byzantine throne and played no decisive role at the Court, while the heraldic double-headed eagle did not originate at the Byzantine Court but probably stemmed from the Roman Empire.

One of Ivan's greatest achievements was to free Moscow from the overlordship of the Golden Horde. In 1480 he ceased payment of tribute to the Tatar Khan, thus shaking off the Mongol yoke; and seven years later he even succeeded in bringing the Khanate of Kazan under the authority of Moscow.

The expansion of the Muscovite kingdom made it necessary to reorganise the administration of the country. From 1500 onwards, therefore, Ivan installed administrative offices (*prikazy*) in towns and villages, with wide powers of control over the inhabitants and direct responsibility to him. He was assisted by a council (*duma*) of nobles (*boyars*) and high dignitaries, but this had little real influence on his decisions.

This strengthening of the royal authority, territorial expansion and consolidation of the princely State was accompanied, however, by a deterioration in the conditions of life for the peasants. In 1497 a new code of law (*sudebnik*) came into effect, in which, at Ivan's behest Russian customary law had been codified; thereafter free peasants were able to change masters on payment of the appropriate due only during the week before and the week after St George's Day (26 November). This made them almost totally dependent on the boyars and landowners and prepared the way for the later institution of serfdom.

In addition to his successes in external policy and these domestic policy measures Ivan is remembered also for the large-scale building activity of his reign which brought many architects, mainly Italian, to Moscow.

Ivan the Great died in Moscow at the age of sixty-five and was buried in the Cathedral of the Archangel Michael in the Kremlin. He had appointed as his successor – perhaps following Byzantine practice – not the relative next in seniority to him but the son of his second marriage who became Vasily III (from his second marriage to Sophia of Byzantium).

Boris Godunov

Vladimir I. Lenin

Alexander S. Pushkin

Ivan IV, son of Grand Prince Vasily III (1505–33), was the first Russian ruler to be crowned as Tsar. His reign saw the development of the Russian "sacred absolutism". Apart from his domestic and external policies, his successes and, predominantly in his later years, failures, he is remembered mainly for the personality which made him one of the most unbalanced of Muscovite potentates and earned him the name of Ivan the Terrible ("grosnij", meaning "The Feared One" or "The Strict One").

Ivan's suspicious nature, persecution mania, violent temper and brutal cruelty are often explained as the result of a childhood during which he witnessed bloody conflicts between kinsmen, murders, arrests and bitter palace intrigues. He lost his father and became Grand Prince at the age of three, his father having followed the example of Ivan III in designating his eldest son rather than his next oldest relative to succeed him. His guardians were his grandfather Prince M. L. Glinsky and Prince D. F. Belsky. Ivan's mother Elena Glinskaya, as Regent, put an end to his uncle Yury's claims to the throne by having him arrested, whereupon his uncle Andrey took the oath of loyalty to his nephew.

When Prince Belsky fled to Lithuania in 1534, Ivan's grandfather attempted to seize power for himself but was arrested by Prince Shuisky and died in prison. The murder of Ivan's mother in 1538, when he was seven years old, was followed by a palace struggle which went on for several years, mainly between the Belskys and the Shuiskys. After the arrest of Prince I. Belsky in 1542 the Shuiskys were for a time in the ascendant. In 1542 Ivan came under the influence of the new Metropolitan of Moscow, Makary (Macarius). A year later he had Prince A. M. Shuisky torn to pieces in the dog pound, and the Glinskys thereupon returned to power.

In 1547 Metropolitan Makary crowned the sixteen-year-old Ivan Tsar of All Russia, in a ceremony which showed Byzantine influence (as did the later style of "Tsar i Samoderzhets", corresponding to the Byzantine "Basileus and Autokrator"). During a great fire in Moscow in the same year the mob lynched Ivan's uncle Prince Y. V. Glinsky.

In 1549 Ivan deprived the boyars of their jurisdiction in matters of taxation, justice and military service over the "boyars' children" (the impoverished and dependent members of the boyar class) and thus considerably reduced their power. In the same year he appointed his own henchmen to key positions in government, a further blow to the authority of the boyars, and the Council of Boyars was now replaced by a "Select Council" presided over by Ivan's confessor Silvester. This displacement of the boyars was accompanied by the advancement of the "service nobility" (granted noble status as servants of the Crown) and the gradual establishment of serfdom on a legal basis. The new legal provisions were incorporated in the Sudebnik (Code of Law) in 1550.

Ivan IV, the Terrible (1530–84) Grand Prince of Moscow 1533–47 Tsar of Russia 1547–84

The system of central government offices (*prikazy*) introduced in the reign of Ivan III was now further developed. The increased status of the service nobility was paralleled in the army by the special role of the regiments of Streltsy as the military élite. This consolidation of the absolutist autocracy within Russia made possible the successes of Ivan's expansionist policies in the conquest of the khanates of Kazan (1552) and Astrakhan (1556). But when the push towards the Baltic was crushed in the Livonian War (1558–82/83) Russia was politically and economically ruined.

In 1560 Ivan dismissed his confessor Silvester and departed from the moderate line of the "Select Council". Three years later, on the death of Makary, he was unable to find a Metropolitan prepared to support the Government. In 1569 he removed Metropolitan Filipp (Philip), who had openly condemned his despotism, from his post and had him murdered by a member of his private army, the Oprichniki; Philip was later canonised. In 1564 Prince Kurbsky fled to Lithuania and from there denounced Ivan's reign of terror. The Tsar then left Moscow, accusing the boyars of treason, but in 1565 returned to the capital, having assumed full powers to liquidate the "traitors". Then followed a further reign of terror by the Oprichniki, involving the destruction of whole towns and the crushing of the boyars. Ivan died in Moscow at the age of fifty-three. Some eighteen months earlier he had killed his eldest son Ivan, designated as his heir, in a fit of wild rage, and the throne, therefore, passed to his feeble-minded younger son Fyodor. The *de facto* ruler of the country was Boris Godunov, later to become Tsar.

Ivan was buried in the Cathedral of the Archangel Michael in the Kremlin. The Church of the Intercession of the Virgin, now St Basil's Cathedral, was built during his reign.

Vladimir Ilyich
Lenin
(1870–1924)
Soviet politician

Lenin, founder of the world's first Soviet state, a giant figure who changed the face of international politics in the 20th c., was born on 22 April 1870 in Simbirsk (now Ulyanovsk), the son of a school inspector named Ulyanov. A happy childhood in a strictly religious household and a successful school career came to an end in 1886 with the death of his father. Fifteen months later his elder brother Alexander was hanged in the St Petersburg fortress of Schlüsselburg as a member of a revolutionary group which had planned to assassinate Tsar Alexander III. The execution took place while Vladimir Ilyich was sitting his final school examinations. His sheltered life in a Lutheran family home was now at an end: as Lenin afterwards wrote, "My way in life was marked out for me by my brother".

The rest of the family moved to Kazan, where Vladimir Ilyich became a student at the University. As the brother of a convicted revolutionary he was kept under surveillance by the Tsarist secret police, and, after taking part in student demonstrations, was exiled to Kokushkino. In 1891 he was allowed to sit the State examinations at St Petersburg University as an external student, and in 1892 he took his degree.

In 1894 Lenin published his first work, "What are the 'Friends of the People'?", a critical analysis of the populist movement.

In 1895, during visits to Germany, France and Switzerland, he established his first contacts with Russian exiles, and in the autumn of that year he founded the St Petersburg League of the Struggle for the Emancipation of the Working Class. There upon he was arrested and spent the years 1897–1900 in exile in Siberia, where he married Nadezhda Krupskaya on 22 July 1898. The works written during his period of exile were concerned not with a theoretical treatment of Marxism but with the attempt to evolve a practical scheme for agrarian Russia.

From 1900 to 1905 Lenin lived outside Russia. In 1902 he published (in Stuttgart) his "What is to be done?", in which he called for an organisation of professional revolutionaries. The Marxist party he had in mind must act as the vanguard of the working class; a socialist consciousness must be introduced into the masses from outside. At a congress held in London in 1903 the Social Democratic Workers' Party of Russia was split into the Bolsheviks (the men of the majority) who supported Lenin and the Mensheviks (the minority) who supported Martov. With the support of the Bolsheviks Lenin became *de facto* leader of the party.

After returning to Russia during the revolutionary uprising of 1905 Lenin spent a further period in exile from 1907 to 1917, during which the Bolsheviks consolidated their position as the leaders of a future revolution. After the outbreak of the February Revolution Lenin returned on 16 April 1917 to Petrograd (as St Petersburg was now called), where he was given a triumphal reception by the workers. In the same month he published his "April Theses", in which he saw the Russian Revolution as the prologue to world revolution. After the October Revolution he was elected head of the Government.

Lenin continued as leader of the party until his death, in spite of being crippled by two strokes (in 1922 and 1923). He died on 21 January 1924 of cerebral sclerosis, brought on, according to the official medical report, by "excessive intellectual activity". His embalmed body can be seen in the Lenin Mausoleum in Red Square (see entry).

Every visitor to Moscow is confronted with the name of the Russian genius Mikhail W. Lomonosov. The largest university in the country is named after Lomonosov who founded Moscow's first university in 1755.

Lomonosov came from a Russian peasant family. As a young man he left his village on the White Sea and was admitted to the Slavic-Greek-Latin Academy in Moscow. Later he transferred to the Academic Grammar School in St Petersburg. He continued his studies in Marburg and Freiberg (Saxony). After five years he returned to St Petersburg and carried on working at the Academy of Sciences.

Lomonosov was the first Russian to become professor of chemistry in 1745. He also pursued intensive studies in physics, astronomy and Russian grammar and literature. His writings on rhetoric and poetry laid the foundations for the stylistic rules of a new Russian literary language. His "Russian Grammar" (1755) is regarded as an epochal achievement. Lomonosov died in St Petersburg in 1765.

Mikhail W. Lomonosov (1711–65) Russian poet and scientist

One cannot visit Moscow without coming across Pushkin: monuments, street names, squares and places of cultural interest (in particular the world famous Pushkin Museum of Fine Art) commemorate the poet who is regarded as the creator of Russian literary language. The majority of his work was lyric poetry but he also wrote several dramas and after 1830 devoted himself to prose.

Alexander S. Pushkin was born on 26 May 1799 in Moscow. From 1811 to 1817 he attended the Lyceum in Zarskoye Selo (near St Petersburg), the most famous elitist school in Tsarist Russia. Here he made friends, some of whom later took part in the Decembrist uprising. His largely satirical and political poetry resulted in his having to leave St Petersburg in 1820. He was in exile until 1826. Afterwards he lived mainly in Moscow and St Petersburg. His works were subject to the direct censorship of the Tsar and their publication was often subject to delay with Pushkin continually finding himself short of money. This was intensified by his way of life. Periods of deep depression alternated with periods of ecstatic enthusiasm for life. He had a considerable number of lovers.

Even after his marriage in 1831 his life was marked by unrest. The couple spent the honeymoon in Moscow (in a house on the Arbat), then lived in Zarksoye Selo and later mostly in St Petersburg. Attacks on the honour of his wife, who was admired for her beauty not least by the Tsar Nicholas I, forced Pushkin into a duel on 27 January 1837 which had fatal consequences for him. He died two days later in his St Petersburg flat.

A museum in Moscow is devoted to the life and work of the poet (Ulitsa Prechistenka) and the above-mentioned house on the Arbat is also a museum.

Alexander S. Pushkin (1799–1837) Russian poet

Ilya Efimovich Repin is the leading representative of the Russian Realist school. His genre scenes, historical pictures and portraits aroused not merely interest but enthusiasm and emotion both in Russia and abroad.

Ilya Efimovich Repin (1844–1930) Russian painter

After studying at the Academy in St Petersburg Repin painted his best-known work, the "Volga Boatmen" (1872). His realistic approach caused a sensation in the art world of the day and was soon taken as the "programme" of the group who called themselves the Peredvizhniki (Itinerants). Although the official Press criticised his "profanation of painting" his importance was recognised and he was awarded a bursary for study abroad. After spending the years 1873–76 abroad, mainly in Paris, Repin returned to Russia and joined the artists' colony which the industrialist and art patron Savva I. Mamontov had established on his estate at Abramtsevo, near Zagorsk. From 1884 to 1907 he taught at the St Petersburg Academy (becoming a professor in 1893), and from 1895 to 1898 also directed the St Petersburg Art Studio run by Princess Maria K. Tenisheva, another generous patron of art.

Repin's sympathy with the poor and downtrodden ("Religious Procession", 1880–83) and with revolutionaries ("Arrest of a Political Agitator in a Village", 1878; "Unexpected Return of a Political Exile", 1884) can be felt in almost every picture he painted. The best example of the violent reactions which his unsparing realism could arouse is perhaps his picture of Ivan the Terrible with the son whom he had fatally injured (1885), which had to be protected by glass after a visitor slashed it with a knife.

History of Moscow

Calendar

Many people are surprised when they discover that the anniversary of the October Revolution is celebrated not in October but in November (see Public holidays). The explanation is that Russia switched from the Julian to the Gregorian Calendar only after the Revolution, long after the rest of Europe.

The Julian Calendar was introduced in Russia by Peter the Great on 1 January 1700 as part of his programme for Europeanising his country. It replaced the old Byzantine era calendar (see below) to which Russia had clung long after the fall of the Byzantine Empire.

Julian Calendar (Old style)

The Julian Calendar introduced by Julius Caesar from the beginning of the year 45 B.C. had eleven months of 30 or 31 days and one month (February) with 28 days and 29 in every fourth year. This gave an average length for the year of 365·25 days.

In the course of the centuries the Julian year diverged significantly from the astronomical year, and in 1582, after long discussions and negotiations, Pope Gregory XIII brought the two into line in the reformed calendar which bears his name. Ten days were dropped from the Julian Calendar, so that 4 October 1582 was immediately followed by 15 October. The average length of the year thus became 365·2425 days, and there was no longer any significant divergence between the calendar and the astronomical year.

Gregorian Calendar (New style)

Italy, Spain and Portugal adopted the new calendar at once, and the other Catholic countries soon followed. The Protestant countries were more hesitant about adopting the "Papal" calendar; sometimes both methods of dating were used concurrently. By 1700, when Russia was just switching to the Julian Calendar, the Gregorian Calendar had been accepted in the German-speaking Protestant countries. It was adopted in Britain in 1752.

The Gregorian Calendar was introduced in the Soviet Union on 14 February 1918. By this time the difference between the Julian and the Gregorian Calendar had increased to 13 days: thus 25 October (Old Style), the day on which the Bolsheviks seized power, was 7 November according to the Gregorian Calendar, and this is, therefore, the day on which the anniversary of the October Revolution is celebrated.

Historians normally give dates of events in Russia before the calendar reform of 1918 according to the Julian Calendar (Old Style). Sometimes it may be convenient to give both Old Style and New Style dates.

The Byzantine era calendar used in Russia before 1 January 1700 took as its starting-point the date of the creation of the world, which was determined to be 1 September 5509 B.C. (according to the Gregorian calendar). Thus the supposed founding of Moscow took place, according to the chroniclers, in the year 6655 (i.e. this number of years from the creation of the world). The conversion from a Byzantine-era date to a Julian date can be exact, however, only if the month is given. For dates between January and August, 5508 years have to be subtracted from the Byzantine date to give the Julian date; between September and December 5509 years have to be subtracted. Where the month is not known 5508 years are subtracted: thus the first mention of Moscow, dated 6655 in the Byzantine era, becomes A.D. 1147 (6655 minus 5508) in the Julian Calendar.

Byzantine era calendar

The Varangians from Sweden are appealed to for help by the inhabitants of north-western Russia and enlisted as mercenaries in their internal conflicts. The term Varangian is derived from the Russian *varyag*, which itself comes from Old Norse *væring* (confederate).

From c. A.D. 700

The Varangians advance over the rivers Memel, Dvina, Velikaya, Volkhov and Dnieper and from Lake Ladoga into the interior of Russia, setting up fortified trading settlements and establishing their dominance over the local population. Their principal strongholds are Ladoga (on the lake of that name), Novgorod on the River Volkhov, Pskov on the Velikaya, Polotsk on the Dvina and Kiev on the Dnieper.

In the Frankish royal annals for the period 830–882, the Annales Bertiniani (named after the Monastery of St Bertin in Flanders where they were found), the "Rhos" are mentioned among those accompanying the Byzantine Emperor. It has been established that this mean Swedes, the term being applied by the Byzantines to the Swedes settling in eastern Europe. The Chronicle of Nestor also equates "Rhos" with Varangians.

The philologist W. Thomsen derives the Greek word "Rhos" from the Finnish *ruotsi* (rower, oarsmen). The Eastern Slav equivalent is "Rus", which has given us the term "Russian".

The names of the first Princes of Kiev are Scandinavian. Since the non-Scandinavian population paid tribute to their new masters the name "Rus" ("Russians") was at first confined to the Scandinavian ruling classes but was gradually extended to cover the whole population and the country.

The fact that the word "Russians" originally meant Scandinavians and that the first Russian State was established by these Viking "oarsmen" gave rise to furious controversy among scholars, since the "Anti-Normanists" regarded the idea – broadly confirmed though it was – as defamatory of the Russian people.

852	This first date in the Chronicle of Nestor (a frequently inaccurate record) marks the beginning of the written history of "Rus".
c. 1080	The finding of a timber roadway dating from about 1080 within the area of the Kremlin suggests that there was a settlement on the site of Moscow in the second half of the 11th c. (Later research suggests an even earlier date: a book from the second half of the 10th c. contains a reference to "the flourishing, properous town of Moscat" which was on the same site as present day Moscow.)
1113–25	In the reign of Vladimir II the principality is once again largely united under a single ruler. Vladimir's II's crown, the Crown of Monomakh, was worn by later Tsars of Russia. After Vladimir's death the political, cultural and economic decline of the principality of Kiev begins.
1147	First reference to Moscow in the Chronicle of Ipatyev, which records a feast given by Prince Yury Dolgoruky (Long Arm) in honour of the Prince of Novgorod. Yury Dolgoruky has since been regarded as the founder of Moscow, and the year 1147 has been taken as the date of its foundation.
c. 1156	Prince Yury Dolgoruky surrounds the Kremlin hill with a defensive palisade.
1223	The army of the Russian princes who have joined forces against the Mongols is routed in the Battle of Kalka. But when these mounted nomadic tribesmen – wrongly called Tatars – unexpectedly withdraw, the alliance of princes falls apart. Thereafter the history of Russia is fraught with rivalries and conflicts between the princes.
1235	Great Khan Ogodei, son of Genghis Khan, resolves in a council held at Karakorum to march against the west. The Mongol army is led by Batu Khan, grandson of Genghis Khan.
1237	Batu Khan takes Moscow. During the next hundred years Russland is exposed to widespread devastation and is completely isolated from Europe.

Batu Khan takes Kiev. The Metropolitan flees.	1240
Batu defeats a knightly German-Polish army in the Battle of Liegnitz and the Hungarian army in the Battle of the River Sayo, but then unexpectedly withdraws, returning to Karakorum to take part in the election of a new Great Khan following the death of Ogodei.	1242
After returning from Karakorum, Batu establishes the capital of the Golden Horde at Saray on the Volga. The rulers of the various Russian principalities are required to appear before the Khan of the Golden Horde at Saray, where, subject to good behaviour, they are invested with the style and dignity of prince. The princes thus appointed by the Khan rule under the supervision of a *baskak*, an envoy or governor representing the Khan, who watches over their conduct of affairs and reports any deficiencies to the Khan.	1252
The Russian population is registered by the Khan's officials and is obliged to pay high taxes. The Church submits to the Mongol rulers, retains freedom of worship and is exempted from payment of tribute. Since no one can become Grand Prince unless he is acceptable to the Mongols there is bitter rivalry and much intrigue between the princes. The Khan plays one off against the other.	1257–59
Daniil Aleksandrovich, youngest son of Alexander Nevsky, Grand Prince of Vladimir, is granted the principality of Moscow.	1276
Maksim, the refugee Metropolitan of Kiev and All Russia, takes up residence in Vladimir, capital of the principality of that name, not far from Moscow.	1299
The only candidates for the dignity of Great Prince are the Princes of Tver and Moscow. The other Russian principalities are extensively devastated. Moscow, protected by its situation amid dense forests, receives a great influx of workers fleeing before the Mongols.	From c. 1300
Yury Danilovich, Prince of Moscow since 1303, marries the Khan's sister and is granted the dignity of Grand Prince.	1317
Yury Danilovich is compelled to yield up the title of Grand Prince to Tver.	1322
The Grand Prince of Tver murders Yury Danilovich, Prince of Moscow, and is executed by the Khan.	1325
Reign of Ivan I Kalita (Money-Bags)	1325–40
Metropolitan Pyotr transfers his residence to Moscow, thereby increasing the prestige of the Princes of Moscow. The foundation-stone of the Cathedral of the Dormition in the Kremlim is laid.	1325/26
Ivan I skilfully exploits a rising in Tver against the Mongol poll tax. The Mongol reprisals, in which Ivan himself takes part, entail the political and economic ruin of Tver, eliminating Moscow's only serious rival. Ivan's policies are directed towards good relations with the Mongols.	1327
Ivan Kalita becomes Grand Prince. The highest secular and religious authorities in Russia (the Grand Prince and the Metropolitan) are now both in Moscow. By securing large tribute payments Ivan gains the favour of the Mongols. He buys up towns and villages, becoming the "first collector of Russian soil".	1328
A great fire devastates much of Moscow, which is almost entirely built of wood.	1331

Calendar

1339	Rebuilding of Moscow and the Moscow Kremlim.
1354–78	Reign of Metropolitan Aleksky, who seeks to promote the national and ecclesiastical unification of Russia under the leadership of Moscow.
From 1357	Internal struggles among the Mongols strengthen the position of Moscow, which throws off the Khan's right to grant the style of Grand Prince.
1359	Grand Prince Ivan III is succeeded by his three-year-old son Dimtry. Metropolitan Aleksey takes over the government of the principality.
c. 1360	Aleksey founds the fortified Andronikov Monastery.
1362	On Aleksey's urging the six-year-old Prince Dmitry becomes Grand Prince of Vladimir.
1380	Grand Prince Dmitry defeats the Mongols in the Battle of Kulikovo, on the Don – the first Russian prince to defeat a Mongol army. Moscow becomes the leader in the struggle to achieve national unity and the symbol of the fight against the infidal. Dmitry is now known as Dmitry Donskov (of the Don).
1382	To avenge their defeat at Kulikovo the Mongols lay siege to Moscow and burn it to the ground. Nevertheless Moscow remains the symbol of the national unification of Russia. The hereditary domains of Vladimir, and with them the dignity of Grand Prince, have now, *de facto*, passed into the hands of Moscow, which is the residence of the Grand Prince, although the title is officially attached to Vladimir.
1395	To protect the city against Mongol attack the wonder-working icon of the Mother of God of Vladimir is brought from Vladimir to Moscow.
1453	The conquest of Constantinople by the Ottomans means that the Russian Orthodox Church is now free of Byzantine control.
1459	The Synod of Russian bishops resolves that the appointment of the Metropolitan of Kiev and All Russia, residing in Moscow, no longer requires the approval of the Oecumenical Patriarch of Constantinople; the approval of the Grand Prince of Moscow is sufficient. The "autocephaly" of the Russian Church is thus established, but the Metropolitan is now dependent on the Grand Prince. At the same time the status of the Grand Prince is enhanced, putting him in the same position as the Greek Emperor in relation to the Patriarch. This development leads a hundred years later to the theocratic autocracy of the Tsars.
1461	The Metropolitan of Kiev and All Russia, residing in Moscow, assumes the new title of Metropolitan of Moscow and All Russia.
1460–1505	Reign of Ivan III, the Great.
1472	Ivan the Great marries Zoe (Sophia), niece of the last Byzantine Emperor.
From 1475	Ivan the Great summons Italian architects to Moscow; rebuilding of the Cathedral of the Dormition, building of the Kremlin walls, the Palace of Facets, etc.
1480	Ivan the Great ceases the payment of the tribute to the Golden Horde.
1492	Metropolitan Zosima declares Moscow to be the new Constantinople.
1505	Ivan the Great dies and is succeeded by Vasily III, his son by the Byzantine princess Sophia.

The Pskov monk Filofey puts forward the theory of Moscow as the "third Rome" – "and a fourth there shall not be". This follows on Zosima's affirmation in 1492 that Moscow is the new Constantinople (which was the second Rome). — Early 16th c.

Reign of Ivan IV, the Terrible. — 1533–84

Ivan is crowned as Tsar by Metropolitan Makary. — 1547

The serfdom of Russian peasants is gradually given legal force.
In parallel with the creation of a centralised adminstration and the granting of property to the "service nobility", the regiments of Streltsy (Marksmen) were built up as the èlite of the army and the Tsar's personal bodyguard. Originally recruited from the urban and village population, they undertook a commitment to life-long service but enjoyed a fixed rate of pay and economic privileges. Service in the corps became hereditary. — From 1550

Livonian War. Ivan the Terrible at first achieves great successes, but under a treaty with Poland in 1582 and with Sweden in 1583 he is compelled to give up all his conquered territory. Moscow has now no access to the Baltic and is politically and economically ruined. — 1558–82/83

Ivan the Terrible abolishes the "Select Council" presided over by his confessor Silvester and abandons the moderate line recommended by the Council. — 1560

After his earlier "abdication" Ivan the Terrible returns to Moscow, armed with wide powers to liquidate "traitors".
In order to ensure his possession of adequate resources Ivan takes over extensive areas around Moscow and in north-east Russia to form a personal domain, the Oprichnina. The boyars in these areas are expelled or killed, their property confiscated and distributed to Ivan's henchmen, the Oprichniki, who form a kind of private army. — 1565

Tartars from the Crimea capture Moscow and burn it to the ground. Russia is again required to pay tribute. — 1571

Ivan the Terrible executes leading Oprichniki and dissolves the organisation which he had himself created.
The Tartars are defeated and compelled to withdraw. — 1572

Ivan the Terrible fatally injures his son and designated successor. — 1582

Ivan the Terrible dies, leaving his principality weakened both politically and economically, mainly as a result of the Livonian War. His feeble-minded son Fyodor is crowned as Tsar, but the real ruler of the country is Boris Godunov, who does not belong to the high nobility and is exposed to constant attack by the aristocracy. — 1584

Dmitry, Ivan the Terrible's youngest son, dies in mysterious circumstances. — 1591

With the death of Tsar Fyodor the male line of the Rurikid dynasty dies out. The "Time of Troubles" begins. Boris Godunov is elected Tsar by the Imperial Assembly, in which the service nobility is strongly represented. His election is thus probably due to his non-aristocratic origins and his good relations with the service nobility. He is the first non-Rurikid to occupy the throne. — 1598

Famine throughout Russia leads to severe social unrest, particularly among peasants and Cossacks. — 1601–03

A Russian convert to Catholicism in Poland declares himself to be Dmitry, the son of Ivan the Terrible who was thought to have died in 1591. With — 1604

Polish military help and a rapidly growing army of discontented peasants and Cossacks he advances on Moscow.

1605	Boris Godunov inflicts a crushing defeat on the False Dmitry's army but dies two months later. His son Fyodor is proclaimed as his successor but is quickly deposed. The Muscovite army, led by Vasily Shuisky, goes over to the False Dmitry, who is crowned in Moscow as the "rightful" Tsar.
1606	The False Dmitry marries a Polish girl, a Catholic. This triggers off a revolt by the boyars, and he is murdered. A second False Dmitry now comes forward, and like the first receives Polish military assistance. Vasily Shuisky becomes Tsar; but since he owes his election to the boyars, not to the Imperial Assembly, he is faced with rapidly growing opposition from the service nobility, peasants and Cossacks. The rebel army, led by a runaway serf named Ivan Bolotnikov, lays siege to Moscow. The rebels are defeated, but then rally under the banner of the second False Dmitry.
1608	Ivan Bolotnikov is taken prisoner, blinded and drowned. The second False Dmitry establishes a rival government at Tushino, just outside Moscow. He becomes labelled as "The Rogue of Tushino".
1609	The Romanov family enter into an agreement with King Sigismund III of Poland in the camp of the second False Dmitry: they are prepared to see the election of Sigismud's son Vladislav as Tsar.
1610	Tsar Vasily Shuisky is banished to a monastery and dies soon afterwards. Vladimir is elected Tsar. When the Poles occupy Moscow and Sigismund, with his own eye on the throne, seeks to prevent the coronation of his son there is a rising against the Catholic Poles, based on both national and religious feeling.
1612	The Russian armies take Moscow and the Kremlin; the Poles capitulate.
1613	The sixteen-year-old Mikhail Romanov, a boyar without princely status, is elected Tsar by the Imperial Assembly, founding the Romanov dynasty which is to rule Russia until 1762.
1652	Foundation of the suburban settlement of Nemetskaya Sloboda, on the River Yauza to the east of Moscow. The name is derived from the Russian word *nemets*, a dumb person, then applied to all foreigners who could not make themselves understood (it is now the normal word for "German"). On the insistence of the Church all foreigners are required to live in the new settlement. Nikon, a reformer, becomes Patriarch in succession to Filaret.
From 1653	Under Patriarch Nikon, following the reforming Synod of 1653, a schism develops in the Russian Orthodox Church. The liturgical texts are brought into conformity with the Greek originals.
1666/67	Patriarch Nikon is relieved of his office by the Synod, but his reforms are made binding on the Russian Orthodox Church. The Old Believers reject the reforms and are thereupon excommunicated and persecuted.
1670/71	Stenka Razin leads a rising of peasants, Cossacks, Old Believers and the urban lower classes. He is taken prisoner and executed in Red Square.
1676	Tsar Aleksey dies and is succeeded by his eldest son Fyodor.
1682	Tsar Fyodor's early death leads to a struggle for the succession. The feeble-minded Ivan V and his brother Pyotr I (Peter the Great) are proclaimed joint Tsars, with their sister Sofya as Regent. The commander of the Streltsy leads a revolt and gains control over the government, but after a brief period of power is executed on the orders of the Regent.

The "Table of Ranks", setting out the hierarchy of the nobility, service nobility, etc., is abolished and replaced by the principle of advancement according to merit.

Reign of Peter the Great.	1689–1725

After banishing his sister Sofya to the Novodevichy Convent, Peter becomes *de facto* sole ruler (though his feeble-minded half-brother Fyodor continues to act as Tsar until his death in 1696). **1689**

Peter has the rebellious Streltsy publicly executed in Red Square and dissolves the corps. **1698**

Adoption of the Julian Calendar in place of the Byzantine era. **1.1.1700**

After the death of Patriarch Adrian, Peter leaves the post vacant. **1700**

Moscow is superseded as capital by St Petersburg (founded 1703). **1712**

Peter prohibits the use of stone for building except in St Petersburg. **1714**

The Patriarch is replaced by the Holy Ruling Synod, an ecclesiastical college controlled by the Procurator General, who in turn is responsible to the Tsar.
Peter assumes the title of Emperor of All Russia. **1721**

Introduction of a tax on beards. **1722**

Death of Peter the Great, who had nominated no successor. His wife Catherine becomes Empress with the help of the Guards regiments commanded by Aleksandr D. Menshikov. **1725**

Death of Catherine I. Menshikov is exiled. Peter the Great's grandson becomes Emperor as Peter II. **1727**

A great fire destroys much of Moscow and the Kremlin. **1737**

Foundation of Lomonosov University. **1755**

Reign of Peter III, also a grandson of Peter the Great. He is killed at the behest of his wife Catherine, a princess of Anhalt-Zerbst; but the belief persists among the people that he is still alive and will return to drive the "new Whore of Babylon" from the throne. **5.1.–27.7.1762**

Reign of Catherine II, the Great, the "foreign woman on the throne of the Tsars". **1762–96**

Church property is transferred to the ownership of a "College of Ecclesiastical Property" – amounting in effect to complete secularisation. **1764**

The Pugachov Rising: a rebellion by peasants, impoverished Cossacks and Old Believers led by Pugachov, a Don Cossack who claimed to be Peter III, Catherine's murdered husband. Pugachov publishes a manifesto against serfdom, which attracts further supporters to his cause. He is captured and publicly executed in Moscow. **1773–75**

Establishment of a censorship office in Moscow to check all publications. Catherine the Great is succeeded by her son Paul I, a believer in absolutist autocracy. **1796**

After Paul is murdered by a group of conspirators, including high officials and officers, Alexander becomes Emperor and introduces liberal reforms. **1801–25**

The nobility recover their old rights, foreign books are permitted to be brought into Russia, a general amnesty is declared, the use of torture in the trial of criminals is prohibited and the secret police is abolished.

1812 Napoleon's Grand Army of some 160,000 men crosses the Niemen without any declaration of war, defeats Russian forces in the battles of Smolensk and the Borodino and occupies Moscow. Kutuzov, the Russian Commander-in-Chief, avoids decisive battles and uses the tactics of mobile warfare, taking advantage of the vast area of the country.

On 1 September Kutuzov evacuates Moscow, and during the next two weeks Napoleon enters the city with some 110,000 men. Difficulties of supply, the burning of Moscow, including the Kremlin, and the approach of winter lead to the withdrawal of the French forces, now numbering 100,000 in October. Under constant attack from the pursuing Russian armies the Grand Army is reduced to 37,000 men by the time it reaches Smolensk; after the crossing of the Berezina, it now numbers only 30,000 and completely disintegrates (November). Alexander is hailed as the "liberator of Europe".

The nobility and the officer class are influenced by the German idealist philosophers (Hegel, Schelling) and poets and writers (Pushkin, Gogol, Lermontov) by the European Romantic movement.

From 1816 The growth of secret societies aimed at securing a constitution on the European pattern and the abolition of serfdom leads Alexander to abandon his liberal and reforming policies; he becomes the "gendarme of Europe".

1825 Opening of the Bolshoy Theatre (January).

After Alexander's sudden death the secret societies take advantage of the turmoil over the succession to launch the Decembrist Rising in St Petersburg. Alexander's successor Nicholas I crushes the rising within a few hours; five of the conspirators (Pestel, Muravyov, etc.) are hanged and the others are exiled to Siberia. The Decembrists provide the model for all revolutionary movements aimed at liberation from Tsarism.

1826 Nicholas prohibits all discussion of the abolition of serfdom and re-establishes the secret police. Pushkin, Russia's greatest poet, sees the task as the "education of the people".

1849 The death sentences passed on the members of the Petrashevsky group (including Dostoevsky) are commuted to exile in Siberia.

1851 Opening of the railway between Moscow and St Petersburg.

1855 Death of Nicholas I. He is succeeded by Alexander II.

1861 Alexander's manifesto on the abolition of serfdom (leaving the ownership of land unchanged) leads to protests by peasants and students demonstrations, which are brutally repressed.

1862 Turgenev's novel "Fathers and Sons" is published in Moscow. The principal character becomes a symbol for the "Nihilists" fighting Tsarism and social injustice.

1866 Unsuccessful attempt on Alexander's life.

From 1877 Show trials of Nihilists, who are executed or sent to Siberia. Increasing numbers of secret societies are established (Land and Freedom, Northern League of Russian Workers, etc.).

1881 Alexander is assassinated in a bomb attack by the People's Will group and is succeeded by Alexander III. The terrorists are arrested and executed. Establishment of the Okhrana (political police).

Student unrest in Moscow leads to the promulgation of "Rules for Students".   1885

October Revolution: fall of Tsarism.   1917

Moscow becomes capital of Soviet Russia.   1918

Opening of the Moskva–Volga Canal.   1937

On 22 June Hitler attacks the USSR without declaring war. In October the   1941
German troops advance as far as Moscow (the position of the front is
marked by a memorial in the suburb of Chimki, through which you pass on
the way from the Seremetjevo-II airport to the city centre). The city is under
siege, but the onset of winter and the exhausted state of the German troops
leads to their withdrawal in December.

The second Plan for the Development of Moscow is adopted (tower blocks   1951
in "wedding-cake" style).

A new General Plan for the Development of Moscow comes into force.   1971

The 22nd Summer Olympic Games are held in Moscow.   1980

With the opening of the Moskovskij Univermag (Moscow Department   1983
Store), the world-famous GUM store is no longer the store with the largest
floor area in the Soviet Union.

The municipal area of Moscow is increased by 100sq.km/39sq. miles, with a   1986
corresponding increase in the population to nine million.

The attention of the world is focussed on the landing of the nineteen-year- 1987
old amateur pilot Mathias Rust in Red Square on 28 May. The adventurous
pilot is sentenced in September to four years' hard labour (in August 1988
he is allowed to return to Germany).

June sees the celebration of 1000 years of Christianity in Russia. The   1988
Patriarch of Moscow and All the Russias and his Holy Synod mark the
occasion by moving their seat from Zagorsk (now Sergyev Possad) to the
newly-restored Danilov Monastery in Moscow.

The former metropolitan of Leningrad and Novgorod, Aleksei, is elected   1990
new patriarch, the head of the Russian Orthodox Church.

In August a coup by the military and politicians opposed to reforms fails not 1991
least because of the decisive action of the Russian president, Boris Yeltsin.
On 21st/22nd December eleven republics of the former Soviet Union found
the Community of Independent States (CIS) thereby sealing the fate of the
USSR.

In April the Congress of People's Deputies decides on a new name for the   1992
country: the Russian Federation – Russia.
On the orders of the Russian Central Bank the ruble becomes convertible,
the opening rate is set on 1 July at 125 rubles to 1 US dollar. However, with
galloping inflation in Russia the exchange rate changes daily (see
Economy).

In July monetary reforms are announced which provoke widespread   1993
resentment among the population. All notes issued before 1993 are to be
withdrawn from circulation as soon as possible. This does not slow down
inflation: the exchange rate in August is 1000 rubles to 1 US dollar (the
minimum pension in the same month is 14,620 rubles!).

The struggle for power between President Boris Yeltsin and parliament, which is boycotting his reforms, comes to a head in September. Yeltsin dissolves parliament and calls new elections for the 11/12th December 1993 sparking off a crisis. On 4 October Russian elite troops put down the uprising with bloody fighting; Yeltsin's opponents Ruskoy and Chasbulatov, are arrested. Yeltsin emerges from the dispute as the victor, yet the divisions within Russian society have not been overcome.

Architecture

The buildings which originated in the centuries following the founding of Moscow – 1147 is taken as the date of its foundation – were mainly wooden together with the first stone churches built in Byzantine style. However, no traces of this period in the city's history remain. The oldest buildings, which survived events in and around Moscow, are from the first half of the 15th c.

In contrast with architecture in Western Europe in Russia there was no uniformity of style from the 15th to the 17th c. Several styles existed alongside each other, which are referred to here under the generic term "Old Russian architecture".

Old
Russian
architecture
(15th–17th c.)

Around the year 1400 churches were constructed in the plan of a cruciform adapted from the Byzantine type where the simple exterior stands in contrast to the luxuriously decorated interior. Inside the believer was quite cut off from the outside world (no windows!) and was able to concentrate completely on the icons (see Baedeker Special p.14/15). An example of this early type of church is the Cathedral of the Trinity in Sergiyev Possad (known as Zagorsk for a time). Since the beginning of the 15th c. more prestigious churches with rich external decoration were built. Windows were let into their mighty limestone walls.
A model for later buildings was the Cathedral of the Saviour in the Andronikov Monastery (built 1410–27) which rises in stages and has eye-catching rows of "kokoshniks" (ogee-shaped gables) which surround the central dome.

A new era in Moscow architecture began in 1470. The modest churches and fortified buildings did not correspond with the image of the capital of a powerful state into which Moscow had since developed. Ivan the Great and his successors sent for Italian architects including Aristotle Fioravanti, from Bologna, and Alovisio Novo. The latter was responsible for the rebuilding of the Kremlin walls together with Pietro Antonio Solari. Inside the Kremlin the Cathedral of the Dormition 1475–79 was designed by Fioravanti and between 1505 and 1508 the Cathedral of the Archangel by Novo. Along with other sacral buildings of the period the influence of the Renaissance is indeed visible but primarily they display typical Russian architectural features.

The cruciform plan with a central dome and four corner domes was adopted. Impressed by the work of their Italian colleagues Russian architects used details from the Kremlin cathedrals in their own buildings. The Cathedral of the Novodevichy Convent and the main church of the Trinity Monastery of St Sergiy are adapted from the Cathedral of the Dormition in the Kremlin.

The Italians were able to show off Renaissance forms more to advantage with palaces and fortifications. This is particularly apparent on the Palace of Facets (1487–91 by Marco Ruffo and Pietro Antonio Solari) and on the rebuilding of the Kremlin Walls, the work of Pietro Antonio Solari and Alovisio Novo. The influence of the Kremlin's mighty defences can be seen not only in other parts of the Russian Kremlin but is echoed in the defensive walls of the monasteries which surround Moscow.

A new indigenous style of church, the tent-roof church, which perhaps had its origins in the early wooden buildings, emerged for the first time in

Cathedral of the Archangel Michael in the Kremlin

Kolomenskoe in 1532. This style was maintained in various forms until the end of the period of Old Russian architecture (Nikon, elected Patriarch in 1652, banned tent roofs and all attractive decoration in church building in order to protect the monastery and monks from the temptations of the world – but he was forced to abdicate in 1658 and tent-roofs continued to be built, if less often).

This tent-roof style is also found in St Basil's Cathedral in Red Square, built by Ivan the Terrible in 1555–61 to commemorate the capture of Kazan. The central domed tower is surrounded by not just four but eight domed chapels.
With its heterogenous assortment of architectural elements and vivid colours St Basil's Cathedral is the supreme achievement of 16th c. architecture. The small chapels which can only accommodate a small number of people stand in sharp contrast to the magnificent fairy-tale exterior, which accounted for its being described as the "town of churches".

In the 17th c. a uniform style gradually developed in Russia. Churches consisted of a bell tower with a tent-roof, a refectory, several side chapels and the main church (an example of this is the Trinity Church in Nikitniki). They featured sumptuous, ornate colourful decoration which stood out from the mainly white or red walls.

From the end of the Sixties brightly coloured ceramic tiles were a popular form of decoration. The customary five domes were closely bunched with tent roofs rising over the front of the buildings. These architectural elements are also found in secular buildings which grew in importance in the 17th c. Churches, palaces and castles together with their working quarters were also carpeted in ornate decoration (such as the Terem Palace in the Kremlin which was later to be altered).

An architectural change took place at the end of the 17th c. with the advent of the Baroque style in Russia. The principal builder of secular buildings was the boyar Naryshkin, a relative of Peter the Great (whose mother was a Naryshkin), and accordingly the term "Naryshkin Baroque" is commonly applied to this period. The first examples of this style are from the 1680s. Churches became symmetrical in their ground plans. Semi-circular porches, which correspond to the apse, were added on all sides. Often the church was built on a pedestal floor surrounded by a terrace. The decorative features – window surrounds and doorways – were increasingly simplified. The finest example of a tower church built towards the end of the 17th c. in Moscow is the Church of the Intercession in Fili (1690–93). This desire for symmetry is also apparent in the defensive monasteries around Moscow. These often took the form of a square base with the main cathedral in the centre (Don Monastery).

In the first half of the 18th c. foreign architects began to introduce Western European styles. Yet few important buildings remain in Moscow from this period. This was because Peter the Great forbade the building of houses in stone anywhere except in the new capital St Petersburg (this ban was only lifted in 1741). However, one example is Archangel Gabriel Church (1704–07), commonly known as the Menshikov Tower.

The Baroque buildings from the middle of the 18th c. were intensely colourful, dark green, azure blue and orange being the dominant shades. The façades were decorated with columns, half columns, pilasters, window surrounds and gables. The corners were often emphasised by columns, often joined (Apraksin House, 1766–69; bell tower of the Trinity Monastery of St Sergiy, 1740 to 1770).

In 1762 Tsar Peter III issued a declaration abolishing compulsory service for the nobility. In the same year several decrees were proclaimed abolishing the crown's monopoly on trade. Following her coup d'état in June 1762 Catherine the Great continued this policy of promoting Russian trade. As a result the aristocracy became involved in trade and architecture showed a movement away from the decorative and Baroque styles towards a more balanced and clearly articulated style of building.

Classical styles of building can be clearly detected from the 1760s, reaching full expression in the 1780s and 1790s. In keeping with ancient tradition the most important architectural element was the order of columns. The columns are no longer only decorative but functional. The central part of the building is nearly always emphasised by a portico (a porch supported by columns) crowned by a triangular gable. There is little ornament or decoration, window and door openings have only simple surrounds. The colour schemes are restrained, chiefly a pale yellow or grey with columns and window surrounds depicted in white. The principal architects of this period in Moscow are W. I. Bashenov (Pashkov House, 1784–86) and his pupil M. F. Kasakov (Senate building in the Kremlin 1776–88; Old University 1782–93).

The manor houses built by the aristocracy in the vicinity of Moscow (Ostankono, 1791–98; Arkhangelkoe, 1780–90) consist mostly of a splendid Classical palace surrounded by an extensive park with pavilions, ponds, summerhouses and statues.

The great fire of 1812 was a decisive point in Moscow's architectural history. 80% of all residential dwellings (mostly wooden) and some prestigious buildings were destroyed. Rapid rebuilding took place until the city was almost completely restored by 1825. As in the rest of Europe the original Greek style, in particular the Doric, was favoured more than the Roman tradition. Simplicity, strength and severity were the dominant qualities with the columns becoming stronger and shorter (Manege, 1817–25).

Russian Baroque
(Naryshkin
Baroque; end 17th
to mid-18th c.)

Classicism
(1760s to first
half of 19th c.)

Architecture

Historicism (second half of the 20th c.)

As with the rest of Europe the demise of Classicism was followed in the middle of the 19th c. by the so-called neo-styles, in Moscow the Old Russian architecture of the 17th c. was revived. K. A. Thon incorporated Old Russian motifs in the façade of the Great Kremlin Palace (1838–49). The building of the Historical Museum (1874–83) is a typical example of neo-Old Russian style. Historicist features can also be found on the old building of the Tretyakov Gallery (around 1900), the GUM department store (1888 to 1894) and also at the Kazan Railway Station (1913–41), a "town within a town".

Art Nouveau (around 1900)

Art Nouveau or "modern style" as it is known in Russian was a reaction against Historicism around 1900. Although it only lasted for a little over a decade numerous traces of this architectural style have been left behind. The principal examples of Art Nouveau are the Old Arbat quarter and the streets east of the GUM department store. Its characteristic features include a free ground plan, window openings of different types and sizes and differing façades: alongside plastered surfaces are some of coarsely hewn stone, brick or clinker. The Hotel Metropol is a typical Art Nouveau building, built in 1899–1903 by V. Valkota. Without doubt the best known architect of this period is Feodor Shekhtel. He constructed quite a variety of buildings in Moscow: railway stations (Yaroslavl Railway Station, 1902–04), villas (nowadays the Gorky Museum, 1900–02) and banks. They display a relatively severe rational variation of Art Nouveau which was to pave the way for Constructivism.

Constructivism (1920s)

After the October Revolution architecture followed the principles of Constructivism. Initially, however, owing to a shortage of finance more buildings were planned than actually were built. Some were constructed from functional materials which were intended to meet the needs of the people (the Rusakov Club by the architect Meinikov in the Stromynka Ulitsa is an example).

Shchusev was awarded the contract in the Twenties to rebuild the new (old) capital of Moscow. The Lenin Mausoleum (1924–30) is indicative of his

Hotel Metropol, a prestigeous Art-Nouveau building

rejection of the neo-Old Russian fairy-tale style in favour of a simple, austere monumental style.

Under Stalin monumental blocks of flats and giant towers in "wedding cake style" were built from the Thirties to the Fifties which still determine the skyline of Moscow. This movement began with an architectural competition from 1931–33 for the "Palace of the Soviets". The gigantic, 400m/1312ft high construction decorated with a huge statue of Lenin, the "most important building of our time", was to be built opposite the Kremlin (on the site of the present day "Moskva" swimming pool. After the end of the war building was not resumed on the Palace of the Soviets, instead eight tower blocks were to be built to commemorate the 800th anniversary of the city in 1947, of which seven were realised in the years that followed. These towers in the so-called "wedding cake style" were intended to be an architectural tribute to Socialism. The largest and most important is the Lomonosov University on the Lenin Hill south of the Moskva (built 1949–53).

An important achievement of this period was the construction of the Metro. Stalin wanted to give the workers the feeling of being in a "palace" while travelling to work.

From the mid-Fifties building styles became more functional and economic. The Congress Palace in the Kremlin (1964) was built in relatively conventional style. The confidence of this period finds expression in what was intended as a showpiece, Kalinin Avenue (now New Arbat: 1964–69). In an attempt to meet the demand for housing (which still has not succeeded today) giant new housing estates sprang up on the edge of the city. During the Seventies artists and architects increasingly worked together. For some years now efforts have been made to try and preserve the "historic face" of the city. Not only individual buildings, as was the case in the past with churches and monasteries being restored, but entire areas of

Apartment building by the Moskva, in "wedding-cake style"

41

the city are to regain their original appearance. A striking example of this is the (old) Arbat.

It remains to be seen whether the finances will be available to realise this project. The problems of this metropolis only came to light through perestroika: the housing shortage is still immense, out-of-date industrial concerns are polluting the air in the city centre, some architectural monuments are falling into decay and many new buildings are already dilapidated.

Quotations

"As a result of the inevitable incursion into Moscow of Europeanism on the one hand, and the wholly surviving element of old-world conservatism on the other, it has emerged as rather an odd city, in which European and Asiatic features combine to dance in a gaudy haze before your eyes. It has spread and stretched over a vast area; what an enormous city, you might say . . .! Yet you have only to take a walk to discover that this sense of space is greatly favoured by the existence of long, exceedingly long, fences. There are no huge buildings; the more substantial houses are not exactly small, but then again they are not exactly large. They do not boast any particular architectural merit. Still striving faithfully towards the goal of domestic felicity, the genii of the ancient Muscovite kingdom quite clearly meddled in their architectural design. After an hour's walk through Moscow's crooked, slanted streets you will soon realise that this is a patriarchal, a family city; the houses stand apart, almost every one in possession of its own wide courtyard, surrounded by outbuildings and overgrown with grass."

V. G. Belinsky (1811–48) Russian literary critic

The Kremlin:
"Fantastic one has always known it to be from photographs. But the reality embodies fantasy on an unearthly scale – a mile and a half of weathered, rose-coloured brick in the form of a triangle that rises uphill from its base along the river. These airy walls, which in places attain a height of forty feet, are hedged with deep crenellations, cloven and coped in white stone after the Venetian fashion. Their impalpable tint and texture might suggest rather the protection of some fabled kitchen-garden than the exigencies of medieval assault.
But from their mellow escarpments bursts a succession of nineteen towers, arbitrarily placed, and exhibiting such an accumulation of architectural improbability as might have resulted had the Brobdingnagians, during a game of chess, suddenly built a castle for Gulliver with the pieces. . . . Within the walls rose a white hill, as it were a long table covered with a cloth of snow, lifting up to the winter sky the residences of those vanished potentates, Tsar and God: to the west the two palaces, nineteenth-century Russo-Venetian, cream-coloured against the presage of snow in the sky; the little Italian palace of the fifteenth century, whose grey-stone façade of diamond rustications conceals the tiny apartments of the early Tsars; and then the Cathedrals: that of the Annunciation, with nine orange domes; that of the Dormition, where the coronations took place, with five helm-shaped domes; and that of the Archangel Michael, whose central bulb stands high above its four smaller companions; nineteen domes in all, each finished with a cross, most of them thinly gilt; and then, higher than all, the massive belfry, crowned with a flat onion; yet still overtopped by the ultimate cupola of the tower of Ivan Veliki, colossal in solitude, the climax of this Caesearopapist fantasia. I looked down to the river below me; I looked up to the sky; I looked to the right and I looked to the left: horizontally and vertically, towers and domes, spires, cones, onions, crenellations, filled the whole view. It might have been the invention of Dante, arrived in a Russian heaven."

Robert Byron "First Russia, then Tibet" (1933)

"We gave five or six hours to a stroll through this wonderful city, a city of white houses and green roofs, of conical towers that rise out of one another like a foreshortened telescope; of bulging gilded domes, in which you see, as in a looking-glass, distorted pictures of the city; of churches which look, outside, like bunches of variegated cactus (some branches crowned with green prickly buds, others with blue, and others with red and white) and which, inside, are hung all round with *eikons* and lamps, and lined with

Lewis Carroll (1832–98) English writer Diary (August 1867)

illuminated pictures up to the very roof; and finally, of pavement that goes up and down like a ploughed field, and *drojky*-drivers who insist on being paid thirty per cent extra to-day, 'because it is the Empress's birthday'."

William Coxe
(1747–1828)
English historian
"Travels" (1792)

"A city so irregular, so uncommon, so extraordinary, and so contrasted, had never before claimed my astonishment. The streets are in general exceedingly long and broad: some of them are paved; others, particularly those in the suburbs, are formed with trunks of trees, or are boarded with planks like the floor of a room; wretched hovels are blended with large palaces; cottages of one storey stand next to the most superb and stately mansions. Many brick structures are covered with wooden tops; some of the wooden houses are painted; others have iron doors and roofs. Numerous churches presented themselves in every quarter, built in a peculiar style of architecture; some with domes of copper, others of tin, gilt, or painted green, and many roofed with wood. In a word, some parts of this vast city have the appearance of a sequestered desert, other quarters of a populous town; some of a contemptible village, others of a great capital."

Nikolay V. Gogol
(1809–52)
Russian writer
"Dead Souls"

A Russian meal:

"'Yes; pray come to table,' said Sobakevich to his guest; whereupon they consumed the customary glass of vodka (accompanied by sundry snacks of salted cucumber and other dainties) with which Russians, both in town and country, preface a meal . . .

"'My dear,' said Sobakevich, 'the cabbage soup is excellent.' With that he finished his portion, and helped himself to a generous measure of *nyanya*– the dish which follows *shchi* and consists of a sheep's stomach stuffed with black porridge, brains and other things. 'What *nyanya* this is!' he added to Chichikov. 'Never would you get such stuff in a town, where one is given the devil knows what.' . . .

"'Have some mutton, friend Chichikov,' said Sobakevich. 'It is shoulder of mutton, and very different stuff from the mutton which they cook in noble kitchens – mutton which has been kicking about the market-place four days or more. All that sort of cookery has been invented by French and German doctors, and I should like to hang them for having done so. They go and prescribe diets and a hunger cure as though what suits their flaccid German systems will agree with a Russian stomach! Such devices are no good at all.' Sobakevich shook his head wrathfully. 'Fellows like those are for ever talking about civilisation. As if *that* sort of thing was civilisation! Phew!' (Perhaps the speaker's concluding exclamation would have been even stronger had he not been seated at table.) 'For myself, I will have none of it. When I eat pork at a meal, give me the *whole* pig; when mutton, the *whole* sheep; when goose, the *whole* of the bird. Two dishes are better than a thousand, provided that one can eat of them as much as one wants.'

"And he proceeded to put precept into practice by taking half the shoulder of mutton on to his plate, and then devouring it down to the last morsel of gristle and bone."

Aleksandr
Ivanovich Herzen
(1812–70)
Russian publicist
and revolutionary
"My Past and
Thoughts"
(tr. Constance
Garnett)

The French entry into Moscow, which took place in the year Herzen was born. (He describes it in the words of his nurse): "At the beginning we got along somehow, for the first few days, that is; it was only that two or three soldiers would come in and ask by signs whether there was something to drink; we would take them a glass each, to be sure, and they would go away and touch their caps to us too. But then, you see, when fires began and kept getting worse and worse, there was such disorder, plundering and all sorts of horrors. At that time we were living in the lodge at the Princess Anna Borissovna's and the house caught fire; then Pavel Ivanovitch said, 'Come to me, my house is built of brick, it stands far back in the courtyard and the walls are thick.' So we went, masters and servants all together, there was no difference made; we went out into the Tverskoy Boulevard and the trees were beginning to burn – we made our way at last to the Golohvastovs' house and it was simply blazing, flames from every window. Pavel Ivanovitch was dumbfounded, he could not believe his eyes. Behind the house there is a big garden, you know; we went into it thinking we should be safe there. We sat there on the seats grieving, when, all at once, a mob of drunken soldiers were upon us; one fell on Pavel Ivanovitch, trying to pull off his travelling coat; the old man would not give it up, the soldier pulled out his sword and struck him on the face with it so that he kept the scar to the end of his days; the others set upon us, one soldier tore you from your nurse, opened your baby-clothes to see if there were any money-notes or diamonds hidden among them, saw there was nothing there, and so the scamp purposely tore your clothes and flung them down. As soon as they had gone away we were in trouble again. . . ."

"The Citie of Mosco is great, the houses for the most part of wood, and some of stone, with windowes of Iron, which serve for Summer time. There are many faire Churches of stone, but more of wood, which are made hot in the Winter time. The Emperours lodging is a faire and large Castle, walled foure square of Bricke, high, and thicke, situated upon an Hill, two miles about, and the River on the South-west side of it, and it hath sixteene gates in the walls, and as many Bulwarkes. His Palace is separated from the rest of the Castle, by a long wall going North and South, to the River side. In his Palace are Churches, some of stone, and some of wood, with round Towres fairely gilded. In the Church doores, and within the Churches are Images of Gold: the chiefe Markets for all things are within the said Castle, and for sundry things, sundry Markets, and every Science by it selfe. And in the Winter there is a great Market within the Castle, upon the River being frozen, and there is sold Corne, earthen Pots, Tubs, sleds, &c. The Castle is in circuit two thousand and nine hundred paces."

Anthony Jenkinson (d. 1611) English merchant "The First Voyage . . ." (1557)

The district between Kalinin Avenue and Kropotkin Street:
"Life went on quietly and peacefully – at least for the outsider – in this Moscow Saint-Germain. In the morning nobody was seen in the streets. About midday the children made their appearance under the guidance of French tutors and German nurses, who took them out for a walk on the snow-covered boulevards. Later on in the day the ladies might be seen in their two-horse sledges, with a valet standing behind on a small plank fastened at the end of the runners, or ensconced in an old-fashioned carriage, immense and high, suspended on big curved springs and dragged by four horses, with a postillion in front and two valets standing behind. In the evening most of the houses were brightly illuminated, and, the blinds not being drawn down, the passer-by could admire the card-players or the waltzers in the saloons. 'Opinions' were not in vogue in those days, and we were yet far from the years when in each one of these houses a struggle began between 'fathers and sons' – a struggle that usually ended in a family tragedy or in a nocturnal visit of the state police. Fifty years ago nothing of the sort was thought of; all was quiet and smooth – at least on the surface."

Pyotr Alekseevich Kropotkin (1842–1921) Russian revolutionary "Memoirs of a Revolutionist"

"The earth, as we all know, begins at the Kremlin. It is her central point."

Vladimir V. Mayakovsky (1893–1930) Soviet poet

A letter to the Empress Marie-Louise from Moscow, 6 September 1812: "I had no conception of this city. It possessed fifty palaces of equal beauty to the Palais d'Elysèe Napoléon, furnished in the French style with incredible luxury, several imperial palaces, barracks, fine hospitals. All this has disappeared, for since yesterday fire has been devouring the city. Since all the little houses of the middle ranks are built of wood they catch fire like tinder. Furious at the defeat they have suffered, the Governor and the Russians have set fire to this beautiful city. Two hundred thousand citizens are in the streets, in despair and in wretchedness. For the army, however, sufficient is left; they are finding treasures of all kinds, for in this disorder everyone takes to plundering. The loss for Russia is immense; Russian trade will be

Napoleon Bonaparte (1769–1821)

Quotations

ruined. These wretches have gone so far as to remove or destroy the fire brigade's pumps. I have got over my cold; my health is good. . . ."

Adam Olearius (1603–71) "Travels to Muscovy and Persia" (1656; tr. S. H. Baron)

"The Russians also greatly love tobacco, and formerly everyone carried some with him. The poor man gave his kopek as readily for tobacco as for bread. However, it was presently remarked that people got no good whatever from it, but, on the contrary, appreciable ill. Servants and slaves lost much time from their work; many houses went up in smoke because of carelessness with the flame and sparks; and before the ikons, which were supposed to be honoured during church services with reverence and pleasant-scented things, the worshippers emitted an evil odour. Therefore, in 1634, at the suggestion of the Patriarch, the Grand Prince banned the sale and use of tobacco along with the sale by private taverns of vodka and beer. Offenders are punished very severely – by slitting of the nostrils, and the knout. We saw marks of such punishment on both men and women. . . ."

Aleksandr S. Pushkin (1799–1837) Russian poet

"And now at last the goal is in sight: in the shimmer
Of the white walls gleaming near,
In the glory of the golden domes,
Moscow lies great and splendid before us!
Ah, how I trembled with joy
When this be-towered, shining city,
Bright-hued, imposing,
Once again, of a sudden, stood before my eyes!
How often, in profoundest grief,
In the night of my wandering fate,
O Moscow, have I thought of you!
Moscow: how violently the name
Plucks at any Russian heart!"

Lev Nikolaevich Tolstoy (1828–1910) Russian writer "War and Peace" (tr. L. and A. Maude)

"It would be difficult to explain why, and where to, ants whose heap has been destroyed are hurrying: some from the heap, dragging bits of rubbish, eggs and corpses, others back to the heap; why they jostle, overtake one another, and fight; and it would be equally difficult to explain what caused the Russians, after the departure of the French, to throng to the place that had formerly been Moscow. But when we watch the ants round their ruined heap, the tenacity, energy, and the immense number of the delving insects prove that, despite the destruction of the heap, something indestructible, which though intangible is the real strength of the colony, still exists; and similarly though in Moscow in the month of October there was no government, and no churches, shrines, riches, or houses – it was still the Moscow it had been in August. All was destroyed, except something intangible yet powerful and indestructible.
"The motives of those who thronged from all sides to Moscow after it had been cleared of the enemy were most diverse and personal, and at first, for the most part, savage and brutal. One motive only they all had in common: a desire to get to the place that had been called Moscow, to apply their activities there.
"Within a week Moscow already had fifteen thousand inhabitants, in a fortnight twenty-five thousand, and so on. By the autumn of 1813 the number, every increasing and increasing, exceeded what it had been in 1812."

Lev Davidovich Trotsky (1879–1940) Russian revolutionary and Soviet politician "My Life"

"The transfer of central government authority to Moscow was naturally a blow to Petrograd. There was great, almost universal, opposition to the move . . . The majority were mainly afraid that it would make a bad impression on the Petrograd workers. Enemies spread the rumour that we had agreed to cede Petrograd to Wilhelm. I believed, with Lenin, that the move to Moscow would not only ensure the safety of the government but also that of Petrograd. There would have been a great temptation to Germany, and also to the Entente, to gain possession, by a rapid stroke, of both the revolutionary capital and Petrograd. It would be a very different matter to take the starving city of Petrograd without a government. Finally the opposition was overcome, the majority of the Central Committee favoured the move, and on 12 March (1918) the government left for Moscow . . . With its medieval walls and its countless golden domes the Kremlin seemed a paradoxical place to establish a stronghold of the revolutionary dictatorship . . . Until March 1918 I had never been inside the Kremlin; and indeed I knew nothing of Moscow except one building – the Butyrki prison, in the tower of which I had spent six months during the cold winter of 98/99. "As a visitor one can admire at leisure the historical monuments of the Kremlin, the bell-tower of Ivan the Great or the Palace of Facets. But we had to instal ourselves here for a long period. The close daily contact between two historic poles, between two irreconcilable cultures, was both astonishing and amusing. Driving past Nicholas's palace on the wooden paving, I would occasionally glance over at the Emperor Bell and the Emperor Cannon. All the barbarism of Moscow glared at me from the hole in the bell and the mouth of the cannon. Here Hamlet would have cried out, 'The time is out of joint; O cursed spite, that ever I was born to set it right!' But there was nothing of Hamlet about us . . . .

"The carillon in the Saviour's Tower was now altered. Instead of playing "God preserve the Tsar" the bells played the "Internationale", slowly and deliberately, at every quarter-hour."

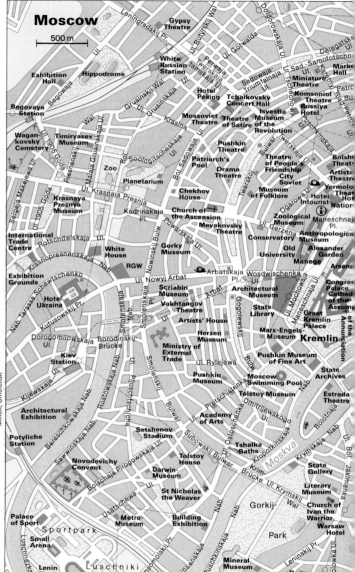

Plan of the Inner City

Plan of the Inner City

49

Moscow from A to Z

From 1991 numerous streets, squares and buildings have assumed their original historical names (for example Gorky Street is again Tverskaya Ulitsa). The renaming process, more may still follow, has not been carried out in any particular order – the former Lenin Library is now officially called the Russian Library, while the metro station is still called Biblioteka Imeni Lenina.

Suggestions for a short stay in Moscow can be found under "Sightseeing Programme" in the Practical Section of the guide.

Note

Abramtsevo

Excursion

Абрамцево
Abramtsevo

Russian

The former estate of Abramtsevo situated about 70km/43 miles north of Moscow is remarkable more for its cultural atmosphere than outstanding buildings. A visit to Abramtsevo can be combined with the famous monastery in Sergyev Possad (see Sergyev Possad; formerly Zagorsk).

The writer and theatre critic S. T. Aksakov acquired the property in 1843 and several important literati stayed here including Gogol, Belinski, Herzen and Turgenev. After Aksakov's death (1859) the estate fell into disrepair and it was only restored in 1870 when it was taken over by the industrialist and arts patron Savva Mamantov Abramtsevo. Well known painters such as Ilya Repin, Valentin Serov, Victor Vasnezov and Mikhail Vrubel spent time here as did the singer Feodor Shalyapin (Chaliapin) and the sculptor Mordechai Antokolski.

The main house of the estate, a simple 18th c. wooden building, is open to visitors. Still with the original furnishings the personal possessions of the former owner together with numerous works of art are on display. In the park are a small chapel built in Novgorod style in 1882 (the iconostasis was painted by Mamantov's artist friends) and some original wooden cottages. Mamantov had ceramics and carpentery workshops, a studio and various cottages built for the artists under his wing. The design for the so-called cottage on chicken legs originates from the fairy-tale teller Vasnezov (see Vasnezov House).

Location
70km/43 miles
north of Moscow

Rail
from Yaraslovl
Station

Open
Wed.–Sun.
11am–5pm

---

*Alexander Garden

H 12 (C 1)

Александровский Сад
Aleksandrovsky Sad

Russian

The Alexander Garden, an oasis of peace amid the turmoil of the city, lies below the north-west side of the Kremlin, between Borovitskaya Ploshchad and the Corner Arsenal Tower. The gardens were laid out in 1821 for Tsar Alexander I, after whom they are named, by Osip I. Beauvais.

Before the gardens were laid out, a little stream, the Neglinnaya, flowed by the Kremlin walls, forming a natural moat. It was bricked over in 1817/1819 and now flows underground. A bridge built over the stream in 1516 can still be seen in the gardens, linking the Kutafya Tower in Manezhnaya Ulitsa with the Trinity Tower of the Kremlin.

Location
Manezhnaya Ulitsa

Metro
Aleksandrovsky
Sad/Biblioteka
Im. Lenina/
Borovitsky

◄ *Church of the Ascension in Kolomenskoe*

Tomb of the Unknown Soldier

At the north entrance of the Alexander Garden is the memorial, in black and red granite, of the Unknown Soldier, commemorating all the nameless dead of the Great Fatherland War (1941–45). The memorial, unveiled in 1967, contains the remains of soldiers who died during the defence of Moscow in 1941. On the black granite slab burns the "eternal flame of glory". The inscription reads "Your name is unknown, but your deed is eternal". The porphyry blocks, beside which the guard of honour stands, contain earth from the cities which were awarded the designation "hero city" after the Second World War.

Corner Arsenal Tower

Above the Tomb of the Unknown Soldier rears the largest of the Kremlin's corner towers, the Corner Arsenal Tower, named after the arsenal which lies immediately behind the walls (see Kremlin).

This 60m/200ft high brick tower, with walls up to 4m/13ft thick, was built by Pietro Antonio Solari in 1492. The original superstructure of 1680 was damaged in 1812 when the French tried to blow up the whole of the Kremlin, but was restored in its original form by Osip I. Beauvais.

A secret spring in the basement of the tower still survives. Its outflow into the Neglinnaya was walled up.

Middle Arsenal Tower

The Middle Arsenal Tower was built in 1495 under the direction of Alevisio the Younger (Alovisio Novo), who, after the death of his fellow countryman Pietro Antonio Solari, built the whole of the north-western section of the Kremlin walls with the exception of the Corner Arsenal Tower. The tower

Tomb of the Unknown Soldier and . . .

. . . Grotto in the Alexander Garden

was originally known as the Faceted Tower (Granovitaya Bashnya) after its striking faceted masonry.

The artificial tower at the foot of the Middle Arsenal Tower was constructed by Osip I. Beauvais.

Grotto

Obelisk of the Great Revolutionaries and Thinkers

This triangular obelisk in the Alexander Garden was Moscow's first monument to the Great October Revolution. It was originally erected in 1913 to commemorate the 300th anniversary of the Romanov dynasty, but in 1918 the double-headed eagle which was the heraldic emblem of imperial Russia was removed and the obelisk was transcribed with the names of the great revolutionaries and thinkers of Socialism and Communism (the term "Socialism", coined in France, was synonymous with "Communism" until the 20th c.).

All Russian Exhibition Centre J 18

Всероссийский Выставочный Центр
Vserossyski Vystavochny Zentr

Russian

A visit to the All Russian Exhibition Centre, the former exhibition of the national economy of the USSR, was until recently included on the itinerary of every group visit. About 100,000 constantly updated exhibits demonstrated the latest development in Soviet industry, science and culture over an area covering approximately 310ha/766 acres. Most of the 80 pavilions have since been acquired by private companies. The interested public can

Location
Prospekt Mira

Metro
VDNKh

All Russian Exhibition Centre . . .　　　　*. . . and the Sputnik Monument*

Andronikov Monastery

Open
Mon.–Fri.
9am–8pm, Sat.,
Sun. 9am–9pm;
Pavilions:
daily 10am–8pm

look at highly polished limousines, electrical goods, clothes and much more. However, for most visitors the prices of these luxury goods are astronomical.

A visit to the All Russian Exhibition Centre is still of interest to the western visitor. Its greens, avenues, flower beds, ponds, fountains, cafes and restaurants together with the monstrous buildings illuminate the contradictions within modern Russia. It is still an experience to see how the USSR wanted to portray itself.

"Worker and Woman Collective-farmer"

Close to the main entrance of the exhibition centre stands the 24m/79ft high monumental sculpture weighing 75 tonnes "Worker and Woman Collective-farmer". Made from rustfree high-grade steel it was created in 1937 by Vera Mukhina for the Paris Exhibition.

Sputnik Monument (Museum for Cosmonauts)

The Sputnik Monument near the VDNKh metro station is a rocket taking off with a trail of titanium. The decorated base houses the Cosmonaut Museum (open: Tue.–Sun. 10am–7pm).

In the avenue in front of this monument to space travel, leading to Prospekt Mira, are sculptures to the "heroes of the cosmos".

---

*Andronikov Monastery M 11/12

Russian

Андроников Монастырь
Andronikov Monastyr

Location
Andronyevskaya Ploshchad

Metro
Ploshchad Ilyicha

Open
Thur.–Sun.
11am–6pm

The greatest of Russia's medieval icon-painters, Andrey Rublyov, lived and worked in the former Andronikov Monastery above the River Yauza on the east side of the city. In 1960 the Andrey Rublyov Museum of Old Russian Art was opened in one of the monastery buildings. The Rublyov monument in front of the entrance was completed by N. Komova in 1985.

According to the old chronicles the monastery was founded about 1360 by Metropolitan Aleksey. It is believed to be named after its first abbot, Andronik. Between 1410 and 1427, in the time of Abbot Alexander, the original timber-built monastery was replaced by new limestone buildings. It now served a defensive function, protecting the south-eastern approach to the capital. Andrey Rublyov, who spent his last years in the monastery and was probably buried here (d. 1430), almost certainly contributed to the decoration of the new buildings, the original painting of which is not, however, preserved.

The entire site has undergone several phases of rebuilding but was restored to its original form in the 1950s. Services are again held in the churches.

Cathedral of the Saviour

The Andronikov Monastery, built more than half a century before the buildings of the Italian period in the Kremlin, offers an excellent opportunity of studying the pattern of early Moscow church-building. The best example is the Cathedral of the Saviour, built on a cruciform plan, with three apses and four pillars dividing the interior into nine compartments. The vaulting of the nave is higher than that of the aisles, and the corner compartments are lower still, so that, seen from the outside, the church rises in stages to its culminating point in the tall dome.

Other buildings

The most interesting building after the Cathedral of the Saviour is the brick-built Refectory, which dates from the reign of Ivan the Great (1504–06). Adjoining this on the east is the Church of the Archangel Michael and St Alexius (1694–1739), in the style known as Naryshkin Baroque. The tower was built by the neo-Classical architect Rodion R. Kazakov.

Andrey Rublyov Museum for Old Russian Art

Andrey Rublyov himself, the greatest Russian icon painter, is represented in the museum which bears his name only by copies (of excellent quality);

Cathedral of the Saviour

Church of Archangel Michael and St Alexius

most of the originals are in the Tretyakov Gallery (see Tretyakov Gallery), and there are other icons by Rublyov in the Cathedral of the Annuciation in the Kremlin (see Kremlin). The large collection of original icons includes a "John the Baptist" which is attributed to Rubylov's school and a "Death of a Virgin" by Dionisy (end of 15th c.). Associated with the museum is a restoration workshop.

*Arbat F 11 – G 12

Арбат
Arbat

Russian

The Arbat is one of Moscow's oldest streets and appears more frequently than any other in Russian literature. First mentioned in the 15th c. the Arbat was a favourite residential area with the nobility and upper classes. At the beginning of the Sixties large areas of this quarter were sacrificed to the New Arbat (see New Arbat). Nowadays all that remains of the former grandeur is Arbat Street (Ulitsa Arbat) and its surrounding side streets. Until the middle of this century it formed the main shopping and business street in Moscow. After the 1960s it became somewhat overshadowed: the paint peeled off the walls of the houses and the area became dilapidated. Following expensive restoration completed only in 1987, the Arbat is now Moscow's only pedestrian precinct. Numerous small shops and cafés, as well as two rows of decorative street lamps and hanging baskets invite you to spend time strolling through it. Here street musicians sing their songs, artists do lightning portraits of passers-by, and ordinary citizens, freaked-out youngsters and artists all meet and mix.

Location
Centre, west
of the Kremlin

Metro
Arbatskaya/
Smolenskaya

The villas and residences along both sides of the street have been reno-vated in their original style. Many of these houses, with their stucco mould-

Buildings along
the Arbat

The only pedestrian precinct in Moscow . . .   . . . and Pushkin House

ings and pastel-coloured façades, are linked with the names of famous people. The poet Alexander S. Pushkin (see Famous People), for example, spent his honeymoon in No. 53 in 1831. A museum has been opened here in his honour (open: Wed.–Sun. 11am–6pm). On the ground floor a small museum is dedicated to the writer Andrei Belye. Less appealing is the stern greyness of the Vakhtangov Theatre (No. 26). However, its architecture is not detrimental to this artistically renowned street. Its productions, which include classics from the West, are becoming more and more popular. The two ends of the Arbat are architecturally contrasting: while writers had sung the praises of the two-storey Praga restaurant in Arbatskaya Square way back at the start of the century, it was not until the 1950s that the multi-storied building housing the Ministry of Overseas Trade was built, in the so-called "wedding-cake" style, at the junction of the Arbat and the road around the gardens.

As a rule the tourist sees only the "icing on the cake" when he visits the Arbat. However, the brightly-painted house fronts conceal a number of run-down back yards and apartments, with several families sharing one bathroom and kitchen.

Arkhangelskoye   Excursion

Russian   Архангельское
                        Arkhangelskoye

Location
23km/14 miles
west of Moscow

The country mansion and estate of Arkhangelskoye situated 23km/14 miles west of Moscow in the town of the same name is an interesting destination for an excursion (the buildings are currently being restored and are not open to visitors, however, it is possible to walk in the park).

From 1703 to 1810 the estate was owned by the Golitsyn royal family and then came into the possession of the Yusupovs until the Revolution. Golitsyn had a two-storey Classical stone palace built in 1780–90, designed by the French architect Charles de Guerné, on the site of a wooden building. Following the destruction of the mansion by Napoleonic troops and a fire in 1820 comprehensive restoration took place between 1813 and 1830. The estate is famous primarily for the art collection acquired by the Yusupovs, one of the richest families in the country. Although they later transferred many paintings to their palaces in St Petersburg and various works were moved to the St Petersburg hermitage the art treasures which remain in Arkhangelskoye are still extremely impressive.

Metro
Tushinskaya
(then by bus
541 or 549)

**currently
undergoing
restoration**

A gateway with cast-iron gates (early 19th c.) leads to the palace courtyard. The main façade is decorated by a four-columned portico above which rises a belvedere surrounded by Corinthian columns. The façade overlooking the park has a semi-circular bay with pairs of Ionian columns.
After the fire in 1820 the rooms of the palace were restored by J. D. Tyurin. The sumptuous furniture was chiefly made in Russian workshops, the porcelain mostly produced in the Arkhangelskoye factory belonging to the Yusupovs, the majority of the paintings remaining in the palace are by European masters (including Anthonis van Dyck, François Boucher, Claude Vernet and Hubert Robert; among the most valuable works are "Anthony and Cleopatra" and "Cleopatra's Feast" by Giovanni Battista Tiepolo). The upper floor housed the library which used to contain 24,000 volumes making it one of the largest in Moscow.

Palace

The palace is surrounded by a regularly laid out park which is terraced down to the Moskva. Numerous sculptures (mainly copies of ancient originals) and smaller pavilions are found within the park. A monument from 1903 commemorates Alexander Pushkin who stayed at Arkhangelskoye on occasions.

Park

In 1817 Yusupov, who had been director of the imperial theatre for several years, built a theatre in Late Classical style not far to the west of the palace. The actors and singers were serfs who appeared here. The famous stage curtain and decorations designed by the Italian Gonzaga between 1818 and 1825 are on display.

Theatre

---

*Bolshoi Theatre

J 13 (D 2)

Большой Театр
Bolshoy Teatr

Russian

The Bolshoi Theatre (meaning "Great Theatre") epitomises absolute perfection throughout the world. Founded in 1776, the Bolshoi moved two years later into its own theatre, which was subsequently burned down on more than one occasion. The present home of the opera and ballet company is a neo-Classical building erected in 1856. It is fronted by a portico of eight columns with a low pediment bearing a bronze quadriga. The interior is lavishly decorated with white, red and gold predominating. The auditorium seats more than 2000.

Location
Teatralnaya
Ploshchad

Metro
Teatralnaya/
Ochotnyi Ryad/
Ploshchad
Revolutsii

The new productions of the Bolshoi have a rarity value; its repertoire actually includes 70 items. Many of the productions and much of the choreography dates from the 19th c. However, the standard of the dancing in its ballet performances means it has no peers. Since the ensemble is often on tour abroad, however, Moscow theatregoers frequently see only the second or third cast.

Boulevard Ring

Russian

Бульварное Кольцо
Bulvarnoye Koltso

Location
around the centre

Metro
Kropotkinskaya

A stroll around the Boulevard Ring allows the visitor to see Moscow from a different, somewhat quieter perspective. This 9km/6 mile long green belt with traffic lanes running along either side forms a horseshoe shape around the city centre. Here the Muscovites go for a walk, meet, read or enjoy the sunshine on the park benches. A massive city wall up to 6m/19ft thick (designed in 1586–93 by Fyodor Kon) which circled the so-called White City has stood on the site of this "green lung" of the Russian capital since the end of the 16th c. It was reinforced with 37 towers, nine of which had gateways. A moat encircled the walls. Under Catherine the Great the city walls were pulled down having lost their strategic importance. They were replaced in 1775 by the Boulevard Ring with its prestigious buildings interrupted in several places by wide-open spaces where the city gateways once stood.

The oldest and most famous section of the Boulevard Ring is the Tverskoy Bulvar. The section with the architecturally most interesting buildings stretches from the "Moskva" swimming pool to Pushkin Square.

**"Moskva"
Open-air
swimming pool**

The Boulevard Ring begins in the south-west with the Gogolevski Bulvar at the Kropotkinskaya metro station. The heated "Moskva" open-air pool is even open in winter. This was the site of the huge Saviour Cathedral built at the end of the 19th c. which Stalin had demolished in 1931. He wanted to replace it with the tower-like Palace of the Soviets which was to declare the superiority of Communism from a height of 400m/1312ft. The work was interrupted by technical difficulties and the Second World War and the project was eventually abandoned. In 1960 the huge hole was converted into a swimming pool. Recently the Russian Orthodox church has started a campaign to rebuild the Saviour Cathedral and set up a donations fund. But no exact plans of the church have been kept and neither was it one of the architectural treasures of the Russian capital.

House No. 10

This Classical villa was built at the end of the 18th c. by the architect Matvey Kasakov. Members of the secret Decembrist movement used to meet here at M. Naryshkin's house.

**Gogol
monument**

A monument to the writer Nikolai Gogol (1809–52) was erected in the Fifties at the end of the the the Gogolevski Bulwar.

Arbat Square

The old Arbat (see Arbat) and the New Arbat (see New Arbat), formerly Kalinin Avenue, open into Arbat Square.

House No. 7

The next section of the Boulevard Ring is known as Nikitski Bulvar (formerly Suvorowski Bulwar). Nikolai Gogol lived and died in a side wing of house No. 7. Another monument here depicts the writer deep in thought (1909).

**Museum of
Oriental Art**

One of the most splendid houses on the Boulevard Ring is No. 12, which today houses the Museum of Oriental Art. It was built in 1818–22 in Classical style for General P. M. Lunin. A portico with eight Corinthian columns stands on the main façade behind which are the exhibition rooms. The museum, which has been situated here since the Seventies, contains Chinese roll paintings from the 8th–17th c., Chinese porcelain (10–18th c.), Japanese wood carving from the 12th–15th c., various examples of Indian art and above all exhibits from the former Soviet republics of Central and Middle Asia.

At the end of the Nikitski Bulvar on the left soars the Great Church of the Resurrection. In February 1831 Alexander Pushkin married Natalya Gontsharova, a woman renowned for her beauty, in this Late Classical church, built around 1800 and later rebuilt in 1820–40.

Great Church of the Resurrection

At the end of the 18th c. the Tverskoy Bulvar was a popular place for Moscow society to stroll. It is described in the works of Pushkin, Tolstoy and Turgenev.
A monument to the Russian naturalist Kliment Timiryassev (1843–1920) stands at the beginning of this section.

Tverskoy Bulvar

The former living rooms (house No. 11) of the popular actress Maria Yermolova (1853–1928) have been turned into a museum. Through her outstanding acting ability she was a decisive influence on an entire era of Russian theatre.

Yermolova Museum

House No. 25 has made history on more than one occasion. The writer and publicist Alexander Herzen (1812–70) was born here and in the Twenties it was a famous restaurant for writers. It features in Bulgakov's novel "The Master and Margarita" (the devil sets it on fire).

House No. 25

Beyond Pushkin Square (see Tverskaya Street) the Boulevard Ring continues as Strastnoy Bulvar. Its name is taken from the Sufferings of Christ monastery which once stood here.

Strastnoy Bulwar

The Palace of Princess Gagarin (now a hospital) is a notable building on the Strastnoy Bulvar. It is a Classical which was built at the end of the 18th c. by Kasakov. Between 1802 and 1812 the Moscow aristocracy used to meet here in the English Club.

Palace of Princess Gagarin

The Petrovski Bulvar which follows owes its name to the Upper Monastery of St Peter which soars up from the Ulitsa Petrovka. It was founded in 1380 by Dmitri Donskoy, most of the buildings still in existence today are from the 17th c.
A palace in Naryshkin Baroque style houses a literature museum with first editions, manuscripts and portraits of 18th and 19th c. writers.

Upper Monastery of St Peter

Next follows the busy Trubnaya Ploshchad, meaning pipe square. Its name commemorates the pipe which was part of the canalisation of the Neglinnaya. The Tsvetnoy Bulvar continues north with one of the largest peasant markets in Moscow. The building of the traditional Moscow Circus (there is a "new circus") was rebuilt next to it.

Tsvetnoy Bulvar

Rozhdestvensky Bulvar is also named after a convent: the Convent of the Nativity of the Virgin (Rozhdestvensky Ul. 2). It was founded at the end of the 14th c. The main cathedral originates from the beginning of the 16th c. and the narrow bell tower was added in 1835.

Convent of the Nativity of the Virgin

The "boulevard of the clean pond" owes its name to the artificial pond laid out in the centre. Originally there were two ponds here. People used to throw rubbish into them and they became known as the "Dirty Ponds". Following a cleaning-up operation by Alexander Menshikov, a favourite and close confidant of Peter the Great, who acquired the land at the end of the 18th c., they were known as the "Clean Ponds".

Chistoprudny Bulvar

The Cathedral of the Archangel Gabriel, commonly known as the "Menshikov Tower" rises on the west side of the boulevard. Menshikov, who, as can be seen from his palace in St Petersburg, loved large-scale dimensions, built the church in 1704–07 on the site of a predecessor from the 17th c. Its tower was 3.2m/10ft taller than the bell tower on the Kremlin. However, the joy at the high building was short-lived: in 1723 it was struck by lightning and the bell tower was burnt down, the church destroyed. It was not rebuilt until the end of the 18th c. this time with a smaller tower. Despite its altered proportions the church is still an impressive example of Early Baroque.

Cathedral of Archangel Gabriel

Apraskin House | The last building of interest on the Boulevard Ring is Apraskin House at Pokrov Gate (Ulitsa Pokrov 22). Built in 1766–69 the mansion is one of the finest Baroque palaces in Moscow.

Central Lenin Museum — J 12/13 (D 1)

Russian | Центральный Музей В. И. Ленина
Tsentralny Muzey V. I. Lenina

Location
Ploshchad
Revolutsii 2

Metro
Ploshchad
Revolutsii

Open
Tue.–Sun.
10am–5pm

The Central Lenin Museum is housed in the old Duma (Parliament) building, erected in 1890. Since it was opened in 1936 it has had some 50 million visitors. Lenin's life and achievements are fully documented in the Museum's thirty-four rooms, which contain almost 13,000 exhibits – photocopies of his manuscripts, drafts of articles, notes, letters to relatives and associates, editions of his works in 118 languages, photographs, records, personal mementoes, models of the houses in which he lived, etc. On the second floor there is also a full-scale model of his study in the residence of the Russian President in the Kremlin (see Kremlin), which can only be seen with special permission.

Church of the Holy Trinity in Nikitniki — E 1

Russian | Церковь Троицы в Никитниках
Cherkov Troizy v Nikitnikakh

Location
Nikitnikov
Pereulok 3

Metro
Kitay-Gorod

One of the finest Moscow churches, the Church of the Holy Trinity in Nikitniki, lies hidden away in a side street a short distance south-east of the GUM store. A merchant Grigory Nikitnikov had it built in 1631–34 on the territory of his trading estate. Its red wall surfaces, green domes and variagated ceramic friezes are very picturesque. The central cube-shaped main building stands on a tall base and is crowned by the traditional five domes. On the south and north sides of the main church are chapels (the south chapel served the Nikitnikovs as a family mausoleum). The tent-roofed bell-tower is joined to the main church by galleries. For the first time in Russian architecture a tent-roofed stepped portico forms the entrance to a church.

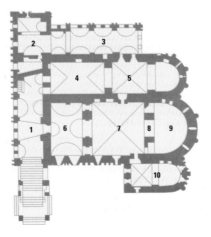

Trinity Church in Nikitniki

1 West Gallery
2 Bell-tower
3 North Gallery
4 Refectory
5 Chapel of St Nicholas
6 Vestibule
7 Community Room
8 Iconostasis
9 Sanctuary
10 Nikita Chapel

© Baedeker

Don Monastery: the West Gate

Trinity Church in Nikitniki

The well-preserved frescoes on the internal walls and cupola date from the middle years of the 17th c.; they show scenes from the life of Jesus and surprisingly the characters represented wear contemporary Russian clothing. The iconostasis, by some of the best icon painters of the 17th c., is noteworthy.

---

*Church of the Intercession in Fili

C/D 12

Церковь Покрова в Филях
Tserkov Pokrova v Filyakh

Russian

The Church of the Intercession in Fili is one of the finest gate churches in Naryshkin Baroque style. It was built in 1693/94, commissioned by an uncle of Peter the Great. The arched base houses the winter church (as is usual for many Russian Orthodox churches) which could be heated. Three large sets of stairs lead up to the main floor, surrounded by a terrace, and the upper church which cannot be heated.

Location
Novosavodskaya
Ulitsa 47

Metro
Fili

Designed by an unknown architect, the square plan has four apsidioles and each apse is crowned by a gilded dome on an octagonal base. Above the central square tower are two tapering octagonal tiers in turn surmounted by a gilded dome with a cross. The white limestone decor is in striking contrast with the red brick walls.

The interior is even more impressive than the exterior. The iconostasis of the upper church, consisting of nine tiers and ornately decorated in gold carvings, reaches up to the vaulting. It was the work of well-known masters of the 17th c., including K. Solotaryov and K. Ulanov. Even the Tsars' box – supposedly used several times by Peter the Great – vaulting and window surrounds are also decorated with gilded carvings.

61

Danilov Monastery

Danilov Monastery

Danilov Monastery

Russian

Даниловский Монастырь
Danilovski Monastyr

Location
Danislovski Val

Metro
Tulskaya

In 1988, on the occasion of the celebration of 1000 years of Christianity in Russia, the Patriarch of Moscow and All the Russias, together with his Holy Synod, moved his seat from the Monastery of the Holy Trinity in Zagorsk to the Danilov Monastery in Moscow.

The monastery was founded at the end of the 13th c. by Prince Daniil Alexandrovich, son of Alexander Nevskiy. The first church was dedicated to St Daniil Stolpnik and the cloisters were also named after him. In 1330 Ivan Kalita dissolved the Danilov Monastery. It underwent a revival during the reign of Ivan the Terrible (1547–84) and new church buildings were constructed. In the 17th c. the cathedral precincts were encircled by a wall with towers. The Cathedral of the Holy Trinity, which dominates the complex today, was built in the 19th c. in neo-Classical style.

After the October Revolution the monastery was closed and used for a time as a children's home and as a prison for young offenders. In 1963 the state handed the cathedral back to the church, which restored it fully with state help.

The four church buildings now shine forth in all their ancient splendour and quite a few new buildings have been constructed, including the patriarch's residence, the administrative wing of the Holy Synod and accommodation for the monks. A modern press-centre was opened in 1988 and a hotel has been added.

*Don Monastery

Донской Монастырь
Donskoy Monastyr

Russian

The fortress-like Don monastery with its seven churches and twelve towers was the southern outpost in the defensive ring of six fortified monasteries designed mainly to protect Moscow from Tartar raids. By the end of the 17th c. it had developed into an important political centre.

Location
Donskaya
Ploshchad

Metro
Shablovskaya

The monastery was founded by Boris Godunov, later to become Tsar, in 1591, during the reign of the feeble-minded Fyodor I Ivanovich. It stands on the site of the Russian armies' position during the decisive battle with the Tartars in 1591, the last time the Tartar army advanced as far as Moscow. The monastery takes its name from a wonder-working icon of the Mother of God of the Don to which the Russians attributed their victory.

Open
Tue., Wed., Thur.,
Sat., Sun.
10am–6pm

The Old Cathedral, built in 1591–93, remained until the end of the 17th c. the monastery's only building. The New Cathedral, in the centre of the square area enclosed by the defensive walls built between 1686 and 1711, was founded in 1684 By Sofya Alekseevna, Regent for her brother Peter I, and consecrated in 1698. Of the 18th c. buildings the most notable are the Gate Church of the Virgin of Tikhvin and the West Gate, both in Naryshkin Baroque style.

The five-domed New Cathedral (1684–98) is in the form of a Greek cross, with each arm of the cross terminating in a large apse and apsidoles flanking the apse on the east side.

New Cathedral

The beautiful interior has a fine Baroque iconostasis with eight tiers of late 17th c. icons. Until the October Revolution the icon of the Don Virgin, now in the Tretyakov Gallery (see Tretyakov Gallery), was on the lowest tier. The frescoes on the pillars and walls, like the icons, date from the late 17th c.

On the south side of the monastery is the park-like cemetery, notable particularly for its burial chapels and tombs of the Baroque period. A board at the entrance lists well known people buried here (the architect Osip. I. Beauvais, the historian Vasily Klyutchevsky, the painter Vasily Perov, relatives of Tolstoy and Turgenev, among others).

Cemetery

Until the beginning of the Nineties the New Cathedral housed a branch of the Shchusev Museum of Architecture. Scattered about the monastery precints are pieces of sculpture from monasteries and cathedrals which have been destroyed or demolished.

Shchusev
Museum
of Architecture

Gorky Museum

Музей А. М. Горького
Musey A. M. Gorkogo

Russian

The Gorky Museum is housed in one of the most splendid Art Nouveau buildings in Moscow, Shekhtel House, which is worth a visit on its own.

Location
Ulitsa Kachalova
6/2

The architect Fyodor Shekhtel built the house in 1900–02 for the banker and industrialist Ryabushinsky. With its asymmetrical balconies and the mosaic frieze it is a typical example of an Art Nouveau villa, or "modern style" as it is known in Russia. The interior also designed by Shekhtel has been preserved. The rooms are grouped around the elegant curved staircase.

Metro
Arbatskaya/
Pushkinskaya

Open
Fri. noon–6pm,
Thur., Sat., Sun.
10am–5pm
Closed last Thur. of
month

In 1931 the house was put at the disposal of Maxim Gorky (1868–1936), who had meanwhile become the greatest revolutionary writer in the USSR. Gorky lived here together with his son, daughter-in-law and their children until he died. Famous literary figures and politicians, including Stalin, were guests here. The museum has been open to visitors since 1965. The interior has been left as it was when Gorky lived here.

Gorky Park

Russian

Парк Культуры и Отдыха Имени Горького
Park Kultury i Otdycha Imeni Gorkogo

Location
Krimski Val

Metro
Park Kultury/
Oktyabrskaya

Gorky Park, situated almost in the centre of Moscow, is one of the many public gardens large and small scattered throughout Moscow (see Practical Information, Parks and Gardens). The gardens, originally laid out in 1938, today offer the visitor 110 hectares/275 acres of varied leisure pursuits. There are large lawns and flower beds where you can relax as well as several small lakes (boats for hire). The attractions include roundabouts, a giant wheel, an open-air theatre (rock concerts take place from time to time) and a bowling alley. In winter, when it freezes, the park becomes a veritable skater's paradise, for large areas are flooded and the whole area turns into a giant ice-rink.

Gorky Street

See Tverskaya Street

*GUM

Russian

Государственный Универсальный Магазин (ГУМ)
Gosudarstvenny Universalny Magazin (GUM)

Opposite the Lenin Mausoleum, on the north-east side of Red Square is Russia's largest department store, Gosudarstvenny Universalny Magazin

The GUM store in Red Square

(State Universal Store), or GUM for short. This huge glass-roofed complex, 252m/825ft long by 90m/295ft across, was built between 1888 and 1894, replacing the old "Trading Rows" which had previously occupied the site. Restored in the 1950s, its three storeys now house 200 shops, over an area of 70,000sq.m/753,480sq.ft, which attract some 200,000 customers every day.

GUM is very different from a Western department store: a more appropriate comparison would be with a Western shopping centre. But instead of American-style glass and concrete architecture GUM has ornate bridges and gangways, Old Russian shop-fronts, chandeliers, mirror walls and much stucco ornament.

A general view of the interior can be had from the balustrade above the fountain in the centre of the complex. The swarming crowds of shoppers from different nationalities make a spectacle which will be one of the visitor's memories of Moscow.

At the moment GUM – together with other major department stores in Moscow – is still state-owned, but a lot of the floor space is being let out to private companies.

Location
Red Square
(Krasnaya
Ploshchad)

Metro
Pl. Revolyutsii

Open
Mon.–Sat.
8am–10pm

---

*Historical Museum

J 12/13 (D 1)

Государственный Исторический Музей
Gosudarstvenny Istorichesky Muzey

Russian

The Historical Museum, first opened in 1883, borders the north side of Red Square. Its 44,000 exhibits, in forty-eight rooms, document the history of Russia and the former Soviet Union from the Palaeolithic period, Kievan Russia, the dominance of the Golden Horde and the beginnings of the principality of Moscow to the consolidisation of the centralised State, the

Location
Red Square
Krasnaya
Ploshchad

Historical Museum

Metro
Pl. Revolyutsii

Open
Closed at
present

cultural history of Russia in the 17th–19th c. and the Communist movement centred on Lenin.

Following the founding of the Historical Museum on 22nd February 1872, work began on the present building, designed by Aleksandr A. Semyonov and Vladimir O. Sherwood, with its façade in the Old Russian style. The architects were concerned to fit the building into the architectural pattern of Red Square, taking as their models St Basil's Cathedral (see St Basil's Cathedral) and the Kremlin Walls (see Kremlin). The interior was designed by Aleksandr P. Popov, and the museum was opened to the public in 1883. The holdings of the museum have swollen – by gifts and donations, but mainly by acquisition of material from all over the former USSR following the nationalisation of land and property – to such an extent that it cannot display one tenth of what it possesses.

Kitay-Gorod   J/K 12/13 (D/E 1)

Russian

Китай-Город
Kitay-Gorod

Location

East of the
Kremlin

Metro
Pl. Revolyutsii/
Kitay-Gorod

The Kitay-Gorod quarter east of the Kremlin – bordered in the south by the Moskva, in the east by Novaya and Staraya Ploshchad, in the north by the remains of the old town wall near the Ulitsa Nikolskaya – is together with the Kremlin one of the oldest parts of Moscow. There is evidence of a settlement dating from the 11th c. In 1543 the quarter was fortified with an earthen wall and a palisade and work began one year later on a red stone wall. It was strengthened by 14 towers and was linked to the Kremlin walls. The origin of the name Kitay-Gorod (literally translated "Chinese town") is still unexplained today. It is thought that "Kitay" is derived from the Old Russian word "kit" which meant woven baskets (these were used to scoop up and carry the earth used in the building of the town wall).

At first it was chiefly the nobility, rich merchants and high officials of the church who settled in Kitay-Gorod followed by artisans and poorer traders. Up until the 18th c. Kitay-Gorod was the only district of Moscow where trading was permitted. Towards the end of the 19th c. large banks and business houses were built and the stock exchange was located here. In time other parts of the quarter became dilapidated, especially the area near the Moskva which with its run-down tenements and cheap dives was a slum area before the Revolution. This area was thoroughly "renovated" at the beginning of the 1960s: one of the largest hotel complexes in the world, the Rossiya, was built here. The tone of the area was completely changed: many old residential and merchant houses, churches and other buildings in Kitay-Gorod were restored and are now listed buildings creating an impression of the atmosphere of past centuries; in addition Kitay-Gorod is also the administrative centre of the Russian capital, many institutions and ministeries have their headquarters here.

A round tour of the quarter could end in the Ulitsa Nikolskaya, on the northern end of Red Square (see Red Square).

Nikolskaya Ulitsa

The old and new name of the Nikolskaya Ulitsa is taken from the monastery of the same name. From 1935 to 1992 it was known as the Street of 25th October commemorating the fighting which took place in 1917 around the Kremlin.

The beginning of Nikolskaya Ulitsa is dominated by a side façade of the GUM department store (see GUM), on the opposite side the former Kazan Cathedral (see Red Square) is being rebuilt.

Zaikonospasskiy Monastery

In the courtyard of No. 7 is the Saviour Cathedral of the former Zaikonospasskiy Monastery. Founded in 1600 the monastery housed the Slavic-Graeco-Latin Academy; one of its most famous pupils was the scientist Mikhail Lomonosov. Of the former monastery, which was dissolved in 1917, apart from the 17th c. cathedral (later rebuilt several times) only a 17th c. house and the former school from 1882 have been preserved.

No. 15 with its magnificent white and green façade dates from 1814. It once housed the Synodal Printing House, nowadays it is the School of History and Archivism. Two 17th c. buildings have been preserved in the courtyard of the Synodal Printing House. They belonged to the Imperial Printing House. In an earlier building the first book in Russia was printed in 1564, the "History of the Apostle"; in 1702 the first edition of the newspaper "Vedomosti" appeared.

Synodal Printing House

Diagonally opposite the printing house in the side street (Bogoyavlenski Pereulok) the dome of the Epiphany Monastery (Bogoyavlenski Monastery) is visible. Founded in the 13th c. the remaining buildings date from the 17th c. and are a striking example of Baroque architecture in Moscow. During excavations recently carried out what is thought to be the earliest stone church in Moscow (14th c.) was discovered. Services still take place in the monastery cathedral.

Epiphany Monastery

No. 17 the Slavyanski Bazar is one of the most well known restaurants in Moscow. Various famous personalities have eaten here in the past including Tchaikovsky, Chekhov and Turgenev.

Slavyansky Bazar

No. 21 Nikolskaya Ulitsa is the oldest chemist's shop in Moscow, opened in 1701. A new building was constructed by the German chemist Ferrein who took it over in 1895.

Old Chemist's shop

The Sherkasky Bolshoy Peroylok leads to the Ulitsa Ilyinka which runs parallel (until recently known as Ulitsa Kuybysheva). Magnificent buildings which were built as banks and insurance companies at the end of the 19th c. and beginning of the 20th c. dominate the street. Nos. 7 and 9 built in Art Nouveau style still house the Finance Ministry. The Stock Exchange (No. 6) was built in 1839 and rebuilt in 1875 (nowadays Chamber of Trade and Industry).

Ulitsa Ilyinka

As a change from the magnificent façades the visitor can stroll from the east end of the Ulitsa Ilyinka in a southerly direction along the Staraya Ploshchad. The narrow Nikitnikov Pereulok leads to the Trinity Church in Nikitniki (see Trinity Church in Nikitniki).

Trinity Church in Nikitniki

There are numerous interesting buildings on the Ulitsa Varvarka (formerly Ulitsa Razina) which runs parallel to the Ulitsa Ilyinka. It was named in the 16th c. after the Church of St Barbara (Barbara = Russ. Varvara).

Ulitsa Varvarka

The first is the Church of St George (No. 12) built in 1657. The bell tower was not added until 1818. Today it is used as an exhibition hall.

Church of St George

Inside the entrance to the Rossiya Hotel is the former Monastery of the Manifestation (Znamenskiy Monastery). This monastery was founded by the first Romanov Tsar Mikhail on the site of his mansion (thus the name Old Tsar's Palace). The cathedral, a red brick building with five domes, dates from 1681. The adjacent bell tower is from the second half of the 18th c.

Monastery of the Manifestation/ Old Tsar's Palace

The House of the Boyars also belonged to the complex of the former Monastery of the Sign (Old Tsar's Palace). It is now a museum (No. 10; entrance directly opposite the Rossiya Hotel; open: Mon., Thur.–Sun. 10am–5pm, Wed. 11am–6pm). It is one of the oldest preserved residential houses in Moscow, the oldest parts are from the 15th c. The Romanov family had the building restored in 1857–59 and the upper floor, which had been destroyed, rebuilt in wood. The rooms of the Boyar House (work room, dining room, ladies quarters, etc.) give a good idea of what life was like in the 17/18th c.

House of the Boyars

The Old Bazaar (No. 3) on the other side of the street occupies a whole block of houses. The influential architect Giacomo Quarenghi designed the Classical building built in 1790–1805.

Old Bazaar

In the Church of St Maxim (No.6; end of 17th c.) are remains of a 18th c. wall painting.

Church of St Maxim

Monastery of the Manifestation

House of the Boyars

Old English House

Set back is the Old English House (No. 4). Ivan the Terrible gave the building to English merchants. The lower floor was used as a warehouse, the main floor consists of reception and ceremonial rooms.

Church of St Barbara

The last building on the left side of the Ulitsa Varvarka is the Classical Church of St Barbara (1794).

*Kolomenskoe   L 5

Russian

Коломенское
Kolomenskoe

Location
Prospekt
J. Andropova 39

Metro
Kolomenskaya

Open
Park: daily
10am–7pm;
Museum: Wed.–
Sun. 11am–5pm

The history of the village of Kolomenskoe can be traced back to the 14th c. In the 15th c. it was owned by the Grand Prince of Moscow, and in the 16th c. became the summer residence of the Tsars. Peter the Great spent his childhood here and the Tsars Catherine I, Anna and Elisabeth stayed here.

Unfortunately nothing remains of the magnificent wooden palace buildings erected in the 17th c. in Kolomenskoe. They were demolished by Catherine the Great as they had fallen into disrepair (the Tsars meanwhile preferred the summer residences around St Petersburg).

Kolomenskoe was declared an open-air museum in 1923 with its churches, towers and gates. As a result other wooden buildings were added from different parts of the country. The charm of Kolomenskoe lies not just in its impressive wooden buildings but in its situation on the Moskva and the beautiful park with its old trees.

Church of the Mother of God of Kasan

Through the entrance gate (Saviour Gate) stands the Church of the Mother of God of Kasan. The church with its blue domes, decorated with stars, was built in the middle of the 17th c., at the same time as the Tsar's palace which was mentioned above. As it was the Tsars' private church it was connected

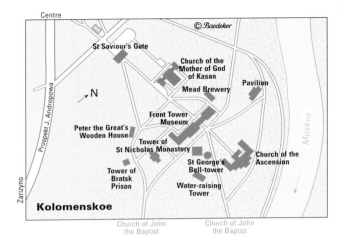

Church of John   Church of John
the Baptist   the Baptist

to the palace with an underground passage. The wall paintings inside the church (church services) date from the 19th c.; the iconostasis contains the icons of the Mother of God of Kasan (early 17th c.).

The Front Tower built in 1672/73 is crowned by a tent-roofed bell tower. The adjoining buildings were the working quarters and administrative buildings of the palace (17th c.). Today they serve as exhibition rooms. A special attraction is the model of the 17th c. Tsars' palace. It was recreated in the second half of the 19th c. by the woodcarver Smirnov according to plans and views of the façades which were made before the place was demolished. Other exhibits include a 17th c. writing room (windows of mica schist), an exhibition labelled "Russian Metallic Art (15th–18th c.)" and various wooden implements of the 17th–19th c. Compared to other Moscow museums the exhibition rooms are very well labelled (in four languages).

Front Tower/ Museum

The oldest and most impressive building in Kolomenskoe is the Church of the Ascension, towering up on a high terrace above the Moskva. It is believed that Vasily III had it built in the years 1530–32 in order to give thanks for the birth of a successor to his throne (the later Tsar Ivan the Terrible). This imposing sacred building does not follow the traditional cruciform domed church style; it is, in fact, the first Russian church with a pyramidal tent-roof to be built in stone. The cruciform plan is surmounted by a tall base structure, followed by an octagonal structure crowned by the pyramidal roof. The very top forms a small dome. The church is surrounded by arcades with steps at various levels. As the walls had to be 3–4m/10–13ft thick for constructional reasons, the interior is very small.

Church of the Ascension

The St George bell tower near the Church of the Ascension is 16th c.; the tower which provided the estate with water is from the 17th c.

Bell tower, water tower

Looking out from the arcades of the Church of the Ascension, the Church of St John the Baptist can be seen up on a hill in the neighbouring village of Djavako (within comfortable walking distance through the park). The architecture of this church, built in the middle of the 16th c., anticipates that of St Basil's Cathedral (see St Basil's Cathedral). The central octagonal tower is surrounded by eight octagonal chapels which are linked by galleries.

Church of St John the Baptist

Kolomenskoe: Bell-tower and Water-tower

Wooden house of Peter the Great	The wooden house of Peter the Great, which he lived in for several months in 1702 while supervising the construction of the Russian fleet at Arkhangelsk, was moved to Kolomenskoe in 1934. The three small rooms which the Tsar could only enter by stooping have been reconstructed in detail.
Other buildings	Other buildings which have in the course of time been sent here include the tower of the Bratsk prison (Siberia, 1652), the tower of the St Nicholas Monastery in Karelia (1692) and the mead brewery from the village of Preobrazhenskoe (near Moscow, also 17th c.).

Kremlin

H/J 11/12 (C/D 1)

Russian	**Кремль** Kreml
Location Centre	A citadel looming over Moscow from its commanding position 40m/130ft above the River Moskva, with the city's main streets radiating from it in all directions; a stronghold in the form of an irregular quadrilateral with an area of 28 hectares/70 acres; palaces and cathedrals, enclosed within a wall 2235m/2445yd long, up to 19m/62ft high and up to 6.5m/21ft thick; a fortress ringed by twenty towers and gates: the Kremlin is the heart and soul of Moscow, once the seat of the highest authority – over whom in the words of a Russian proverb, there was only God – and still the centre of government, since the end of 1991 with the Russian red-blue-white tri-colour flying overhead. The Russian president is based here and the Parliament of the People's Deputies meets at least twice annually in the Kremlin. The Kremlin is bounded on the south-east by the Moskva, on the north-east by Red Square (see Red Square), on the north-west by the Alexander
Metro Bibl. Im. Lenina/ Borovitskaya/ Alexandrovski Sad	
Open Fri.–Wed., 10am–7pm (1 May–30 Sept.) Fri.–Wed. 10am–5pm (1 Oct.–30 Apr.)	

Kremlin

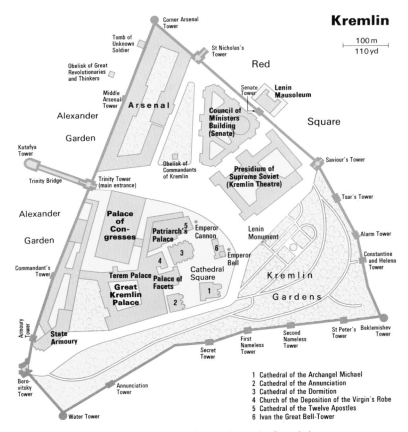

Scale: 100 m / 110 yd

Corner Arsenal Tower
Tomb of Unknown Soldier
St Nicholas's Tower
Obelisk of Great Revolutionaries and Thinkers
Middle Arsenal Tower
Arsenal
Red
Senate Tower
Lenin Mausoleum
Council of Ministers Building (Senate)
Alexander Garden
Square
Kutafya Tower
Trinity Bridge
Trinity Tower (main entrance)
Obelisk of Commandants of Kremlin
Presidium of Supreme Soviet (Kremlin Theatre)
Saviour's Tower
Alexander Garden
Palace of Congresses
Patriarch's Palace
5 Emperor Cannon
Lenin Monument
Tsar's Tower
Alarm Tower
4 3
6 Emperor Bell
Constantine and Helena Tower
Commandant's Tower
Terem Palace
Palace of Facets
Cathedral Square
Kremlin
Great Kremlin Palace
1
Gardens
2
State Armoury
First Nameless Tower
Second Nameless Tower
St Peter's Tower
Beklemishev Tower
Secret Tower
Armoury Tower
Borovitsky Tower
Annunciation Tower
Water Tower

1 Cathedral of the Archangel Michael
2 Cathedral of the Annunciation
3 Cathedral of the Dormition
4 Church of the Deposition of the Virgin's Robe
5 Cathedral of the Twelve Apostles
6 Ivan the Great Bell-Tower

Garden (see Alexander Garden) and on the south-east by Borovitsky Square (Borovitskaya Ploshchad).

In 20th c. usage the term "Kremlin" has come to be used as a synonym for the "government", but it was originally a general term applied to a fortified stronghold or district of a town (analogous to the acropolis of a Greek city), usually situated on high ground above a river or between two rivers (the Moscow Kremlin lay between the Moskva and the Neglinnaya, which has flowed underground since 1817/19). The word "kremlin" may be derived from the Greek "kremnos", a crag or steep escarpment.

The medieval Kremlin contained within its circuit of walls and towers the seats of secular and ecclesiastical authority and the residences of the country's rulers – a palace, government offices, a monastery, a church or cathedral, etc. This was the capital of the principality of Moscow as described in the first quarter of the 16th c. by an emissary of the Holy Roman Empire, Sigmund von Herberstein: "On account of its size the castle may well be called a small town, for within its walls are not only the large and magnificent houses of the Princes but also the residences of the Metropolitan, the Grand Prince's brother and the principal members of

View of the Kremlin from the bank of the River Moskva

the Council, who all have large wooden mansions here, and within the castle there are many churches."

When the Kremlin was rebuilt from 1475 onwards the highest secular and ecclesiastical authorities in the land, the Tsar and the Metropolitan, had their residences here; and the architecture of the Moscow Kremlin became the standard model for kremlins throughout Russia.

The huge area of the Kremlin reflected the requirements of defence at the time it was built. With the development of the cannon in the 14th c. the Kremlin had to be capable of withstanding artillery. The palace, churches and government offices had as far as possible to be outside cannon range, and accordingly an area of open space was left between the walls and the buildings within them.

It was only at the beginning of the 17th c., after the occupation of the Kremlin by Polish forces and their subsequent surrender, that the old defensive structures began to give place to the palatial buildings which give the Kremlin its distinctive character today.

Tour

The main entrance to the Kremlin for tourists is the Kutafya watch tower on the edge of the Alexander Garden (the opening times given above relate to the Kremlin area and the visits to the cathedrals and museums). The ticket offices for the Kremlin, cathedrals and museums together with a cloakroom and toilets are located here (if you are undecided which cathedral or museum to visit then it is best to buy a ticket to the Kremlin area; tickets can be bought at the individual cathedrals or museums). Visitors who only wish to see the State Armoury should enter by the Borovitsky Tower.

Only part of the Kremlin is open to visitors. Closed off areas are marked by a white line and guards are often on duty. Entry to these areas is forbidden. Access to the interior of the cathedrals, the Museum of Russian Folk Art and Culture in the 17th c. housed in the Patriarch Palace and the Armoury containing the diamond collection is allowed. The other buildings, the government buildings, are – as in almost every other state in the world –

Kremlin: Kutafya Watchtower . . .   *. . . and Trinity Gate-tower*

closed to visitors. In the evenings plays, concerts and films may be seen in the Congress Palace (see Practial Information, Theatres and Concerts).
The entrance fees to the Kremlin area and the cathedrals are relatively low. However, entrance to the Armoury and diamond treasury is quite expensive (Armoury: 10 US dollars, diamond treasury 16 US dollars). Guided tours around the Kremlin and the museums are expensive and the visitor must decide whether to join one of these for him/herself (Intourservice offers these tours, see Practical Information, Information). All the buildings open to the public can be visited on an individual basis.
Photography is allowed in the areas not cordoned off but is forbidden in the cathedrals and museums.

History

The earliest fortified structure is mentioned in 1156, during the reign of Yuri Dolgoruky, who is regarded as the founder of Moscow. It lay near the present Borovitsky Tower and covered perhaps a tenth of the area now occupied by the Kremlin. When Batu Khan captured Moscow in 1238 the Tartars burnt down the Kremlin. One year later the high ground between the Moskva and the Neglinnaya was surrounded by an oak palisade. The Metropolitan of "Kiev and All Russia" moved his seat from Vladimir to the Kremlin in 1325/26. Prince Ivan I Kalita erected the first stone building in the Kremlin, the Cathedral of the Dormition in 1326/27. Following fires in 1331 and 1337 the Kremlin was rebuilt in timber in 1339.

Early wooden buildings

Grand Prince Dmitri – later to be known as Dmitry of the Don after his victory over the Tartars – built the first stone Kremlin. The white limestone of the the walls led many travellers to call Moscow "the white city". Subsequently various government buildings and churches were erected, including the Cathedral of the Annunciation between 1397 and 1416. Its interior was decorated in 1405 by Feofan Grek, Andrey Rublyov and Prokor

White Kremlin

the Elder of Gorodets. In 1445 the Kremlin was almost completely destroyed by fire.

Italian period

The years from 1474 to about 1530, during the reigns of Ivan III (the Great) and his son Vasily III, were a period of great building activity which largely gave the Kremlin its present appearance. Ivan the Great summoned architects to Moscow not only from other towns in Russia but also from northern Italy (the Milan school). The following buildings were designed by Italian architects: 1475 to 1479 the Cathedral of the Dormition (A. Fioravanti), 1485–1516 the walls (Pietro Antonio Solari, Alovisio Novo), 1487–91 Palace of Facets (Marco Ruffo, Pietro A. Solari), 1505–08 Ivan the Great Bell-Tower (Bon Fryasin) and the Cathedral of the Archangel (Alovisio Novo). Russian architects from Pskov built the Cathedral of the Deposition of the Robe 1484/85 and between 1484 and 1489 the Cathedral of the Annunciation.

The buildings of this period, however, cannot be classified as belonging to the Italian Renaissance. To meet the requirements of the time and place the foreign architects had to find a synthesis between the Italian architecture with which they were familiar and the general style of the Kremlin as it had developed over the centuries. In addition, the Kremlin now not only had to meet the requirements of defence, but also to reflect the power and dignity of the strongest state in Eastern Europe and the Russian Orthodox Church as the head of the "third Rome".

The walls along the Red Square side of the Kremlin (see Red Square) were completed in 1500. Between 1508 and 1516 a moat 32m/105ft wide and 12m/40ft deep was dug below the walls on the Red Square side, linking the Moskva with the Neglinnaya. At first sight the Kremlin and the town of Moscow seemed two quite separate entities: on the one hand the brick-built fortress looming over the town with its white cathedrals, on the other the low wooden houses of the ordinary people. In fact, however, the town fitted into the general plan centred on the Kremlin: its streets radiated from this central point and surrounded it in successive rings. These circles are still recognisable in the Boulevard Ring and Garden Ring.

The late 16th and early 17th c. were a period of decline: in 1547 much of the Kremlin was destroyed by fire, in 1571 the Tartars of the Crimea took Moscow and devastated the town and Kremlin, in 1610 Polish troops occupied the Kremlin. Two years later Russian troops and partisans recovered the Kremlin; the Polish occupying forces surrendered.

Russian "fairy-tale" style

After the destruction wrought by the Tartars and the Poles the rebuilding of the Kremlin began, with more emphasis on decorative quality and less on the military aspects. The feature characteristic of this period is the tall pyramidal tent roof, first seen in the Cathedral of the Ascension, Kolomenskoe (1532) (see Kolomenskoe) and found also on the central tower of St Basil's Cathedral (1555–1560; see St Basil's Cathedral).

A further characteristic is the liking for decoration already mentioned. Stylistic elements, both external and internal, were taken over from palace architecture and used in building churches, with the object of creating a house of God which should surpass all secular buildings in splendour and magnificence. Buildings in this style are: 1624–25 Saviour's Tower superstructure (Christopher Halloway), 1627 St Catherine's Church, 1635/36 Terem Palace (Trefil Sharutin), 1635/36 Upper Cathedral of the Saviour and 1652 the Pleasure Palace. During the reign of the Patriarch Nikon, who had banned tent roofs and ornate decoration in the 1650s as being profane, the Patriarch's Palace and the Cathedral of the Twelve Apostles were built between 1653 and 1656.

In 1658 Nikon abdicated and two years later he was officially relieved of his post. Although in subsequent years tent roofs were little used, the decoration became still more lavish and more fantastic. The towers on the Kremlin walls were given tent roofs between 1670 and 1685.

Naryshkin Baroque

After a time the stock of ideas of the decorative period were obviously exhausted and the first intimations of Europeanisation were unmistakable;

and in the 1680s the Baroque style came to Russia. The principal builder of secular buildings was a boyar named Naryshkin, a relative of Peter the Great, and accordingly the term "Naryshkin Baroque" is commonly applied to this period. Models were provided by architectural works imported from the West. The surviving examples of this style in the Kremlin are mainly of the late 17th c., since after the transfer of the capital from Moscow to St Petersburg in 1712 Peter the Great forbade the building of houses in stone anywhere except St Petersburg (1714). Examples of Naryshkin Baroque in the Kremlin are: 1680/81 the Church of the Resurrection (Terem Palace), 1681 the Church of the Crucifixion (Terem Palace) and 1702 to 1736 the Arsenal.

In 1773 a general rebuilding of the Kremlin in Classical style was planned by Catherine the Great, It was, fortunately, not carried out, but some of the towers on the Moskva side are destroyed during preparatory work. From 1776 to 1788 the Senate (now the residence of the Russian president) was built.

Classicism

In 1812 Napoleon, before leaving the smoking ruins of Moscow with his Grand Army, ordered the Kremlin to be blown up. The people of Moscow sabotaged most of the operation, but the Water Tower, the First Nameless Tower and the Ivan the Great Bell Tower were blown up. The restoration of the Kremlin followed between 1813 to 1818 and the moat on the Red Square side was filled in. The damaged towers were restored under the direction of Osip I. Beauvais. After the Neglinnaya was covered over in 1817–19 so that it flowed underground through a brick conduit, the Alexander Garden (see Alexander Garden) was laid out in 1821 by Osip I. Beauvais. By 1825 the restoration of the Kremlin was for all practical purposes complete.

Later buildings were the Great Kremlin Palace (Konstantin, A. Thon, Nikolay I, Chichagov and others) in 1838–49 and the State Armoury (Thon, Chichagov and others) from 1844 to 1851.

The post-Revolutionary period has been mainly concerned with restoration and renovation work in the Kremlin. This work has restored the Kremlin, not perhaps to its old splendour but to a new splendour which it has not known for centuries. The churches have been restored and frescoes exposed, though the tasteless decorations of Nicholas I's reign cannot be reversed and a number of historic old buildings have been lost. Two monasteries have been demolished, but the other cathedrals are now mostly museums.

20th c.

From 1932 to 1934 the Presidium of the Supreme Soviet (today the Presidium of the Russian Federation), originally designed as government offices, was built with the Kremlin Theatre. In 1937 the towers were topped by five-pointed Soviet stars, which revolve slowly and are illuminated at night. The last building to be built was the Palace of the Congresses in 1960–61.

Borovitsky Gate-tower (Borovitskaya Bashnya)

The Borovitsky Gate-tower, at the west end of the Kremlin walls, was erected in 1490 during the rebuilding of the Kremlin by Pietro Antonio Solari. It is a massive cubic structure built in brick with a series of receding storeys. The tent-roofed superstructure was added in the 1670s, when almost all the Kremlin towers received their present roofs. Like many of the towers, the Borovitsky Gate-tower is topped by a five-pointed Soviet star, 3m/10ft high and weighing 1.5 tonnes, which is illuminated at night. The total height of the Borovitsky Gate-tower is 50.7m/166ft.

The tower occupies the position of the oldest entrance to the Kremlin. Its name is derived from the word "bor" (forest) – suggesting that the original settlement on the site of Moscow was established in this wooded area (now represented by only a few trees), on the Neglinnaya and near the Moskva, by people who lived by hunting and fishing.

Kremlin

Borovitsky Barbican

Great Kremlin Palace

Barbican

In addition to the normal gateway flanked by towers the Kremlin gates originally had the additional protection of a barbican or outwork. These (none of which survive) were usually in front of the gate; in the case of the Borovitsky Gate-tower the barbican was on one side. The chains of the drawbridge over the Neglinnaya ran through openings in the front of the gate.

The passage through the barbican had portcullises, which could be lowered on the approach of an enemy. The space thus enclosed, with embrasures and machiolations, could be kept under surveillance from above.

Walls

The distance between the towers was determined by the range of the firearms then available. The towers also served as buttresses to increase the strength of the walls.

Along the top of the walls between the towers ran wall-walks with swallow-tail embattlements up to 2.5m/8ft high, embrasures and a wooden roof.

**State Armoury (Gossudarstvennya Oruzheinaya Palata)

Open
Mon.–Wed., Fri.
10am–5pm

The State Armoury is the oldest museum in Russia and one of the richest. Among its treasures are the crown jewels and coronation insignia of the Tsars, historic arms and armour, costumes and furnishings, icons and manuscripts, coaches, sleighs, State carriages, objets d'art and much else besides.

The collection includes not only Russian art but the arts and crafts of Western and Northern Europe and the East as well. The Armoury's displays of English silver and German goldsmiths' work of the Baroque period, for example, are among the finest collections of their kind in the world.

History

Although the Armoury has for centuries been a museum it still preserves its old name, here in the time of the Princes, Grand Princes and Tsars arms and armour were made and stored.

Façade of the State Armoury Museum in the Kremlin

The collection dates from the time of Ivan the Terrible. During the "Italian period" a special stone building was erected to house the Tsars' treasures. The original collection of arms and armour, military booty, royal insignia, gifts to the Tsar, carriages, etc., grew to such an extent that when it was moved to Novgorod in 1571 to escape the Tartars no fewer than 450 sleighs were required to transport it.

The heyday of the Armoury was in the second half of the 17th c. In 1654 Bogdan Khitrovo was appointed Director, and under his management the most talented craftsmen and painters in the old Russian art centres (Yaroslavl, Ustyug, Uglich, etc.) were summoned to Moscow to work in the Armoury. When St Petersburg became the capital in 1712 the artists and craftsmen left Moscow for the new capital. In 1812, when Napoleon was advancing on Moscow, most of the Armoury's treasures were evacuated to Nizhny Novgorod (now Gorky) for safety, to be brought back in the following year.

The present Armoury building, in pseudo-Russian style, with features borrowed from Naryshkin Baroque, was erected between 1844 and 1851. It is in architectural harmony with the Great Kremlin Palace, also designed by Thon and Chichagov.

Until the October Revolution the Armoury housed the Court Museum. After the Revolution the collections were enriched by treasures from the Kremlin cathedrals and the Patriarchal Treasury and by the crown jewels. Thereafter the museum was completely reorganised – a process which was completed in 1961. Further rebuilding resulted in its being closed for a period of three years in the 1980s.

Visiting

For a long time the museum was only open to group visits but it is now accessible to individuals. Entrance tickets are on sale on the ground floor. Admission to the Diamond Collection in the State Armoury is extra. The tours usually commence from the first floor.

Kremlin

First floor
Rooms 1 and 2

Russian and Byzantine Art:
The Ryazan Hoard, gold and silver ladles, a goblet belonging to Prince Yuri Dolgoruki, icon mounts (including that of the famous Icon of the Virgin of Vladimir), mass icons, Gospel covers, goldsmiths' work, etc.

Room 3

Arms and armour of the 15th–19th c.
Helmet of the Grand Prince Yaroslav Vsevolodovich of Kiev (reigned 1238–46) with silver ornamentation. The inscription states that the helmet belonged to Yaroslav, father of the famous Alexander Nevsky. Helmet of Tsar Mikhail Romanov, the "Jericho Hat", Moscow work 1621. Also Western armour, horse-armour, flintlocks.

Room 4

Arms, armour and spoils of war:
Golden keys of the city of Riga, Bible belonging to the Swedish King Charles XII, Russian medals awarded during the Nordic War (1700–21), Swedish rifles. The wrought-iron door to Room 4 is decorated with the coats-of-arms of Russian cities.

Room 5

Gifts made to the Tsars by West European ambassadors (arranged in country order):
Magnificent table-settings, bowls, drinking vessels. One showcase alone is filled with Sèvres porcelain, a service presented by Napoleon I to Tsar Alexander I to commemorate the Peace of Tilsit.

Ground floor
Room 6

Church vestments and secular robes:
Vestments of Metropolitans Pyotr, Aleksey and Photius; robe belonging to Peter the Great; coronation robes of Catherine I and Catherine the Great.

Room 7

Thrones of Russian Tsars and royal insignia:
The ivory throne of Ivan the Terrible; Boris Godunov's throne (wood, covered with gold-leaf; more than 2000 precious stones); the throne of Mikhail Fyodorovich, the first Romanov Tsar; the Diamond Throne of Tsar Aleksey Mikhailovich (over 8000 diamonds); the triple throne of the joint Tsars Ivan V and Peter I and their sister and Regent Sofya Alekseevna.
The Cap of Monomakh:
The Cap (or Crown) of Monomakh is believed to have been a gift from the Tartar Khan to Grand Prince Ivan I of Kalita. It was used in the coronation of all Grand Princes of Moscow and Tsars of Russia until Peter the Great's coronation as Emperor in 1721. It is probably 14th c. Oriental work (emeralds and rubies; gold plates with spiral patterns in gold wire; a cross encrusted with pearls).

Ivory throne

Legend has it that this crown was a gift from the Byzantine Emperor Constantine IX Monomachus (1042–55) to Vladimir II Monomakh of Kiev (1113–25), but the dates alone make this impossible. The legend was evidently designed to establish the legitimacy of the Russian princes. The presentation of the Byzantine royal insignia (including the Cap of Monomakh) to the Grand Prince of Kiev is depicted on the sides of Ivan the Terrible's throne in the Cathedral of the Dormition.

Room 8

Riding equipment:
Saddles, bridles and other horse trappings from Russia (Tsar Mikhail Fyodorovich's saddle), the Caucasus, Central Asia, Europe, China, Iran and Turkey.

Collection of State coaches: Room 9

Coach presented to Boris Godunov by Queen Elizabeth I; small coaches and sleighs made for the boy Peter I; the coronation coach of Tsaritsa Elizabeth; the summer coach of Catherine the Great.

Also on the ground floor (extra admission fee) in a special security wing is the diamond treasury of the Russian federation, a unique treasure house containing gold bars, precious stones, jewellery and ornaments of exquisite beauty. The most notable exhibits include the great Tsars' Crown (inlaid with 5000 diamonds), allegedly the largest gold bar ever (36kg) and the so-called Orlov diamond (189.6 carats, one of the largest polished stones in the world); a present to Catherine the Great from her lover Count Orlov. Diamond Treasury

Great Kremlin Palace (Bolshoy Kremlyovsky Dvorets)

The Great Kremlin Palace was formerly the Tsar's Moscow residence. In addition to the Tsar's apartments, which have been left intact, it contains the Assembly Hall of the Supreme Soviet of the Russian Federation. **No admission**
The palace with its 700 rooms was built in place of Rastrelli's winter palace for Tsar Nicholas I between 1838 and 1849 by Konstantin A. Thon and Nikolay A. Chichagov and associates. The main front facing the Moskva is 125m/410ft long, in a style which harmonises with the Armoury and the Terem Palace. At first sight the building seems to have two storeys above the ground floor, but in fact there is only one upper storey with a double row of windows.

In the south wing of the ground floor are the former private apartments of the Tsar. The rather tasteless decoration and furnishings, left untouched after the Revolution for their historical interest, are a mixture of Late Rococo, neo-Classical, neo-Old Russian and other eclectic elements borrowed from the styles of the past. Ground floor

The upper floor with its double row of windows contains the State apartments, named after various Russian orders, including St George's Hall (named after the Military Order of St George, founded by Catherine II in 1769), a hall 61m/200ft long by 20m/65ft wide which is now mainly used for government receptions. Upper floor
St Andrew's Hall (the Old Throne Room) and St Alexánder's Hall were combined in 1933–34 (architect Ilarion. A. Ivanov-Shits) to form the Assembly Hall of the Supreme Soviet of the USSR and RSFSR (Now Assembly Hall of the Russian Federation). On the end wall of this large hall (seating for 3000), which is familiar to the Soviet public through its appearance in television news reports, is a monumental marble statue of Lenin.

Cathedral Square (Sobornaya Ploshchad)

Flanking this square in the centre of the Kremlin are the most important of its historic buildings – as the name of the square indicates, principally the cathedrals.
On the south side, adjoining the Great Kremlin Palace, is the Cathedral of the Annunciation. To the right of this is the Cathedral of the Archangel Michael, the only one of the Kremlin cathedrals to have silver domes (though the central dome has recently been gilded). Next to this rises the Kremlin's tallest building, the Ivan the Great Bell-Tower, at the foot of which is the world's largest bell, the Emperor Bell.
On the north side of the square, set back a little, stands the former Patriarch's Palace with the Cathedral of the Twelve Apostles, now housing the Museum of 17th Century Folk Art and Culture. Between the Patriarch's Palace and the Bell-Tower is another great tourist attraction the Emperor Cannon (Tsar-Pushka).

Also on the north side of the square is the Cathedral of the Dormition, in which the Tsars were crowned. To the left of this, partly concealed, is the Church of the Deposition of the Robe. Between the Church of the Deposition of the Robe and the Palace of Facets to the west extends the east wall of the Terem Palace, with the cluster of golden domes belonging to the Tsar's domestic chapels (Upper Cathedral of the Saviour, Church of the Resurrection, Church of the Crucifixion).

The cathedral square was originally formed at the beginning of the 14th c., in the reign of Ivan Kalita. Since the great building and rebuilding operations of 1475 to about 1530 it has been the central point of the Kremlin, and thus of Moscow.

Cathedral of the Annunciation (Blagoveshchensky Sobor)

The Cathedral of the Annunciation with its nine gilded domes is the smallest of the three main Kremlin cathedrals, but the decoration of the interior (in particular the frescoes and icons by Andrey Rublyov and Feofan Grek) makes it one of the greatest treasures of Moscow.

The cathedral was built in 1484–89 by a team of builders from Pskov as the Court Church of Grand Prince Ivan III. It was connected by a passage at gallery level with the palace of the Grand Prince and later with the Tsar's residence. The passage still leads from the Gallery into the Great Kremlin Palace, which immediately adjoins the cathedral.

The nine domes and the arcade on the south side are reminiscent of the Cathedral of the Dormition in Vladimir, but there are also Renaissance features, since the Cathedral of the Annunciation was influenced by Aristotele Fioravanti's Cathedral of the Dormition, built only a short time earlier.

History

There were two earlier churches on the site – a 14th c. church on the foundations of which the present cathedral is built, and a slightly later one built between 1397 and 1416, during the reign of Vasily I, with paintings by Feofan Grek, Andrey Rublyov and Prokhor the Elder. This latter church, having become unsafe, was pulled down in 1482 and was replaced two years later by the present cathedral, built of brick on the high stone base of the earlier churches. It was in the shape of a cube with four pillars supporting the main dome and two domed apsidioles flanking the main apse. The church was surrounded by galleries – at first open but later given vaulted roofs – on the north, west and south sides.

After the 1547 fire Ivan the Terrible had the church restored and enlarged. Two "blind" domes were added flanking the main dome, and four small chapels with small domes and their own iconostases were built at gallery level, bringing the number of domes to nine. The domes were regilded in 1963.

In 1572, still in the reign of Ivan the Terrible, a further chapel was built at the south-east corner of the church and the steps leading up to the north-east entrance were constructed. In the 19th c. the sacristy was installed in the porch of the south-east chapel.

Interior

The visitor entering the Cathedral of the Annunciation is surprised by its small size, the space being still further reduced by the royal gallery at the west end, and by the paintings which cover every inch of the walls. The pavement of polished jasper dates from the reign of Ivan the Terrible.

Over the years the frescoes were frequently restored and over-painted, but during the thorough restoration of the church which was completed in 1961 the original layers of painting were exposed. An inscription records that the paintings were the work of Feodosy (Theodosius), son of Dionisy (Dionysius) and his assistants (1508). The finest of the frescoes are on the pillars, in the apse and diakonikon and on the gallery. Particularly worth seeing is the picture of the Apocalypse in west part of the rear gallery, as well as

Cathedral of the Annunciation ▶

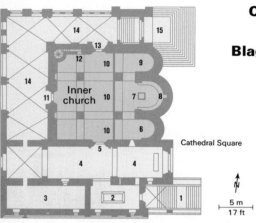

Cathedral of the Annunciation

Blagoveshchensky Sobor

Inner church

Cathedral Square

1 Groznensky Steps
2 Reliquary
3 Sacristy
4 Parekklesion
5 South doorway
6 Diakonikon
7 High Altar
8 Bishop's throne
9 Prothesis
10 Iconostasis
11 West doorway
12 Up to choir
13 North doorway
14 Gallery
15 Steps to gallery

5 m
17 ft

the magnificently coloured fresco of "Christ on a White Horse" in the south-west corner below the gallery.

Iconostasis

The iconostasis is the icon-screen, with three doors, which separates the sanctuary of an Orthodox Church from the body of the church. In Russian Orthodox churches the iconostasis frequently reaches right up to the roof vaulting. The iconostasis originated as a simpler form of separation

Icons in a side-room of the Cathedral of the Annunciation

between the sanctuary and the rest of the church, with images on the beams of the architrave and curtains which later gave place to painted wooden panels. In Russia the iconostasis reached its full development at the end of the 14th c.

The iconostasis of the Cathedral of the Annunciation is the embodiment of a fully developed Russian iconostasis. According to the chronicler the paintings in the earlier church were by Feofan Grek, Andrey Rublyov and Prokhor the Elder from Gorodets. The chronicle also records that Rublyov's iconostasis was destroyed in the great fire of 21st June 1547. The restoration work revealed, however, that only some of the icons were damaged in the fire. The iconostasis is divided vertically into the door level and four tiers above this: the "chin" (rank, dignity) tier; the festival tier; the tier of the Prophets; and the tier of the Patriarchs.

The door level forms the base of the iconostasis: the central or royal door, the north door to the left and the south door to the right. The metal facing of the iconostasis (beaten bronze, gilded), including the ornamental mountings of the royal door and the base, are 19th c. work, to the design of Nikolay A. Sultanov.

The royal door, symbolising the gates of heaven, which led into the sanctuary could be used only by ordained priests and deacons. Formerly the (theocratic) Tsar was also allowed to pass through this door. Between the royal door and the north door there was always an image of the Virgin. In this case it is the famous virgin of the Don painted by Feofan Grek (copy; original in Tretyakov Gallery, see Tretyakov Gallery). Between the royal door and the south door are a figure of the Saviour enthroned (1337) and a 17th c. copy of the Ustyug Annunciation (Tretyakov Gallery, see Tretyakov Gallery).

The north and south doors lead into the two small rooms on either side of the sanctuary, the prothesis on the north side in which the bread and wine for the Eucharist were prepared and the diakonikon on the south side in which liturgical vestments and books were kept.

Immediately above the doors is the principal tier of the iconostasis, the chin tier. The central group of icons on this tier is the Deesis or Intercession, with Christ as the Judge of the world enthroned in the centre and Mary (on left) and John the Baptist (on right) interceding for mankind. This, the basic Deesis, is here extended to include the Archangels Michael and Gabriel, the Apostles Peter and Paul and two Greek Fathers of the Church, Basil the Great and John Chrystostom.

On the festival tier are fifteen icons of the annual Festivals of the Church. It was this tier that suffered most damage in the 1547 fire.

In the centre of the tier of the Prophets is the Mother of God, with icons of the Prophets on either side. The icons were painted after the 1547 fire, probably by artists from Pskov.

On the top tier, under ogee arches, are head-and-shoulder figures of the Old Testament Patriarchs, flanking a central icon of the Trinity. The icons are mostly 19th c.; one or two date from the 16th and 17th c.

*Palace of the Facets (Granovitaya Palata)

The Palace of the Facets, built in 1487–91 by Marco Ruffo and Pietro Antonio Solari, is the only part of the huge complex constituted by the Great Kremlin Palace, the Terem Palace and associated buildings which has been almost completely preserved in its original form.

No admission

The name of the palace, which is almost exactly square in plan, comes from the faceted limestone blocks which pattern the main front – a form of rustication which originated in the early Italian Renaissance. The windows on the second floor, with rectangular framings in Naryshkin Baroque style and ornate columns borne on brackets, replaced the original twin pointed windows after a fire in 1682.

The main entrance to the palace used to be on the south side. From here the "red" or "beautiful staircase" led to the Holy Vestibule. Nowadays the only

Palace of Facets; in the background the East Front of the Terem Palace

entry to the Palace of Facets is from St Vladimir's Hall in the Great Kremlin Palace.

Interior

The wall-paintings in the Holy Vestibule, the ante-chamber to the Great Hall, are 19th c. Two of the six doorways, decorated with carving and gilded, are false doors installed in the reign of Nicholas I.

The historic old Great Hall, on a square plan with four low groined vaults borne on a single pier, creates a powerful impression by its size (just under 500 sq.m/5400 sq.ft) and its magnificent wall-paintings. It served as a throne room and reception room. The original frescoes were destroyed in 1612, during the Polish occupation, and repainted in 1668 by Simon Ushakov. The present paintings were done in 1882 by two icon-painters from Palekh under the direction of the brothers Vladimir and Vasily Belusov, following detailed descriptions of earlier frescoes by Ushakov himself. This restoration was necessary beause the frescoes had been covered with whitewash in the 1670s and the walls hung with red velvet, following Western European models.

The inner doorway, with carved decoration in Renaissance style, dates from the 15th and 16th c. The gilding of the carving and the ogee arch was carried out in the reign of Nicholas I; the canopy over the throne dates from the same period.

*Terem Palace (Teremnoy Dvorets)

No admission

A cluster of golden domes, glimpsed between the Palace of Facets and the Church of the Deposition of the Robe, is all that the ordinary visitor will see of this, the most splendid of the Kremlin's palaces.

In 1681–82 the Tsar's domestic chapels – the Upper Cathedral of the Saviour, the Church of the Crucifixion and the Church of the Resurrection – were given a common roof, out of which rise eleven gilded domes. The ornate crosses and the coloured tiles on the brick drums of the domes were designed by a woodcarver named Ippolit the Elder.

The history of the building can be more easily followed on the south front (described below), which can only rarely be seen by visitors, than on the small section of the east side glimpsed between the Palace of Facets and the Church of the Deposition of the Robe. The following is a brief account. The original Terem Palace was built by a team of architects (Antip Konstantinov, Bazhen Ogurtsov, Ivan Sharutin and others) in 1635–36 for Mikhail Fyodorovich, the first Romanov Tsar. There was much alteration and rebuilding in the 19th c., as a result of which only parts of the two long basement storeys survive from the original palace. Parts of the ground and first floors go back to Ivan III's palace, built by Aleviz Fryazin (Alevisio or Aloisio of Milan) in 1499–1508.

On these two basement storeys, set back, is the cube-shaped residential block, also of two storeys, with a flat roof surrounded by a balustrade which served as a terrace. Above this again, set further back, is the Teremok, a tower or belvedere, with a hipped roof which was originally gilded. In this were the quarters of the royal children.

History

In the basement storey on the east side of the palace is one of the few rooms to survive in its original state, the Golden Chamber of the Tsaritsa, named after its gilded decoration and wall-paintings. The vaulted ceiling of this room, in which the Tsaritsa used to receive high ecclesiastical and secular dignitaries, is borne on a single massive arch. The wall-paintings which have been exposed since 1947 date from the late 16th c.: ''Baptism of Grand Princess Olga'', ''Triumphal Procession of Tsaritsa Dinara after the Defeat of the Persians''.

The three east windows look out on the little square between the Palace of the Facets and the Church of the Deposition of the Robe.

Golden Chamber of the Tsaritsa

On the north side of the Golden Chamber is St Catherine's Church, the Tsaritsa's domestic chapel, built by John Taylor in 1627. It was enclosed by other buildings and spoiled during the construction of the Great Kremlin Palace in 1838–49.

St Catherine's Church

This church, above the Golden Chamber, was built in 1635–36 and served as the Tsar's domestic chapel. The main features of interest are the iconostasis with its facing and royal door of beaten silver (1778) and the 17th c. icons. One of the icons is said to be an authentic portrait of Christ ''not made by the hand of man''.

Upper Cathedral of the Saviour

Between the Upper Cathedral of the Saviour and the residential block is the Stone Forecourt. The staircase which descends from here to the Boyars' Square on the south side of the palace (the Lower Golden Staircase) is closed by a gilded copper grille (1670), decorated with a host of fabulous animals, long-tailed birds, horned heads, etc., within a pattern of spirals.

Stone Forecourt

The Upper Golden Staircase leads to the Church of the Crucifixion, built in 1681. It is notable particularly for the icons on the splendidly decorated iconostasis. Dating from soon after the building of the church, these are embroidered on silk, only the exposed parts of the body (face and hands) being painted in oil. Also of interest are the Crucifix by Ippolit the Elder (1687), a ''Last Judgment'' by Ivan Y. Saltanov and a ''Passion'' from the Armoury workshops.

Church of the Crucifixion

From the Church of the Crucifixion a richly decorated door leads into the Church of the Resurrection (1680–81), with a fine gilded iconostasis (about the turn of the 17th–18th c.).

Church of the Resurrection

The churches described above and the Golden Palace of the Tsaritsa lie behind the east wall of the Terem Palace, which can be seen between the

South front

Palace of Facets and the Church of the Deposition of the Robe. Concealed behind the south front are the royal apartments. The south front is of fantastic effect with its squat pilaster-like features containing recesses and its double-arched windows topped by pediments (mostly broken) and richly carved limestone framings with a pendant between the arches ending in an animal's head. In recesses in the cornice strip under the terrace balustrade are coloured tiles with coat of arms and plant and animal designs. The doorways of the teremok are still more richly decorated: limestone arabesques with winged horses amid swirling foliage ornament, a pelican, winged Cupids armed with bows emerging from blossoms and shooting at birds.

Royal apartments

The apartments on the third and fourth floors are reached from the Stone Forecourt by way of the Lower Golden Staircase. The five private apartments of the Tsars have low vaulted roofs with vaulted windows containing 19th c. stained glass which admits only a dim twilight. The interior apartments, painting and ornament combine to enhance the fairy-tale effect created by the south front. A visitor might well be forgiven for thinking that he had strayed into some Oriental palace from the "Arabian Nights".

Church of the Deposition of the Virgin's Robe (Risopolsensky Sobor)

In front of the eleven domes of the Terem Palace is the Church of the Deposition of the Virgin's Robe, with a single dome. It was built in 1484–85 by the Pskov architects who were also responsible for the Cathedral of the Annunciation (1484–89). The church, which was linked by a staircase with the Patriarch's Palace, served as the domestic chapel of the Metropolitans and Patriarchs.

Exterior

The church is built on the foundations of an earlier church erected in 1451 and burned down in 1473. From Cathedral Square it is seen as a cubic structure on a high base. The three low projecting apses have blind arcading with ogee arches. Barrel vaults, also with ogee arches, form a transition to the dome, its tall drum resting on an octagonal base. The doorway on the south side, which is approached by a flight of steps, is framed in receding ogee arches.

Interior

The Church of the Deposition of the Robe is cruciform, with four pillars supporting the dome. The wall-paintings, which have been completely exposed only since the 1956 restoration, date from 1644 and are almost entirely on themes from the Acathist Hymn, a hymn of four verses in honour of the Virgin which is attributed to Romanus the Melodist, a hymnographer of the 5th/6th c. The fine iconostasis (1627) is from the workshop of Nazary Istoniou.

**Cathedral of the Dormition (Uspensky Sobor)

The Cathedral of the Dormition of the Virgin is the largest and most historic of the cathedrals in the Kremlin. Here Princes, Grand Princes and Tsars were crowned by the Metropolitan or Patriarch, here Metropolitans and Patriarchs were enthroned and buried, and here many a chapter in the history of Moscow and of Russia began or was concluded. From its completion in 1479 until the end of the 17th c. it provided an unmatchable model for all cathedral-building in Russia.

The Dormition (Falling Asleep or Death) of the Virgin, a festival celebrated by the Orthodox Church on 15th August, corresponds to the Roman Catholic festival of the Assumption, also celebrated on 15th August. The Cathedral of the Dormition is, therefore, sometimes referred to – wrongly – as the Cathedral of the Assumption.

In 1325/26 Pyotr, Metropolitan of Kiev and all Russia, moved his seat from Vladimir to Moscow, and in the same year Ivan I. Kalita laid the foundation-stone of the Cathedral of the Dormition, Moscow's first stone church. It was consecrated on 4th August 1427.

In 1475–79 this church was replaced by a new Cathedral of the Dormition built by the Bologna architect Aristotele Fioravanti for Ivan III as a state church. This church has survived substantially in its original form (minor alterations to the façade after the 1547 fire and other small alterations to the interior in the mid 17th c.).

While Fioravanti's cathedral provided a model for all later Russian cathedrals it was itself, according to the chroniclers, modelled on the Cathedral of the Dormition in Vladimir, which in turn had been built in 1158–61 in deliberate rivalry to the Cathedral of the Dormition in Kiev (1073–78). The historical background was as follows:

When, in 1299, Maksim, Metropolitan of Kiev and All Russia, moved his seat from Kiev to Vladimir on account of the Tartar menace, Vladimir inherited Kiev's role as the ecclesiastical centre of the Russian principalities. During the reign of the Metropolitan Pyotr (1307–26) contacts between the head of the church in Vladimir and the Moscow Princes and Grand Princes became increasingly close, and in 1325/26 the Metropolitan moved from Vladimir to Moscow. (Pyotr was subsequently canonised in 1339.) Moscow had thus succeeded Kiev and Vladimir as the seat of the Metropolitan, and its status as the political successor to Vladimir was finally established by Dmitry Donskoy's victory in the Battle of Kulikovo (1380).

But although Ivan Kalita built a Cathedral of the Dormition in the Kremlin immediately after the Metropolitan's move to Moscow this church still fell far short of the Vladimir Cathedral of the Dormition in magnificence and splendour. In order to remedy this Ivan III sent Aristotele Fioravanti to Vladimir, not so much to get ideas for his own new Cathedral of the Dormition as to have a standard of comparison which he could surpass by building a still more sumptuous cathedral. The cathedral in the Kremlin admittedly owes a good deal to imitation but it owes much more to the consummate skill with which Fioravanti developed elements taken from Vladimir into something new and distinctive.

The most striking view of the Cathedral of the Dormition is from the south-east. In spite of the cruciform plan which is revealed by the central

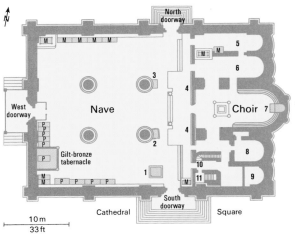

Cathedral of the Dormition
Uspensky Sobor

1 Throne of Monomakh (Ivan the Terrible's throne)
2 Patriarch's throne
3 Seat of the Tsaritsa
4 Iconostasis
5 Chapel of SS Peter and Paul
6 Side chapel
7 Bishop's throne
8 Chapel of St Demetrius
9 Sacristy
10 Staircase to Chapel of the Virgin
11 Staircase to sacristy

M Tombs of Metropolitans
P Tombs of Patriarchs

87

Cathedral of the Dormition

dome and the four subsidiary domes, all gilded, it is seen as a rectangular mass: the five low apses at the east end project only very slightly and do not detract from the compact effect; and the apses are rendered still more unobtrusive by the boldly projecting pilasters at the end of the east front and the greater projection of the three round-headed gables (zakomary) on the east front as compared with those on the south front.

The cathedral, built of limestone and brick, stands on an unusually high base (4m/13ft; but compare the substructure of the Church of the Deposition to the rear), though this is largely concealed by raising the level of Cathedral Square.

The south front was the main front, with the main entrance (there are also doorways on the west end and the north side). The façade is vertically articulated by pilasters with imposts supporting the semicircular arches of the gables. Horizontally it is patterned by the base, a tier of blind arcading and a range of four slit windows like arrow-loops under the gables.

The arched south doorway is the finest of the cathedral's three doorways. It is decorated with frescoes which, like those on the west doorway, date from the 16th c. Painted on sheet copper in gold on a black ground, they depict Biblical scenes; above, the Virgin and Child.

Interior

The interior is of striking effect, thanks to its paintings but even more to its size and lightness. Compare the tiny Cathedral of the Annunciation, built by Russian architects, rendered still smaller by the royal gallery at the west end. In the Cathedral of the Dormition Fioravanti omitted the west gallery and created a spacious hall, with groined vaulting borne on four round piers (and four square pillars behind the iconostasis).

Throne of Monomakh

To the left of the south doorway is the throne of Ivan the Terrible (1551), a magnificent example of Russian woodcarving. It is also known as the Throne of Monomakh, after the carvings on the sides depicting the presentation of the Byzantine imperial insignia by the Emperor Constantine IX

Monomachus to Grand Prince Vldimir of Kiev, symbolising the transfer of Byzantine imperial authority to Russia. The presentation of the "Cap of Monomakh" (now in the Armoury) is also depicted.

Along the north and south walls of the Cathedral are the tombs of Metro-   Patriarchs' tombs
politans and Patriarchs of the Russian Orthodox Church. The last Patriarch was Adrian (1690–1700), after whose death Peter the Great left the Patriarchal throne vacant, establishing instead (in 1721) the Holy Ruling Synod as the Church's highest authority. The Patriarchal constitution was restored by the Soviet Government, and on 5th November 1917 Tikhon, Metropolitan of Moscow, was chosen by lot to be Patriarch of the Russian Orthodox Church.
The gilt-bronze tabernacle in the south-west corner of the church, with a tent-roofed canopy borne on ogee arches, contains the sarcophagus of the Patriarch Germogen or Hermogenes (1606–12). Hermogenes had excommunicated the Polish invaders of Russia, and because of his anti-Latin (i.e. Polish and anti-Catholic) campaigns as imperial administrator and quasi interrex he was murdered by the Polish invaders in 1612. After his death the Patriarchal throne was left vacant for Filaret, a member of the Romanov family, who in 1608 had set up as a rival Patriarch under the second False Dmitry and in 1619 was officially enthroned as Patriarch, assuming the style of Veliky Gosudar (Great Sovereign), hitherto reserved for the Tsar.

The frescoes of 1642–43 underwent extensive restoration between 1911   Frescoes
and 1960. The earliest frescoes in the church were painted by Dionsy in the 1480s; then in 1513–15, when they were already in poor condition, they were overpainted; and finally in 1642–43 more than a hundred icon-painters from all over Russia took part in the third painting of the church, carefully following the originals. In 1773 the frescoes were overpainted in oils, and further overpainting was carried out in the reign of Nicholas I.

In 1812 the cathedral was occupied by Napoleon's Grand Army. The icons   Iconostasis
were used as firewood, and some 250kg/550lb of gold and 5 tons of silver were carried off. Most of this booty was abandoned during the French army's retreat and was recovered and returned to the cathedral. The 16m/52ft high iconostasis dates from 1652; the silver-gilt frame is 19th c. Most of the icons are copies (originals in the Tretyakov Gallery, see Tretyakov Gallery), but a few, particularly on the lowest tier, are original.
At door level are icons of the "Saviour with the Fiery Eye" (14th c.), the "Dormition" and the "Old Testament Trinity" (16th c.; head of right-hand angel 14th c.). To the left of the royal door is the famous "Virgin of Vladimir" (a 17th c. copy; original in the Tretyakov Gallery). Other fine icons are those of Metropolitan Peter, with sixteen scenes from his life (c. 1480), St George (12th c.) and St Alexius the Man of God.

Patriarch's Palace, with the Cathedral of the Twelve Apostles
(Patriarsky Dvorets y Sobor Dvenadtsaty Apostolov)

The three-storeyed palace of the reforming Patriarch Nikon, with the Cathe-   **Open**
dral of the Twelve Apostles which served as his private chapel, now houses   Mon.–Wed.,
the Museum of 17th Century Russian Art and Culture.   Fri.–Sun.
Erected in 1653–56, the building reflects Nikon's objection to the tent roof   10am–5pm
as reminiscent of secular building and his dislike of the Old Russian or "fairy-tale" style: like the Cathedral of the Dormition, it is a compact mass on a high base, with a cruciform plan and five domes.

The principal attraction is the Hall of the Cross, a vaulted hall with an area of   Hall of the Cross
250sq.m/2700sq.ft, its roof supported without the use of columns. This was   (Room 1)
the meeting place of Church Synods and the scene of State receptions. When the Patriarchate was replaced by the Holy Ruling Synod in the reign of Peter the Great the palace was occupied by monks, who produced the consecrated oil in the Hall of the Cross.

Patriarch's Palace

Iconostasis in Twelve Apostles Cathedral

A prominent feature of the room is the stove (1675–80) used in the preparation of the consecrated oil. Another interesting item is the silver basin (1767) in which the oil was kept.

Other rooms of the museum (Rooms 2–5)

In the small side rooms off the Hall of the Cross are Russian and Western European silver (silver chess set, 17th c. silver globe from Augsburg), Oriental fabrics and Russian pearl embroidery.
Among the other exhibits are arms and armour, gold liturgical utensils, tiled ovens and domestic equipment.

Cathedral of the Twelve Apostles (Room 6)

The iconostasis in the Cathedral of the Twelve Apostles (also accessible from upper floor of the Patriarch's Palace) is from the Monastery of the Ascension (demolished after the October Revolution) which was from around 1700. The other icons on display are from various churches and monasteries.

*Emperor Cannon (Tsar Pushka)

The Emperor Cannon is the world's largest cannon, with a calibre of 890mm/35in., 5.34m/17ft long and weighing 40 tonnes, it was cast in 1586 by Andrey Shchokhov. On the barrel is a likeness of Tsar Fyodor I. Ivanovich. The gun carriage (designed by Alexander Bryullov) and the cannon balls lying in front of the cannon are merely decorative, an addition from the first half of the 19th c. The original site of the cannon, which has never had to be fired, was the south end of Red Square, aimed at the Moskva Bridge. Peter the Great had the cannon moved, together with other famous weapons, to the Arsenal in the Kremlin, it was erected in front of the Arsenal in 1835. It has stood on its present site since 1960.

The Emperor Cannon　　　　　　　　*The Emperor Bell*

*Emperor Bell (Tsar Kolokol)

At the foot of the Great Bell-Tower is the world's largest bell, the 210 tonne Emperor Bell "Tsar Kolokol". It is 6.14m/20ft tall and has a diameter of 6.60m/21.6ft.

The Bell ("Zar Kolokol") was cast by Ivan and Mikhail Motorin in 1734–35 during the reign of the Empress Anna Ivanovna and consists of just under 80 per cent copper. It is decorated in relief with portraits of the second Romanov Tsar, Aleksey Mikhailovich, and the Empress Anna Ivanovna, five icons and two inscriptions relating the origin of the Bell.

During the great fire of 1737 the bell was still in the foundry pit and had to be sprayed with water to prevent it melting. However, because of the difference in temperature a piece broke off weighing 11.5 tonnes. For almost 100 years it lay buried in earth until the architect Auguste Ricard Montferrand, who did most of his work in St Petersburg, unearthed it and put it on a granite base. It was he who added the crowning imperial orb and gilded cross.

*Ivan the Great Bell-Tower (Kolokolnya Ivan Veliky)

The Ivan the Great Bell-Tower consists of the Bell-Tower, the adjoining Belfry in the north and the Filaret Building. The lower floor of the Belfry houses temporary exhibitions from the museums of the Kremlin.

The site of the present complex was originally occupied by an early 14th c. church built by Ivan I. Kalita and dedicated to St John Climacus (c. 579–649), a hermit who became Abbot of St Catherine's Monastery on Sinai and wrote a celebrated treatise, the "Ladder of Paradise" ("Klimax tou Paradeisou"). The church was replaced in 1505–08 by a two-storey church built by Bon Fryazin (Marco Bono), also dedicated to St John (Ivan) Climacus. The tower was built at the same time; an additional storey was added in the reign of Boris Godunov.

History

The Bell-Tower itself survived the attempt by Napoleon to blow it up in 1812 but the adjoining buildings were completely damaged. Rebuilding soon followed in 1814/15.

The 81m/266ft high Ivan the Great Bell-Tower, with 329 steps and a view extending over 40km/25 miles (visitors are not permitted to climb the tower), is the tallest building in the Kremlin (Boris Godunov had declared that no other building in Moscow should exceed it and until the end of the Second World War it was the tallest structure in Moscow).
The tower, built of brick, stands on a base of white dressed stone. Successive storeys, octagonal in plan, decrease in size, ending in platforms with arched openings for the bells. The top section, with the dome and its summit cross, was added in 1600, as part of a three-part inscription (regilded in 1967) records: "By the grace of the Holy Trinity and on the order of Tsar and Grand Prince Boris Fyodorovich, autocrat of All Russia, this sacred place was completed and gilded in the second year of their reign."

The Belfry, next to the Bell-Tower, was built between 1532 and 1543 by an Italian architect known as Petrok Maly. The Renaissance features in the lowest storey on the side facing Cathedral Square are unmistakable. In the arched openings hang the bells, the heaviest of which is the 19th c. Dormition Bell (65.5 tonnes).

The third element in the complex, also with tower and arched openings for bells, was built in 1624 during the reign of the Romanov Patriarch Filaret whose name it bears.

Cathedral of the Archangel Michael (Arkhangelsky Sobor)

The Cathedral of the Archangel Michael, built in 1505–08 by Alevisio the Younger, was the burial church of the Tsars. Here all the Princes, Grand Princes and Tsars from Ivan Kalita onwards had their last resting-place, with the exception of Boris Godunov, who, with his wife, is buried in the Monastery of the Trinity at Sergyev Possad (see Sergyev Possad; formerly Zagorsk). After St Petersburg became the capital in 1712 the Tsars and Emperors from Peter the Great onwards were buried in the cathedral in the Peter and Paul Fortress; the exception was Peter II, who died of smallpox in Moscow in 1730.

The present church was built on the foundations of an earlier church built by Ivan Kalita in 1333 in thanksgiving for relief from famine. The original church had frescoes (not preserved) painted by Feofan Grek (Theophanes the Greek) in 1399.
The demolition of the first Cathedral of the Archangel began on 21st May 1505, and the new one built by Alevisio the Younger was consecrated on 8th November 1508: a rectangular structure with a system of five domes displaced towards the east end. The two slightly smaller domes are over the lateral apses. Unlike the other Kremlin cathedrals, the Cathedral of the Archangel has silver domes, apart from the recently gilded central dome. The cathedral was surrounded on three sides by galleries, which were demolished in the 18th c. with the exception of part of the south gallery. The tent-roofed annexe at the south-west corner was built in 1826, and the buttresses on the south side were also later additions. The two single-domed chapels beyond the north and south apses date from the mid 16th c. The cathedral was thoroughly restored in 1955.

The façade, like that of the Cathedral of the Dormition, is divided by pilasters topped by imposts bearing the rounded gables. The five vertical divisions of the north front are of different widths, corresponding to the

◀ *Ivan the Great Bell-tower*

Cathedral Square

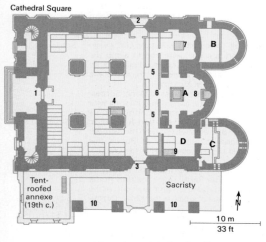

Cathedral of the Archangel

Arkhangelsky Sobor

A Chapel of the Archangel
    Michael (altars)
B Chapel of St Varus
C Chapel of John the Baptist
D Diakonikon

1   West doorway
2   North doorway
3   South doorway
4   Reliquary of Tsarevich Dmitry
    Ivanovich
5   Iconostasis
6   Royal door
7   Altar of Offerings
8   Bishop's throne
9   Tomb of Ivan the Terrible
10 Buttresses

10 m
33 ft

various elements in the plan. The narrow westwork contained the Chapel of St Aquila, with windows opening into the nave, which was originally reserved for ladies of the royal family.

At the east end is the section containing the sanctuary and apses. On the north side is the Chapel of St Varus, a tiny structure with a single dome. Horizontally the building is articulated by an ornamental frieze half-way up the wall, with blind arcading below this and above it a series of blind recesses and – the most striking feature of all – scallop shells under the gable arches.

Interior

The interior appears very narrow, with square pillars breaking it up into three barrel-vaulted aisles. The most notable features are the royal tombs, the frescoes and the iconostasis.

Tombs

The forty-eight brick sarcophagi (some of which are double) contain the remains of fifty-four Princes, Grand Princes and Tsars and some of their sons; they all date from 1636–37. The uniform bronze covers were added in 1903, during the reign of the last Tsar, Nicholas II. The finest tombs are those of Tsarevich Dmitry and Ivan the Terrible.

On the north side of the south-east pier is the reliquary of Dmitry Ivanovich (murdered in 1591), of limestone, partly gilded, which dates from 1638. The silver plate with scenes from Dmitry's life which formerly covered the reliquary is now in the Armoury. Dmitry was killed at Uglich in 1591, when he was eight years old, in circumstances which remain mysterious. Popular opinion blamed Boris Godunov for his death. During the Time of Troubles a number of "False Dmitrys" came forward, each claiming that he was the legitimate heir to the throne who had escaped Boris Godunov's attempt on his life. The best known of the pretenders were the first two, known as Pseudo-Demetrius I and II. The remains of the murdered Prince were transferred to the Cathedral of the Archangel in 1606 by Tsar Vasily IV Shuisky, and thereafter were revered as wonder-working.

Frescoes

Of the frescoes painted by Feofan Grek in the earlier cathedral in 1339 nothing survives. The early 16th c. frescoes of the new cathedral were removed a century later and replaced by new ones. The sequence of the original frescoes was recorded before they were destroyed, and although the new paintings followed the same pattern they were very different in style. Among the painters who contributed to the 17th c. decoration was Simon Ushakov.

These paintings were completely overpainted in the 18th and 19th c., and were not exposed in their original form until the second half of the 20th c. On the north and south walls are scenes featuring the Archangel Michael and Old Testament scenes; below, New Testament scenes and legends of the Emperor Constantine; the west wall features the "Last Judgment".

The lower part of the walls of the Burial Vault has more than sixty portraits of Princes, Grand Princes and Tsars, with the names of the patron below each one (many of them are copies, the originals are in the Tretyakov Gallery (see Tretyakov Gallery).

The iconostasis (1680–81) was the work of a group of artists under the direction of Ivan Nedumov. The icons were restored and the richly decorated royal door was installed in the early 19th c.

Iconostasis

The icon of the Archangel Michael, with eighteen scenes from his legend in panels round the sides, dates from the turn of the 14th–15th c.

Palace of Congresses (Dvorets Syezdov)

The Palace of Congresses, built in 1960–61 by a team of artists led by M. V. Posokhin, is the most modern building within the precincts of the Kremlin – a structure of triangular marble pylons and gleaming glass.

Admission only to events

The architects were awarded the Lenin Prize in 1962, and the Palace of Congresses became the model for modern Soviet urban architecture. The objective of the planners was to create a building which would be in harmony with the late medieval façades of the cathedrals and towers; and accordingly the permitted height of the building, which was the subject of an architectural competition, was restricted, so that much of the accommodation is underground. But at the same time the building – erected within the Kremlin precincts, which until 1958 had been almost sacrosanct – was to be open to all.

The Palace of Congresses is, therefore, also designed as a theatre and public hall, used for congresses, ceremonial occasions, performances by the Bolshoi Company, film festivals, political rallies and meetings.

The main auditorium is the largest in Russia – 50m/165ft long and 20m/65ft high, with seating for 6000. It is equipped with 7000 concealed loudspeakers and has excellent acoustics. Escalators lead up to the Banqueting Hall, which seats 2500 people and in which refreshments are served during the intervals in performances and which affords magnificent views of the Kremlin and Moscow.

Castle of Pleasure (Poteshnyy Dvor)

Behind the Palace of Congresses, between the Commandant's Tower and the Trinity Tower, is the Castle of Pleasure. The original building, built in 1650, was converted by Tsar Feodor in 1679 into a theatre in which festivities were held to amuse the Tsar and his family.

No admission

In the 19th c. it was enlarged and converted into a residence in which the Commandant of Moscow lived for a time. However, the main part of the building has remained unchanged, with decorative window surrounds of white stone.

Trinity Tower (Troitskaya Bashnya)

Between the Palace of Congresses and the Arsenal is the massive Trinity Gate-tower, which gives access to Manezh Street (Manezhnaya Ulitsa), also to the Alexander Garden and the Lenin Library (see Alexander Garden and Lenin Library). It is linked with the Kutafya Tower by the Trinity Bridge.

the seven-storey Trinity Tower, the tallest of the Kremlin towers and the counterpart on the west side of the Saviour's Tower (see Red Square) on the east, was built between 1495 and 1499. The superstructure with its octagonal tent roof dates from 1685, when almost all the Kremlin towers were given their present roofs.

Kutafya Tower

The Kutafya Tower is reached from the Trinity Tower on the Trinity Bridge, built in 1516 over the Neglinnaya (now flowing underground), which then served as a moat; the bridge was renovated in 1901.

The Kutafya Tower was built about the same time as the bridge to protect the river crossing. Like many other Kremlin towers, it was given a new superstructure in 1685, in this case a balustraded wall of open windows.

Arsenal (Arsenal)

No admission

The Arsenal was built between 1702 and 1736, with some interruptions to the work, on the site of the Granary, which was burned down in 1701. The general plan of the building was sketched out by Peter the Great himself; the architects were Dmitry Ivanov, Christoph Konrad and others.

It was given its present aspect between 1815 and 1828, after the French attempts to blow up the Kremlin before abandoning Moscow had made radical rebuilding necessary. The work was begun under the direction of Osip I. Beauvais, who erected a plain neo-Classical building, with wings laid out in trapezoid form around a pentagonal central courtyard. The Baroque portico was added by Dmitry V. Ukhtomsky.

After the rebuilding it was intended to use the Arsenal as an army museum: hence the 875 cannons lining the outside walls. The stucco reliefs of military trophies on the walls reflect the same intention.

Arsenal Corner Tower

The tower to the north of the Arsenal is the Corner Arsenal Tower, which can be seen better from the Tomb of the Unknown Soldier in the Alexander Garden (see Alexander Garden).

Middle Arsenal Tower

For the tower to the north-west of the Arsenal, the Middle Arsenal Tower, also see Alexander Garden.

St Nicholas's Tower

The tower immediately east of the main front of the Arsenal is the St Nicholas's Tower (see Red Square).

Residence of the President of the Russian Federation
(Residentsiya Presidenta Rossiyskoy Federatsiy)

No admission

The Residence of the President of the Russian Federation is a prominent landmark with its huge green dome topped by the red-white-blue tricolour of the Russian Federation. Originally built as the Senate and from 1918 to 1991 it served as the seat of the Soviet Government.

The Senate was built between 1776 and 1788 to the design of Matvey F. Kazakov. A portico in the form of a triumphal arch, with four Ionic columns and a pediment, leads into the inner courtyard, which is divided into three sections by two transverse wings. The main front, set on a high base, has rusticated masonry on the ground floor and Doric pilasters on the two upper floors.

Sverdlov Hall

Directly under the dome, at the apex of the triangle formed by the three main wings of the building, is the Catherine or Sverdlov Hall, one of the finest halls in Moscow (following his death in 1919 the Catherine Hall was renamed after the leader of the Communist Party). Round this circular hall, 25m/80ft in diameter and 27m/90ft high, are closely set Corinthian columns, between which are allegorical reliefs depicting Justice, Philanthropy, Law-abidingness, etc. (copies: originals in the Armoury). On the third floor are reliefs of Russian Grand Princes and Tsars, the originals of which are also in the Armoury.

In the east wing are the two rooms (seen only with special permission) occupied by Lenin and his wife from 1918 to 1922. A reproduction of Lenin's study can be seen in the Central Lenin Museum (see Lenin Museum).

Lenin's Flat

Behind the Residence of the Russian President is the Senate Tower (see Red Square).

Senate Towers

Presidium of the Supreme Soviet of the Russian Federation
(Presidium Verkovnogo Soveta Rossiskoy Federatsy)

The neo-Classical building beside the Saviour's gate houses the Presidium of the Supreme Soviet of the Russian Federation. The building was erected in 1932–34 (I. I. Röhrberg) for use as Government offices. The Kremlin Theatre, which has the most modern equipment and seating for 1200, was opened in 1958 with a performance of a play featuring Lenin, "Bells of the Kremlin". Rebuilding followed after the theatre in the Palace of Congresses was made available in 1962.

No admission

The Saviour's Tower near the Presidium building is described under Red Square (see Red Square) as are the Tsar's Tower which adjoins the Saviour's Tower on the south side, the Alarm Tower, Constantine and Helena Tower and the Beklemishev Corner Tower.

Kremlin towers

On the south-east side of the Presidium building is the spacious Kremlin Square, in which, on the edge of the Tainitsky Garden to the south, is a statue of Lenin by the contemporary sculptor Pintshuk unveiled in 1967 (formerly a statue of Alexander II stood here).

Lenin Monument

The Lenin Memorial in Kremlin Square

97

Towers on the south side of the Kremlin

The towers along the Moskva side of the Kremlin can be seen from the Tainitsky Garden inside the walls or from the Kremlin Embankment (Kremlyovskaya Naerezhnaya) outside the walls. The Beklemishev Tower at the east end of the south side is described under Red Square.

St Peter's Tower

St Peter's Tower (Petrovskaya Bashnya), built about 1500, is named after the first Metropolitan of Moscow, Peter, who was later canonised. it was frequently destroyed in the course of its history – in 1612 by the Poles, in the reign of Catherine II in preparation for the planned rebuilding of the Kremlin, in 1812 by the French – but each time was rebuilt.

Second Nameless Tower

The Second Nameless Tower (Vtoraya Bezymyannaya Bashnya) – its official name – was built about 1500 and has been preserved substantially in its present form. The octagonal tent-roofed superstructure dates, like the superstructures of other towers, from 1680.

First Nameless Tower

The First Nameless Tower (Pervaya Bezymyannaya Bashnya) was also built about 1500. In the reign of Ivan IV it was used for storing powder. An explosion in the powder magazine caused heavy damage, and the tower was pulled down under Catherine II's plan for rebuilding the Kremlin. After being rebuilt it was blown up by the French in 1812 and was again rebuilt by Osip I. Beauvais on the basis of old sketches and plans.

Secret Tower

The Secret Tower (Taynitskaya Bashnya) is named after a secret underground passage leading out of the Kremlin. It was the first of the Kremlin towers, built by Pietro Antonio Solari in 1485. It was demolished in preparation for Catherine II's planned (but never executed) rebuilding of the Kremlin, and was rebuilt by Osip I. Beauvais in 1817–19, broadly in its original form. It was originally a gate-tower, but the gateway was walled up in 1930.

Annunciation Tower

The Annunciation Tower (Blagoveshchenskaya Bashnya) was built in 1487–88, the superstructure about 1700. The name of the tower comes from an icon of the Annunciation which was once displayed on the tower. Many of the Kremlin towers are named after monasteries which no longer exist but were once connected with the Kremlin by a road running from one of the towers. The name of the monastery was given to the road and to the tower, and an icon of the appropriate saint or festival was set up in the gateway of the tower.

Water tower

The Water Tower (Vodovzvodnaya Bashnya), like the other corner towers, is circular so that its guns could cover the whole field of fire. It was built in 1488 by Anton Fryazin ("Fryazin" being the term applied to Italians or "Franks"). The tower acquired its present name in 1633, when a pump was installed in it to bring up water from the Moskva to water the Kremlin gardens, it was badly damaged in 1812 when the French tried to blow it up, but was rebuilt in 1817 by Osip I. Beauvais.

Krutitsky Monastery   M 9

Russian

Крутицкое Подворье
Krutitskoe Podvorye

Location
Perviy Krutsky
Pereulok 4

The Krutitsky Monastery rises up near the banks of the Moskva, south-east of the centre of Moscow. A monastery has stood here since the 13th c. and from 1589 it was the residence of the Metropolitan of Sarai and the Don region. It flourished in the second half of the 17th c. when the magnificent buildings were described by visitors of the time as a "paradise". The monastery was dissolved in 1788 under Catherine the Great. Later the

Krutitsky monastic residence

buildings were used as barracks and a prison. Further decay was prevented by restoration works carried out in 1984.

On the south side a tent-roofed bell-tower adjoins the five-domed Church of the Dormition, dating from the end of the 17th c. The church is connected by a gallery (1693/94) built on a pedestal floor to the teremok (small attic room) above a twin-arched gateway. The teremok (1693/94 by O. D. Starzev and L. Kovalyev) with colourful tiles decorated with plants on the wall facing the courtyard is a masterpiece of Old Russian architecture. Next to the teremok is the two-storey Metropolitan's Palace and the adjoining private church.

Metro
Proletarskaya/
Volgogradsky
Prospekt

Not far south-west of the Krutitsky Monastery are the ruins of the Simonovsky Monastery (Voshnotshnaya Ulitsa). It was built in 1380 as part of the defensive ring of monasteries which surrounded Moscow. One of the finest Russian Baroque buildings, only a section of the monastery wall with its massive towers and the trapesa remain.

Simonovsky
Monastery

*Kuskovo

off the map

Кусково
Kuskovo

Russian

On the south-east edge of Moscow in the centre of beautiful parkland stands the palace of Kuskovo, the former mansion of the Sheremetev family. After the Revolution it was made into a museum, while since 1932 the pavilions of the palace have housed the porcelain museum. There are over 18,000 exhibits including examples of Meissen, Chelsea and Sèvres porcelain together with Russian ceramics and glassware.

Kuskovo belonged to the Sheremetev family as far back as the early 17th c. In the middle of the 18th c. work began on turning it into a summer residence. It is a prime example of an Early Classical mansion house.

Location
Ulitsa Yunosti 2

Metro
Ryazanski
Prospekt
(from here bus 208)

Kuskovo

The museums are open Wednesday to Sunday from 10am to 4pm. Closed last Wed. of month.

Palace

The palace was built between 1769 and 1775 according to plans by Charles de Vailly and K. I. Blank on the bank of a previously excavated pond. The building was supervised by the Sheremtevs' own serf-architects. The wooden building on a stone base is comparatively simple. An Ionic portico of six columns stands in the centre of the façade.

In contrast the interior is richly decorated and furnished. The largest room is the ballroom (or mirror gallery) with its white walls decorated in gold carvings. In this magnificent setting the Sheremtevs' serf-orchestra performed concerts. The other rooms also have exquisite stucco work and display 17th and 18th c. Flemish tapestries and paintings by European artists (mainly unknown).

Park

From the north side of the palace there extends a French style park with herbaceous borders, water gardens and numerous marble statues by Russian and Italian artists. A Minerva statue (1779) was erected in honour of Catherine II's visit to Kuskovo.

Buildings in the park

Close to the house are the former kitchen and the oldest building at Kuskovo, the church (1737–39; bell-tower from 1792). Within the park are other pavilions and smaller buildings which are used for exhibitions. One of the most attractive buildings is the hermitage, built between 1756–71, with Baroque and Early Classical features. The grotto on the Italian lake is from 1756–71 and covered with shells inside. The counterpart of the Italian pond is the Dutch pond with the Dutch cottage (1749–51). This two-storey brick building, built in end of the 16th c. style, is decorated inside with Dutch tiles from the end of the 17th c. The main avenue ends at the stone orangery (1761–63) with the central part of the building being linked to two pavilions by glass-covered galleries.

Lomonosov University

Lomonosov University

D 7

Московский Университет Имени Ломоносова
Moskovsky Universitet Imeni Lomonosova

Russian

South-west of the Moskva, which here describes a wide bend round the Luzhniki Sports Complex (see entry), on the Lenin or Sparrow Hills, is the huge main building (1949–53) of Lomonosov University, the largest university in Russia (before completion it was based in the Old University on Manege Square (see Manege Square)).

Location
Lomonosovsky
Prospekt

Metro
Universitet

The university owes its name to poet and academic Mikhail Lomonosov (1711–65) who founded Moscow's first university in 1755. Like the Hotel Ukraina and certain residences, the main building is in the "wedding cake" style, the skyscraper form most favoured during Stalin's time.

The central tower building is 240m/790ft high, has 31 floors and is topped by a slender 60m/200ft spire. It contains the university's teaching and research departments. It is flanked by residential wings of 17 and 8 storeys respectively. The whole university complex contains 60 buildings and extensive lawns, an excellent library with some 6 million volumes, museums, a cinema, a theatre, several shopping centres, a swimming pool and much more.

From the large square north-east of the university, above the ski-jump there is a magnificent view over Moscow – it was here that Napoleon surveyed Moscow burning.

Luzhniki Sports Complex

E/F 8/9

Лужники
Luzhniki

Russian

The Luzhniki Sports Complex, an extensive area with a number of halls and stadiums, lies in a wide bend of the River Moskva. Many events in the 22nd Summer Olympic Games in 1980 took place here. The complex covers about 180ha/445 acres and has facilities for over 140 different sports.

Location
Luzhnetskaya
Naberezhnaya

Metro
Sportivnaya

In the centre of the area is the immense Lenin Stadium, originally built in 1955 and overhauled for the 1980 Olympics (floodlighting). The stadium can accommodate more than 100,000 spectators, most of them in the open.

The Lenin Stadium, seen from Sparrows Hill

The Palace of Sport and Little Arena lie north-west of the Lenin Stadium. The Palace of Sport, which can seat 17,000 spectators, is designed to accommodate a variety of sports; it can be flooded to form an ice-rink. The Little Arena has seating for 10,000 spectators. Immediately adjoining the Swimming Stadium is the Friendship Hall, one of the few entirely new buildings erected for the Olympics. Its concrete dome with triangular window openings looks like the shell of a large tortoise.

There is also a small Museum of Physical Education and Sport which displays cups and medals, etc. won by Moscow sportsmen and women.

Manege Square   G/H 12/13 (C 1)

Russian

Манежная Площадь
Manezhnaya Ploshchad

Location
west of the
Kremlin

Metro
Ochotnyi Ryad

Manege Square extends north-west of the Kremlin, more precisely Alexander Garden. It is hard to imagine that up until the 19th c. mills were grinding corn here driven by the waters of the Neglinnaya. Manege Square was quite late in acquiring a Communist name. From 1967 to 1991 the official title was "Square of the Fiftieth Anniversary of the October Revolution". Since then efforts have been made to give this busy square a new "face". In the north-east corner of the square is the Hotel Moskva, the first new hotel building of the Soviet period; following in clockwise direction are the Central Lenin Museum (see entry), the Historical Museum (see entry), the Arsenal Corner Tower of the Kremlin (see Kremlin) and the Alexander Garden (see entry). In the south is the Manege and next to it in the west the building of the Old University. Also of interest is the Hotel National several metres further north.

The Manege, in the square of the same name

The Manege, situated opposite the Alexander Garden, was built in the years 1817–25; the plans were drawn up by A. Betancourt and the architect in charge was Osip I. Beauvais.

The classically rectangular building is surrounded by a colonnade of Doric pillars which serves an important function in supporting the building. The roof over the interior was a great technical advance in its time: in spite of the huge dimensions (170m/560ft by 47m/155ft) the building has no internal supports of any kind.

Originally the Manege served as a riding school for officers, but has now been converted into the Central Exhibition Hall. Covering an area of 6500sq.m/70,000sq.ft, it houses exhibitions of Russian and foreign art.

Moscow's first university founded by Mikhail Lomonosov (see Famous People) in 1755 was initially housed in numerous locations. Between 1782 and 1793 the Old University (Mokovaya Ulitsa 18) was built according to plans by M. F. Kasakov and various university departments are still based here (most faculties are, however, located on the Sparrow Hills (see Lomonosov University)).

Kasakov created a Classical building which resembles a traditional mansion house with its side wings and courtyard. During the great fire of 1812 the Old University was almost completely destroyed. Rebuilding took place between 1817 and 1819 keeping broadly to the original plans apart from alterations to the main façade. The previous eight-columned Ionic portico was replaced by massive Doric columns. The central section is crowned by a gently curved dome which covers the hall.

The Hotel National stands on the corner of Manege Square/Tverskaya Street. This five-storey hotel built in 1903 by the architect A. Ivanov is to be refurbished into a luxury hotel. It is renowned for its many famous guests including André Gide, John Reed and Bernard Shaw as well as Lenin who occupied room 107 for several days in 1918.

Manege

Old University

Hotel National

Museum of Applied and Folk Art   H 15

Музей Декоративно-Прикладного и Народного Искусства
Muzey Dekorativno-Prikladnogo I Narodnogo Iskusstva

Russian

The Museum of Applied and Folk Art, first opened in 1981, is housed in an 18th c. building which was renovated in the 19th c. and extended in the 1950s. It gives the visitor a good idea of the everyday art forms, old and new, from the various regions of the CIS.

Particularly worthy of attention are the wooden objects from the 17th–19th c., miniature paintings and toys to be found on the ground floor. In one room on the upper floor there is an exhibition of 19th and 20th c. samovars. You can also follow the development of Russian glass production and see both modern Soviet porcelain together with some valuable 19th c. items.

Some rooms in the museum are reserved for special exhibitions.

Location
Delegatskaya
Ulitsa 3

Metro
Tsvetnoy Bulvar

Open
Mon., Wed., Sat.,
Sun. 10am–6pm;
Tue., Thur.
12.30–8pm
Closed last Thur. of
month

Museum of the History and Reconstruction of Moscow   K 13 (E 1)

Музей Истории и Реконструкции Москвы
Muzey Istorii i Rekonstruktsii Moskvy

Russian

The Museum of the History and Reconstruction of Moscow is housed in the neo-Classical Church of St John the Evangelist (1825). A six-columned limestone portico with a triangular gable adorns the façade above which towers a cylindrical drum with is decorated by a frieze of blind arches.

Location
Novaya Pl. 12

Metro
Lubyanka

A visit underground

When Moscow's first Metro line, 11.2km/7 miles long, with thirteen stations, opened on 15th May 1935 passengers found themselves in surroundings very different from other buildings in the capital – palatial stations, spacious halls with chandeliers, huge concourses decorated with mosaics, constructed by an army of workers, artists and engineers under the direction of Nikita S. Khrushchev, then the city's Party Chief, with a lavish use of 70,000sq.m/750,000sq.ft of multi-coloured marble, precious metals, mosaics, gold and glass.

"Palaces for the People"

These first stations, planned by Stalin as prestige and show buildings, set a standard which the designers of subsequent stations sought to maintain. Although the sumptuous decorations of Stalinist times are no longer in favour, Moscow's Metro must still be the most luxurious underground railway system in the world.

The flat-fare of a few rubles not only covers a journey of any length but also gives admission to a whole series of unique underground museums. While in most cities the underground system aims only to achieve functional efficiency, the Moscow underground stations meet two requirements: they are functional, but they also offer art for the enjoyment of passengers. The decoration of each station is related to a different theme.

Even visitors who do not intend to use the Metro system for the purpose of travel (it carries seven million passengers a day) should at least look into one or two of the principal stations. Seemingly endless escalators – some descend to a depth of 75m/246ft – transport the passengers into the marble halls. "Stand on the right, pass on the left" is the rule on the escalators. Whoever breaks this rule or indeed any other, or pushes or shoves will not get past the often rather corpulent ladies who sit in their glass kiosks at the bottom of the escalator.

Perhaps the most impressive station is Komsomolskaya, in the square of the same name, Komsomolskaya Ploshchad, which is also the location of the three impressive railway stations Leningrad, Yaroslavl and Kazan. Constructed in 1952, it is named after the Russian Communist League of Youth, founded in 1918, which after the death of Lenin was renamed the "Russian Communist Lenin League of Youth" and from 1926 was known as the "All Union Communist Lenin League of Youth".

The main concourse has seventy-two octagonal marble-clad piers supporting small round arches. The central section is dominated by huge chandeliers suspended from the highest point of decorative but non-functional stucco ribs. Between the chandeliers are eight monumental mosaics, each with 30,000 individual pieces, framed in elaborate stucco mouldings depicting scenes from Russian history.

The Kievskaya Metro station, beneath the Kiev railway station, dates from the Stalin period. In addition to mosaics, which document the friendship between Russia and the Ukraine, and chandeliers it is notable for its arcades with sculptural decoration.

The Mayakovskaya Station (1938–39), named after the poet Vladimir Mayakovsky (1893–1930), is notable for its sense of vertical space and its indirectly lit dome mosaics. The lateral arcades and the main arches are supported on stainless-steel pillars. The mosaics, in fluorescent materials, were designed by Aleksandr A. Deineka, an exponent of Socialist Realism; the thirty-five scenes depict the Soviet conquest of space. On 6th November 1941, when a state of siege had been declared in Moscow and the Germans were within 10km/6miles of the capital, Stalin made a famous speech to the Supreme Soviet, at a meeting in the station.

The main attraction of the Novoslobodskaya Station (1952) is its stained glass, with variations on themes from Russian tapestries – vases, rosettes, plants, figures ("Russian reading the newspaper in the study"), etc.

The station Ploshchad Revolutsi (1939) in Revolution Square, conveniently situated for the Central Lenin Museum, Red Square and the Kremlin, appropriately takes the October Revolution as its theme. Under its forty arches are bronze figures, in pairs, of "Heroes of the Revolution" – idealised representations of those who made the Revolution possible and contributed to the building up of the Soviet State. Among them are a kneeling Young Pioneer with his gun slung round his neck; the crew of the cruiser "Aurora"; a frontier guard and his dog, with ears pricked expectantly; a mother and child; and various sportsmen (footballers, a girl discus thrower). Each figure – whether an architect bent over his plans or a young girl reading – is represented in a typical but idealised manner.

Other stations of the Stalin era which are worth seeing include Kropotinskaya, Beloruskaya, Biblioteka Imeni Lenina, Okotny Ryad (which until recently was called Prospekt Marksa), Krasnye Vorota (formerly Lermontovskaya), Paveletskaya, etc. There are also a number of notable newer stations which have a particular theme. Pushkinskaya station has motifs from the works of the great poet and Tsvetnoy Bulvar station, opened in 1988, has circus motifs as is it situated close to the Old Circus. In the Sportivnaya Station is the Museum of the History of the Metro.

Novoslobodskaya Metro station

New Arbat

<table>
<tr><td>

Open
Tue., Thur., Sat.,
Sun. 10am–6pm;
Wed., Fri.
noon–8pm

</td><td>

With its large collection of architectural finds, old prints, pictures, town plans, views, models and photographs, the museum deals with the earliest settlements on the Kremlin Hill, the burning of Moscow in 1812, the replanning and rebuilding after the fire, the October Revolution, the Great Fatherland War of 1941–45, development after the Second World War and building plans for the immediate future.

</td></tr>
</table>

New Arbat F/G 12

<table>
<tr><td>

Russian

</td><td>

Новый Арбат
Novy Arbat

</td></tr>
<tr><td>

Location
West of
Kremlin

Metro
Arbatskaya

</td><td>

The New Arbat with its numerous shops, restaurants and cafés is a good example of the juxtaposition of fine modern development and historic old Moscow buildings in the city. Until 1991 it was known as Kalinin Avenue and consisted of an old and a new part. The older section of this road between the Kremlin and the opening of the old Arbat (see Arbat) is now called Vosdvishenka Ulitsa and still preserves the atmosphere of the past with its buildings from the 18th and 19th c.

Work began on the site of the New Arbat heading west to the Kalininsky Bridge in 1962. The avenue was named after Mikhail Ivanovich Kalinin (1875–1946) who was head of state of the USSR from 1919 to 1946. The team of architects who designed the ultra-modern New Arbat were awarded the Grand Prix of the Paris Centre of Architectural Research in 1966 for this magnificent example of modern town-planning (it is debatable whether every visitor to this mass of concrete would share this opinion). Along the left-hand side of the avenue, which is over 80m/260ft wide, are four huge buildings in the form of open books housing the offices of various Government departments. They are linked by a two-storey gallery 850m/930yd long containing shops, restaurants, cafés, etc.

</td></tr>
<tr><td>

Morosov
House

</td><td>

Still in Vosdvishenka Ulitsa (No. 16) is Morosov House built in 1890 in the style of a Moorish castle by the factory-owner Morosov (now the House of Friendship with Peoples of Foreign Countries). The rooms of this picturesque villa are also elegantly furnished. They are now used for meetings, lectures and discussions between artists and scientists.

</td></tr>
<tr><td>

Church of
St Simeon Stylite

</td><td>

On the right-hand side of the New Arbat is the Church of St Simeon Stylite. Carefully restored this attractive limestone building fits surprisingly well into its new setting of huge tower blocks, each containing 280 flats.

</td></tr>
<tr><td>

White House

</td><td>

At the western end of the New Arbat is the White House (Belye Dom; Krasnopresnenskaya Nab. 2), seat of the Russian parliament. In August 1991 tens of thousands gathered here and through their presence brought the coup d'état to an end in three days. The White House was once again in the public eye in September 1993 when President Yeltsin dissolved parliament. Yeltsin's opponents, the leader of the Supreme Soviet Kasbulatov and vice-president Rutsoy together with their supporters, took refuge in the building. On 4th October élite troops of the Russian army loyal to Yeltsin stormed the building – more than 100 people were killed and the upper floors were destroyed by fire.

</td></tr>
</table>

**Novodevichy Convent E 9

<table>
<tr><td>

Russian

</td><td>

Новодевичий Монастырь
Novodevichy Monastyr

</td></tr>
<tr><td>

Location
Novodevichy
Proezd 1

</td><td>

The Novodevichy Convent (New Convent of the Maidens), situated in a loop of the Moskva, is one of the finest and most interesting of Moscow's old religious houses. It was dissolved in 1922. Seen from some distance

</td></tr>
</table>

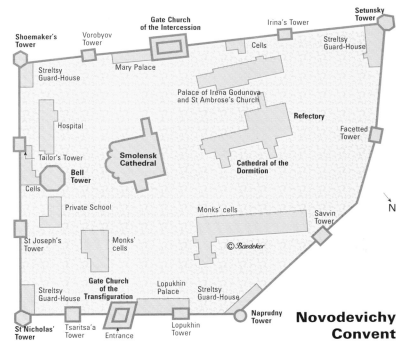

Setunsky Tower
Gate Church of the Intercession
Irina's Tower
Shoemaker's Tower
Vorobyov Tower
Streltsy Guard-House
Cells
Streltsy Guard-House
Mary Palace
Palace of Irena Godunova and St Ambrose's Church
Refectory
Hospital
Facetted Tower
Tailor's Tower
Smolensk Cathedral
Bell Tower
Cathedral of the Dormition
Cells
Private School
Monks' cells
Savvin Tower
© Baedeker
N
St Joseph's Tower
Monks' cells
Gate Church of the Transfiguration
Lopukhin Palace
Streltsy Guard-House
Streltsy Guard-House
Naprudny Tower
St Nicholas' Tower
Tsaritsa'a Tower
Entrance
Lopukhin Tower

Novodevichy Convent

away, with its fifteen buildings of the 16th and 17th c., it looks more like a fairy-tale city than a convent.

The convent was founded by Vasily III in 1514 to commemorate the capture of Smolensk and was designed to form part of the ring of fortified monasteries round Moscow. As in the case of the Don Monastery (see entry), however, only the principal cathedral was built in the first place. This was the Smolensk Cathedral (1524–25), the only early 16th c. building in the complex. The walls and towers were built at the end of the 16th c., following the model of the Kremlin walls, but by then the time for such defensive structures was almost over.

The heyday of the convent was in the 17th and 18th c., particularly during the Regency (1682–89) of Sofya, Peter the Great's half-sister. The "maidens of the convent" – often ladies who were considered by the rulers to be too dangerous or influential – mostly belonged to the higher ranks of society, and although they were prisoners in the convent were generously supplied with money by their noble relatives. The convent was thus able to carry out an active building programme, in the Moscow Baroque manner rather than the Old Russian style.

The finest building in the Novodevichy Convent is the Smolensk Cathedral. Externally it is very similar to the Cathedral of the Dormition in the Kremlin (see Kremlin), on which it is modelled. It is of different proportions, being higher. The pedestal base is surrounded on three sides by covered galleries, the first example of this style of architecture.

Metro
Sportivnaya

Open
Daily
10.30am–5.30pm
Closed Tue. and first Mon. of each month

Smolensk Cathedral

Novodevichy Convent

The Novodevichy Convent, to which noble ladies were once banished

Its main attraction, however, is the interior with its frescoes, icons and magnificent iconostasis. The frescoes (1526–30) are primarily representations of religious themes, but their symbolism goes beyond the religious message to express the Russian State's sense of triumph after the conquest of Smolensk, and they are thus of great historical as well as religious significance.

The main feature in the nave is the five-tiered iconostasis, which dates from 1683–86 commissioned by the Regent Sophia by famous artists from the Armoury (O. Andeyev and S. Sinovyev among others). Each pillar of the iconostasis looks like a climbing vine and is carved out of a tree trunk. The icons of the fourth tier (counting from the bottom) originate from an iconostasis from the end of the 16th c. commissioned by Boris Godunov. Also of interest is a large copper font in the centre of the cathedral which was completed in 1685 in the Armoury.

The oldest tombs of the Novodevichy Convent are in the pedestal base. Sofya, the half-sister of Peter the Great, was buried here in 1704.

Cathedral of the Dormition

The Smolensk Cathedral was the nuns' summer church, with no form of heating. In winter they used the Cathedral of the Dormition, which was heated. This church and the adjoining Refectory were built by Regent Sofya Alekseyevna in the 1780s. The present terraced church roof crowned by a small dome stems from 19th c. rebuilding. Daily services take place in the Cathedral of the Dormition

Other monastery buildings

Above the main entrance is the Gate-Church of the Transfiguration, one of the finest buildings in the monastery. It was built in 1687–89 and has splendid window surrounds. Next to it stands the Lopukhin Palace (1687/88) where the first wife of Peter the Great, Yevdokia Lopukhina, was made to live after he rebuffed her.

Smolensk Cathedral

Cathedral of the Dormition

Novodevichy Convent cemetery: tombstones of Krushchov and Chekov

Novodevichy Convent

The 72m/236ft bell-tower built in 1690 is the focal point of the monastery complex. Built on an octagonal base it consists of six tiers, capped by an onion dome.

Cemetery

The space between the churches is taken up by an old convent cemetery. Noble ladies and church dignitaries were buried here. As the cemetery was sold in the 19th c. none of the old graves has been preserved. Here lie the remains of several Decembrists, participants in the 1812 war and various relatively unknown poets, scientists, politicians and other names of the 19th c.

New Cemetery · Novodevichy Cemetery

Entrance
Lushnetski
Prospekt 2

Open
Wed.–Sun.
11am–4pm

Much more interesting is the New Cemetery on the far side of the defensive walls. This has been open to the public since 1987 and is one of Moscow's main tourist attractions. It was closed for a year as some of the graves belonged to party officials who had since fallen from favour.

Famous people lie buried in the walled cemetery laid out in 1898. Many of the graves are decorated with symbols indicating the fields in which the deceased were once famous. Some of the gravestones were designed by famous artists. There was much controversy concerning the erection of a monument to Nikita Khrushchev, who was refused a grave at the Kremlin walls. The gravestone made from black and white marble blocks is by the equally famous and also for a long time unpopular Ernst Nyesvestnye. Nina Khrushchev is said to have commissioned the headstone on the wishes of her husband. During the Sixties Khrushchev dismissed Nyesvestnye's art as "hideous trash, as distorted subjective interpretation".

Some of the prominent personalities were transferred to the cemetery long after their death. The mortal remains of Gogol were brought here in 1930 from the cemetery of the Danilov Monastery. Shalyapin (Chaliapin), who died in exile in 1938, was only moved here in 1988.

Cemetery of the Novodevichy Convent

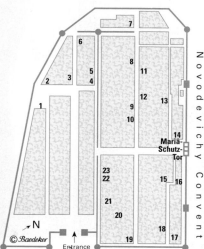

1 Andrei Tupolev (aircraft designer; 1888–1972)
2 David Oistrach (violinist; 1908–74)
3 Serge Ilyushin (aircraft designer; 1894–1977)
4 Ilia Ehrenburg (writer; 1891–1967)
5 Igor Tamm (physicist; 1895–1971)
6 Nikita Khrushchev (politician; 1894–1971)
7 Piotr Kapitza (physicist; 1894–1984)
8 Fyodor Chaliapin (opera singer; 1873–1938)
9 Piotr Kropotkin (revolutionary; 1842–1921)
10 Andrei Gromiko (politician; 1909–89)
11 Serge Prokofiev (composer; 1891–1953)
12 Alexander Scriabin (composer; 1872–1915)
13 Andrei Belyi (poet; 1880–1934)
14 Alexander Dovshenko (theatrical producer; 1894–1956)
15 Pavel Tretyakov (merchant and art collector; 1832–98)
16 Vladimir Mayakovski (writer; 1893–1930)
17 Vyacheslav Molotov (politician; 1890–1986)
18 Nadeshda Allilujeva (Stalin's first wife; 1901–32)
19 Dimitri Shostakovich (composer; 1906–75)
20 Valentin Serov (painter; 1865–1911)
21 Michail Bulgakov (writer; 1891–1940)
22 Anton Chekhov (dramatist, writer; 1860–1904)
23 Nikolai Gogol (writer; 1809–52)

© Baedeker

New Monastery of the Saviour

Новоспасский Монастырь
Novospassky Monastyr

Russian

Another important monastery, the New Monastery of the Saviour, is situated south-east of the Kremlin on the banks of the Moskva. A Monastery of the Saviour had already been founded in 1272 and was moved by Ivan Kalita in 1330 to the Kremlin. Ivan III needed room for a new palace in the Kremlin and had it moved again: in 1462 it was transferred to its present location near the Krutitsky Monastery (see entry).

Location
Krestyanskaya
Ploshchad 10

Metro
Proletarskaya

In the central position stands the Cathedral of the Saviour built in 1640 and 1642 on the site of an earlier cathedral which had been a burial place of the Romanov family. The five-domed church on a pedestal base is modelled upon the Cathedral of the Dormition in the Kremlin. The interior was painted by F. Subov, a master of the Armoury and icon-painters from Kostroma in 1689. Remains of these frescoes were able to be saved from overpainting and were taken to the Tretyakov Gallery and elsewhere.

The walls and towers of the monastery date from the same time as the cathedral. A Baroque bell-tower 78m/256ft high (1759–89) surmounts the main entrance.

Restoration work on the long neglected monastery buildings has only just begun in recent years. Whereas church services take place in the Cathedral of the Saviour the other rooms still house the workshops of the restorers (it is possible to visit the exterior).

Cathedral of the Transfiguration in the New monastery of the Redeemer

*Ostankino Castle (Museum of Serf Art) H/J 18

Russian	Останкинский Дворец Ostankinsky Dvorets
Location Ostankinksaya Ulitsa 5	The noble family of Seremetev, who acquired the Ostankino country seat in the middle of the 18th c., erected a superb building there from 1790 onwards. Based on a design by the Italian Quarenghi the palace, although of wooden construction, appears to be stone because of the artistic plaster finish. The theatre in the main part of the building was constructed between 1791 and 1798.
Metro VDNKh	
Open closed at present	In this, the Seremtev's summer residence, the Museum of Serf Art was set up in 1918. The name is misleading: this 18th c. aristocratic palace in fact contains some magnificent furniture and works of art. The palace and its contents were seized by serfs – hence the name.

The splendid rooms of the palace are well worth seeing, with their doors, ceilings and furniture decorated with gilded carvings, the stucco mouldings and splendid parquet floors. The rooms house a comprehensive collection of paintings, sculptures, porcelain and crystal. The castle's main attraction, however, is the theatre. Within a few minutes the auditorium can be raised to the same level as the stage, so that the theatre can also be used as a dance hall or reception room. Some of the technical equipment used originally to provide lighting and sound effects is still in use today. This is where the Seremtev's own theatre group, composed of more than 200 actors, musicians and singers from among their serfs, used to perform.

Church of the Trinity	Also on the Ostankino estate is the 17th c. Church of the Trinity built of red brick, with green onion domes, turrets, steps and arcades. The bell-tower was added in 1832 (tent roof from 1878). Services are held again in the church.

Peredelkino Excursion

Russian	Переделкино Peredelkino
Location 20km/12 miles south-west of Moscow	This idyllic country retreat from Moscow was and is the home of many well known intellectuals. Most visitors come to Peredelkino to see the house and grave of the writer and translator Boris Pasternak (1890–1960).
Rail from Kiev station (Elektrikishka)	Pasternak, whose early narrative prose and poetry also found recognition in the Soviet Union, fell increasingly out of favour with the political leadership. His most famous novel, first published in Italian, "Doctor Zhivago" in 1957, was not allowed to be published in the Soviet Union until 1988 because of statements on revolution and religion which did not conform to
Open Pasternak House Thur.–Sun. 10am–4pm	the accepted party view. When Pasternak was awarded the Nobel Prize in 1958 he at first accepted but later rejected the highest literary award, owing to political pressure. He was an outcast until his death which caused him great suffering as a poem written shortly before his death shows: "I'm at the end: an animal in the net. Out there are people, freedom, light. Behind me the noise of the rabble. Yet I cannot go outside."
Pasternak House	The house where Boris Pasternak spent his last years and wrote his famous novel "Doctor Zhivago" at Ulitsa Pavlenko No. 3 (coming from the railway station the road branches off from the main road to the right at the beginning of the wood) has been open to visitors since 1991. The rooms have been left in their original condition, Pasternak's coat is still hanging on the hook, thus creating the feeling that he might walk into the room at any moment.

Peredelkino: Pasternak's house . . .   *. . . and the grave of the writer*

In the cemetery 2km/1 mile south lies Pasternak's grave (every local visitor knows it). The simple white gravestone is nearly always provided with flowers.

Pasternak's grave

Polytechnic Museum

K 13 (E 1)

Политехнический Музей
Politekhnichesky Muzey

Russian

The Polytechnic Museum illustrates the technological development of Russia with some 20,000 exhibits in sixty rooms. The exhibits are arranged and explained in exemplary fashion, with dioramas, experiments, machines, models and even robots speaking several languages, all helping to demonstrate and make comprehensible processes of nuclear technology, telecommunications and television, mining, computers, automobile manufacture, etc.

The museum is housed in an imposing building erected in the second half of the 19th c. in a pastiche of Old Russian style.

Location
Novaya Pl. 3/4

Metro
Lubyanka/
Kitay-Gorod

Open
Tue.–Sun.
10am–6pm

Pushkin Museum

G 11

Музей Пушкина
Muzey Pushkina

Russian

In the house of the noble Krushchev family a museum dedicated to Alexander S. Pushkin (1799–1837) was opened in 1961. The house has no connection with the writer apart from his having admired the garden (neither

113

Pushkin Museum of Fine Art

Location
Ulitsa
Pretshistenka 12
(entrance at
Khrushchevsky
Pereulok 2)

Metro
Kropotkinskaya

Open
Tue.–Sat.
10am–8pm,
Sun. 10am–6pm

his birthplace nor any of the houses in which Pushkin spent his childhood have been preserved in Moscow).
The Late Classical building was designed by A. Grigoriev in 1817. It incorporated part of an earlier 18th c. building and consequently has an irregular plan. However, it is among the finest early 19th c. houses in Moscow. Both the façades on Pretshistenka Street (formerly Kropotkinskaya Ulitsa) and Khrushchevsky Peroylok are decorated with Ionic porticoes.
As was usual for mansions of this period the reception rooms are on the sides facing the street while the private living rooms overlook the garden. The house is furnished in 19th c. style. Over 50,000 editions of Pushkin's works, numerous manuscripts, letters, personal possessions belonging to the writer, paintings and sketches are on display here. Some of the exhibits were privately donated.

Tolstoy
Museum

Diagonally opposite Pushkin House in Pretshistenka Ulitsa is the Tolstoy Museum (see entry).

Pushkin Museum of Fine Art   H 11

Russian

Музей Изобразительных Искусств Имени А. С. Пушкина
Múzey Izobrazitelnykh Iskusstv Imeni A. S. Pushkina

Location
Ul. Volkhonka 12

Metro
Kropotkinskaya

In spite of the name the Pushkin Museum of Fine Art has nothing to do with the great Russian poet (see Pushkin Museum). It was named in his honour in 1937. It is housed in a neo-Classical building built for this purpose in 1912 from donations.
The nucleus of the museum was a collection of casts of Classical sculpture established in 1912. Its resources were dramatically increased, however,

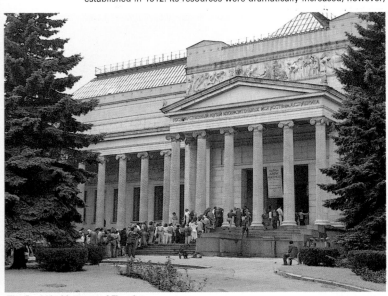

The Pushkin Museum of Fine Art

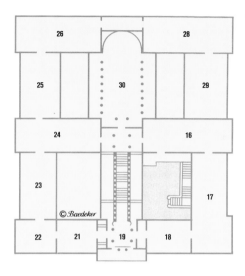

UPPER FLOOR
- 16 Greek art 1st half 5th c. B.C.
- 17–23 European art 19th/20th c.
  - 17 Bonnard, Denis, Derain, Fries, Kandinsky, Léger, Marquet, Matisse, Miró, Picasso, H. Rousseau, Signac, Utrillo
  - 18 Cézanne, Gauguin, van Gogh
  - 19 Sculptures by Emilio Greco, Manzù, Messina
  - 21 Degas, Manet, Monet, Pisaro, Renoir, Sisley
  - 22 Bastien-Lepage, Böcklin, Bonnat, Carrière, Cassatt, Feuerbach, Forain, Fortuny, Liebermann, Loir, Menzel, Meunier, Munch, Munkáczy, Puvis de Chavannes, Raffaelli, Zorn, Zuluaga
  - 23 Bodin, Constable, Corot, Courbet, David, Delacroix, Diaz de la Peña, Dupré, Gérard, Gericault, Gros, Guérin, Lawrence, Millet, Opie, T. Rousseau, Troyon, Vernet
  - 24 Greek art 4th–1st c. B.C.
  - 25 Roman art 6th c. B.C.–4th c. A.D.
  - 26 Medieval European art
  - 28 Italian Renaissance sculptures
  - 29 Sculptures by Michelangelo
  - 30 Special exhibitions

Pushkin Museum of Fine Arts

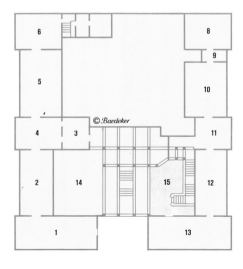

GROUND FLOOR
- 1, 2 Ancient Orient
- 3 Coptic and Byzantine art
- 4 13th–15th c. Italian painting
- 5 15th–16th c. Italian, German and Netherlands painting: Bordone, Cranach Master of Messkirch, Tintoretto
- 6 16th c. Italian painting: Bassano, Bordone, Botticelli, Tintoretto, Veronese
- 8 17th c. Flemish painting: Brueghel, Rubens, van Dyck
- 9 16th c. furniture
- 10 16th–17th c. Netherlands painting
- 11 17th c. Italian and Spanish painting: Benedetto, Castiglione, El Greco, Zurbarán
- 12 17th–18th c. Italian painting: Bellotto, Guardi, Tiepolo
- 13 17th–18th c. French painting: Boucher, Drouais, Fragonard, Greuze, Lorrain, Poussin, Watteau
- 14 Greek art 1st half 5th c. B.C.
- 15 Courtyard (modelled on that of the palazzo del Bargello in Florence) Casts of originals of medieval period and Renaissance

115

Red Square

Open
Tue.–Sat.
10am–8pm
Sun. 10am–6pm

after the October Revolution, when large private collections were taken over by the State and it also acquired many works of art from museums in Leningrad. The Pushkin Museum now possesses a large collection of antiquities from the Near East, Egypt, Greece and Byzantium, as well as numerous casts of Antique and Renaissance works of sculpture. It owes its international reputation, however, to its extensive holdings of European (non-Russian) painting. Its main strength lies in the French schools, from the neo-Classical artists (David, Fragonard, Watteau, Poussin) by way of the Impressionists (Cézanne, Manet, Monet, Gauguin) to the beginnings of modern art (Matisse). Italian painters (Botticelli, Perugino, Tiepolo), Flemish (Rubens, Jordaens, Van Dyck), Dutch (Rembrandt, de Hooch) and Spanish painters (El Greco, Murillo, Velázquez, Zurbaràn, Picasso) are also well represented.

The Pushkin Museum frequently puts on special exhibitions; for instance in 1993 it put on the highly regarded Matisse exhibition.

Priamos
Treasure

It was confirmed in the summer of 1993 that the long-lost "Priamos Treasure" was stored in a secret vault of the Pushkin Museum. This valuable hoard discovered by Heinrich Schliemann in 1872 in Troy had gone missing following the capture of Berlin in 1945 by the Soviet army. Meanwhile four countries (Russia, Germany, Turkey and Greece) have laid claim to the 4000 year old treasure.

Red Square J 12 (D 1)

Russian

Красная Площадь
Krasnaya Ploshchad

Location
Centre

Metro
Ploshchad
Revolutsi

Red Square, with an average length of 400m/440yd and an average breadth of 150m/165yd, is the central square not only of Moscow but of the whole of Russia. Since the time of Ivan III this has been the scene of great public events, mainly political – rallies, demonstrations, processions.

Red Square dates back to the 15th c.; prior to then the buildings almost reached the walls of the Kremlin. At that time it was called "torg" (Russ.= trade), and then in the 16th c. Trinity Square after a church which stood here. The name Red Square arose in the 17th c.; in Old Slavonic "krasnaya" meant both "beautiful" and "red", as red was considered a particularly beautiful colour. The translation "Red Square" instead of "Beautiful Square", which is now universally used, became established only in the 20th c.

Originally the approach to the Kremlin from Red Square was protected by a moat, 32m/105ft wide and 12m/40ft deep between the Neglinnaya and the Moskva. During the reconstruction and rebuilding carried out under the direction of Osip I. Beauvais to make good the damage caused by the French in 1812 the moat was filled in, the Neglinnaya was bricked over and the drawbridges in front of the Saviour's Tower and St Nicholas's Tower were removed.

Before the October Revolution official proclamations were read out in Red Square, and it was also the scene of markets, fairs and religious festivals, including the Palm Sunday procession when the Patriarch, mounted on an ass, and the Tsar, with their retinues, made their way into the Kremlin (see entry) through the Saviour's Gate-tower. Here, too, public executions were carried out; from here Russian forces led by Minin and Posharsky launched the attack which recovered the Kremlin from the Poles in 1612; and here after the Second World War the flags of the German Wehrmacht were brought in triumph and burned in front of the Lenin Mausoleum. During the existence of the USSR every year on 7th November a military parade was held in Red Square to mark the anniversary of the October Revolution, and on 1st May, Labour Day, and on 7th November there were parades of the workers of the Soviet Union which had something of the air of a popular

Pushkin Museum of Art: houses ancient and modern masterpieces (Picasso) (see p. 114)

(see p. 114)

festival. Since the August putsch in 1991 the Russian government has not held military parades, instead Red Square is a showpiece for cultural events.

Red Square is bounded on the south-west by the walls of the Kremlin with their numerous towers and two gate-towers. At the north end is the pictur-esque building occupied by the Historical Museum. Next to it at the entrance to Nikolskaya Ulitsa rebuilding has started on the Kazan Cathedral which was built in 1625 by Prince Posharsky as thanks for the liberation of Russia but demolished in the Thirties. Most of the north-east side of Red Square is occupied by the GUM (see GUM) Department Store, facing the Lenin Mausoleum with the tribunes of honour. Behind are the tombs of prominent citizens below the Kremlin walls, and at the south end soars St Basil's Cathedral (see entry).

Buildings around Red Square

Lenin Mausoleum

The queues in front of the Lenin Mausoleum have definitely grown shorter. It does not involve so much time now to go down into the air-conditioned vault in which the embalmed body of the founder of the Soviet State lies in a glass coffin. In recent years people have called for Lenin to be buried, as laid down in his will, next to his mother in St Petersburg. It looks in-creasingly as if this will happen in the near future. The guard of honour in front of the Mausoleum was withdrawn in October 1993. It is Moscow's loss as a tourist attraction. The hourly changing of the guards with their goose-step and puppet-like gestures always drew a crowd of spectators.

The Lenin Mausoleum occupies the site of the temporary Red Square wooden mausoleum in which Lenin's body was deposited on 27th January 1924 after the official funeral ceremony. The pavilion museum "Lenin Funeral Train Museum" contains models of this temporary structure (see

Open
Tue.–Thur.
10am–1pm;
Summer
Sat. 10am–1pm and
Sun. 10am–3pm
Winter closed Sun.

117

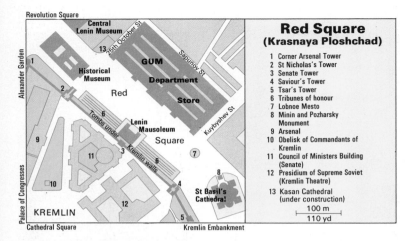

Red Square
(Krasnaya Ploshchad)

1 Corner Arsenal Tower
2 St Nicholas's Tower
3 Senate Tower
4 Saviour's Tower
5 Tsar's Tower
6 Tribunes of honour
7 Lobnoe Mesto
8 Minin and Pozharsky Monument
9 Arsenal
10 Obelisk of Commandants of Kremlin
11 Council of Ministers Building (Senate)
12 Presidium of Supreme Soviet (Kremlin Theatre)
13 Kasan Cathedral (under construction)

100 m
110 yd

Practical Information, Museums). The present mausoleum, on the highest point in Red Square, in front of the Senate Tower of the Kremlin (see entry), was built in 1930 to a design by Aleksey V. Shchusev. On either side are the tribunes of honour, with seating for 10,000 spectators. The mausoleum – which also serves as a reviewing platform for members of the Government – is built of dark red granite in a series of receding tiers, with a mourning band of black labradorite encircling the whole structure.

Interior

From the entrance, which is surmounted by the name "Lenin" in inlaid porphyry letters, twenty-three porphyry steps lead down into the semi-darkness of the air-conditioned burial vault, which is faced with black and grey labradorite, with porphyry pilasters. Lenin's embalmed body dressed in a dark blue suit lies in a glass coffin. Visitors were not allowed to pause before but now the guards are not so strict and there is time to stop and study the mortal remains of the man who changed the world so drastically. The gradual erosion of the Lenin cult has resulted in most myths which surrounded the founder of the State being exploded. Meanwhile it has become known that enormous technical efforts were undertaken in the underground vault to preserve Lenin's body. The temperature in the sarcophagus was a constant 16°C/61°F, special solutions were regularly applied to the body to prevent signs of decay.

Tombs below the Kremlin walls

Behind the Lenin Mausoleum, separated from Red Square by a row of silver firs, the remains of the Soviet Unions's honoured dead are buried (access only from the Lenin Mausoleum). For the main part it is politicians who are buried under the Kremlin walls. Together with Sverdlov, Breshnev and Kalinin, Stalin also was finally laid to rest in a tomb with a stone bust. Originally he was buried, according to his own instructions, in the Mausoleum beside Lenin, but his body had not been there very long (1953–61) when Khrushchev had it moved.

The urns of other worthy Soviet citizens and foreign Communists are buried behind tablets in the Kremlin walls. Among them are Nadezhda K. Krupskaya, Lenin's wife, after the October Revolution the leading figure in

Red Square

Lenin Mausoleum

Tombs in the Kremlin wall

the People's Commission for Education, and Clara Tsetkin, German Communist campaigner for women's rights, on Lenin's recommendation she was accepted into the Moscow "Socialist Academy of Social Sciences". Among the cosmonauts buried here is Yuri A. Gagarin, the first person to circle the earth in a space capsule in 1961. He was killed in a flying accident in 1968, which he and his companion could have survived by ejecting but which they refrained from doing as otherwise the MIG 15 would have crashed into a village.

Lobnoe Mesto · Place of Skulls

The Lobnoe Mesto (Place of Skulls) is a circular stone platform approached by a short flight of steps and closed by wrought-iron gates, from which before the October Revolution heralds proclaimed the decrees of Tsars and Patriarchs. It was also a place of execution, although some executions were carried out not on the stone platform but on temporary wooden scaffolds in front of it.

In the summer of 1606 the corpse of the False Dmitry was burned here and the ashes fired from a cannon towards the west, the direction from which the hated Polish Catholics had come. In 1671 Stenka Razin, leader of the first large peasant rising, was executed and dismembered here. Here, too, 2000 rebellious Streltsy were executed in 1698, when Peter the Great is said to have struck off the first ten heads with his own hand. The public execution of the great Cossack rebel Pugachov also took place here in 1775.

Kremlin towers in Red Square

Corner
Arsenal Tower

The northern Corner Arsenal Tower is best seen from the Grave of the Unknown Soldier (see Alexander Garden).

St Nicholas's
Tower

The 70m/230ft high St Nicholas's Gate-tower was built in 1491 by Pietro Antonio Solari. From this gate a road once led to a monastery (destroyed) dedicated to St Nicholas, and there was a mosaic icon of the Saint on the gateway.

The tower was blown up by the French and badly damaged. It was restored in 1816 under the direction of Osip I. Beauvais, who also filled in the moat between the Kremlin and Red Square and removed the drawbridge which spanned the moat outside St Nicholas's Tower. At the same time Luigi Rusca built the 15m/50ft high neo-Gothic superstructure, modelled on the 13th–15th c. St Mary's Church in Stargard (Pomerania; now in Poland). Like most of the Kremlin towers, St Nicholas's Tower is crowned by a five-pointed star which is illuminated at night and slowly rotates.

Senate Tower

Immediately behind the Lenin Mausoleum is the Senate Tower, also built in 1491 by Pietro Antonio Solari. It was given its name after the building of the Senate (1776–87; now residence of the Russian president, see Kremlin), just inside the walls at this point. The superstructure dates from 1680.

Saviour's
Tower

The 70m/230ft high Saviour's Tower is the most magnificent of the Kremlin towers, the very symbol and emblem of Moscow. From time immemorial it has been the principal entrance to the Kremlin (no admission for tourists). The Saviour's Tower was built in 1491 by Pietro Antonio Solari. The tent-roofed structure was added in 1624/25 by Christopher Halloway and Bazhen Ogurtsov, and a clock and carillon were installed by Halloway. The present clock, by the Butenop brothers, dates from 1852: the gigantic mechanism of the carillon occupies three storeys of the tower. Until the October Revolution the carillon played the Tsarist National Anthem, and between 1917 and 1941 it played the "Internationale". The clock now only strikes the hours (you can be sure that the clock is correct as it is directly linked with the control clock of the state astronomical institute).

St Nicholas's Gate-tower

Saviour's Tower

The tower was given its official name in 1658, when an icon of Christ was set up over the entrance. Before the October Revolution men were required to take their hats off when passing through the gate.

The Tsar's Tower or Tsar's Pavilion, near the Saviour's Tower, was built only in 1680, when the other towers were given their present superstructures.

Tsar's Pavilion

It is said that Ivan the Terrible used to sit in a wooden pavilion here to watch executions in Red Square: hence the name of the tower.

The name of this tower (built in 1495) indicates its function: in case of impending danger the alarm bell (nabat) was rung here. During a rising in 1771 the rebels rang the alarm bell: whereupon Catherine the Great, after crushing the revolt with troops from St Petersburg, had the clapper of the bell removed. Since 1821 the bell has been kept in the Armoury in the Kremlin (see entry).

Alarm Tower

The Constantine and Helena Gate-tower takes its name from a monastery in the Kremlin, now destroyed, which was dedicated to the Emperor Constantine and his mother Helena. The gate-tower was built in 1490 by Pietro Antonio Solari. The superstructure, like those of other Kremlin towers, was added in 1680. In order to level it up with the steep slope to the river the tower has recently had a quantity of soil piled up against it.

Constantine and Helena Gate-tower

The Beklemishev Tower, which is just under 47m/155ft high, was built by Marco Ruffo (Mark Fryazin) in 1487. The superstructure dates from the 1680s.

Beklemishev Tower

The tower is named after a boyar called Beklemishev who had a mansion just inside the Kremlin walls at this point. After Beklemishev was executed in the reign of Ivan III the tower was used as a prison. The tent-roof was partly demolished during the October Revolution but was restored to its original state in the 1950s.

Russian State Library H 12

Russian

Российская Государственная Библиотека
Rossyskaya Gossudarstvennaya Biblioteka

Location
Ulitsa
Vosdvishenka 3

Metro
Biblioteka
Imeni Lenina

The Russian State Library, previously known as the Lenin Library (paradoxically the name of the metro station has not changed), of which the former Pashkov House forms part, with more than 35 million volumes, is the largest library in Europe and one of the largest and most modern libraries in the world.

This gigantic complex, with five library buildings, occupies the whole of a city block. Designed by Vladimir A. Aduko and W. G. Helfreich, it was built between 1928 and 1940, though the interior was not completed until 1958. Particularly impressive are the façades looking towards the Kremlin (see entry) and the Manege, notably the main entrance with its neo-Classical granite-clad colonnades. Also noteworthy is the rich sculptural decoration of the two attic friezes, the allegorical figures, busts and portrait medallions. The leading Soviet sculptors of the day contributed to the decoration of both the exterior and the interior.

*Pashkov House

The former Pashkov House (currently being restored), a mansion in Early Classical style, stands on higher ground behind the State Library. This palatial residence, consisting of a central block and two symmetrical wings linked with it by galleries, was built in 1784–86 according to plans by W. I. Bashenov. The façades of the wings have four Ionic columns, while the main building, which stands higher, is preceded by a Corinthian portico. The whole complex is dominated by a circular belvedere.

The Pashkovs sold the palace in 1839 and it was subsequently used as an educational institute. In 1862 it housed the extensive art collection of the statesman and diplomat Count N. P. Rumyanzev (1754–1826). Among the museum's treasures is a library comprising 25,000 volumes which formed the original stock of the Lenin Library.

**St Basil's Cathedral J/K 12

Russian

Храм Василия Блаженного (Покровский Собор)
Khram Vasiliya Blazhennogo (Pokrovsky Sobor)

Location
Red Square
(Krasnaya Pl.)

Metro
Pl. Revolutsii

Open
Wed.–Mon.
9.30am–5.30pm

Many would think that St Basil's Cathedral alone would justify a visit to Moscow. This extraordinary building – the supreme achievement of 16th c. architecture in Moscow – is now a branch of the Historical Museum. Until 1978 the cathedral, with its ground-plan in the form of an eight-pointed star, its nine churches and its bizarre domes, its vivid colours and its heterogenous assortment of architectural elements, could be seen only from the outside; but the interior has recently been excellently restored and is now open to the public.

History

The church was originally built by Ivan the Terrible in 1555–61 as the Cathedral of the Intercession of the Virgin (Pokrovsky Sobor) to commemorate the capture of Kazan, the capital of the khanate of Kazan, on the festival of the Intercession of the Virgin in 1552.

According to the chronicler the architects of the cathedral, Postnik and Barma, were sent to Ivan the Terrible by God. The story that the Tsar had them blinded after the building was completed, however, is no more than a legend, for in 1558, four years after Ivan's death, Postnik and Barma added

St Basil's Cathedral, the finest 16th c. building in Moscow ▶

GROUND PLAN

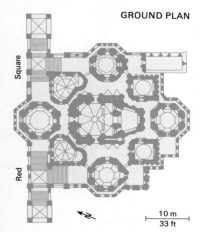

Square

Red

10 m
33 ft

St Basil's Cathedral
Pokrovsky Sobor
Vasiliya Blazhennogo

St Basil's Cathedral, properly the Cathedral of the Intercession of the Virgin, is described in Baedeker's "Russia" (first English edition, 1914) as follows:

". . . It consists of eleven small dark chapels, arranged in two storeys, and combined in a most extraordinary agglomeration. The building is surmounted by a dozen domes and spires, painted in all the colours of the rainbow and of the most varied forms. Some of them are shaped like bulbs or pineapples, some are twisted in strange spirals, some are serrated, some covered with facets or scales. All of them bulge out over their supporting drums and are crowned by massive crosses. The decoration, in which numerous Renaissance details may be detected, is of the most exuberant character. The whole effect is quaint and fantastic in the extreme."

the chapel at the north-east corner of the cathedral housing the tomb of the holy fool Basil (Vasily).

The holy fools, or fools in Christ, were itinerant ascetics who enjoyed great popularity among the ordinary people of Russia, many of them being revered as saints.

The holy fool Basil the Blessed died in 1552, the year of the capture of Kazan. He was well known for his fearless denunciation of Ivan the Terrible's cruelties; and when, after Ivan's death, his chapel was built on to the cathedral the name of the chapel gradually came to be applied to the whole cathedral.

The domes were given their present form at the end of the 16th c. To refer to them as onion domes seems an over-simplification, given their turban-like and tear-drop shapes. Originally the domes were helm-shaped, with eight domes set around the central tower (destroyed at the end of the 18th c.). The colourful painting of the domes dates from the 17th c., when the bell-tower was added and the open galleries round the whole complex were vaulted over.

In 1812 the French stabled their horses in St Basil's Cathedral. Before leaving Moscow Napoleon ordered it to be blown up; but cold, hunger and fear of sabotage by the people of Moscow prevented the order from being carried out.

Ground-plan/exterior

Although St Basil's Cathedral looks such a confusion of chapels, galleries, loggias and domes it is actually based on strictly geometrical principles. In the centre is the principal church with its 57m/187ft high tower, its octagonal tent roof topped by a small dome, rising high above the other structures. Round this central tower are four large and four small chapels, with domes proportional to their size. The four larger chapels are at the ends of an imaginary cross with the principal church at its central point; the smaller chapels lie between the larger ones.

These nine churches stand on a high brick-built base with arcading and pillars. The four larger chapels have an octagonal lower storey topped by a series of triangles enclosing slit windows; the apexes of the triangles point upwards, giving the tower a strong sense of vertical movement. Above these are a cornice and a band of blind semicircular arches, and above these again are more triangles and slit windows, maintaining the upward movement.

The towers of the four smaller chapels begin with tiers of blind semicircular arches, set back above one another. Above these is the drum supporting the dome, with brick mosaic decoration and slit windows.

Since St Basil's Cathedral was conceived as a monument commemorating the capture of Kazan, the interior is less impressive than the grandiose exterior. It is still, however, worth seeing. Its most notable features are the frescoes in the central tower and the passages and galleries, mostly of the 16th c. The icons date from the 15th–17th c.

Interior

In the two rooms under the bell-tower there is an exhibition on the theme "The Prokovsky Cathedral as an Example of 16th century Architecture", with old prints, sketches, plans and drawings illustrating the history of the cathedral.

The Monument to Minin and Pozharsky

The Monument to Minin and Pozharsky, in front of St Basil's Cathedral, was Moscow's first patriotic monument, unveiled on 20th February 1818. It was the work of the neo-Classical sculptor Ivan P. Martos, who spent almost fourteen years, with interruptions, on the task. The cost was met by public subscription.

The monument was moved to its present position after the construction of the Lenin Mausoleum. Note the position of Minin's right arm, pointing towards the Kremlin. Kuzma Minich Minin (d. 1616) was a butcher of Nizhny Novgorod who in 1611 formed a popular militia to fight the invading Poles and persuaded Prince Dmitry Mikhailovich Pozharsky (1578–1642) to become its commander. Pozharsky's forces soon swelled into a considerable army, the so-called Second Force.

In the spring of 1612 he moved to Yaroslavl, and on 26th March set out for Moscow. A Polish army was routed in August, and on 2nd October Pozharsky took Kitay-Gorod (the trading district off Red Square). Soon afterwards the Kremlin was captured, and on 27th October 1612 the Poles surrendered.

On the granite base of the monument are bronze reliefs of "Citizens of Hizhny Novgorod" and "The Surrender of the Poles". The figures of Minin and Pozharsky are also cast in bronze – Minin pointing towards the goal of the patriotic forces, the Kremlin, and Pozharsky still hesitating to take command.

Sergyev Possad   **Excursion**

Сергиев Посад
Sergyev Possad

Russian

For the visitor with several days to spend in Moscow an excursion to Sergyev Possad is highly recommended. It is possible to join an organised (but expensive) excursion but it is only a 90 minute trip by rail from Yaroslavl Station or by hired car.

Location
74km/46 miles
north-east

Sergyev Possad is best known to visitors as Zagorsk, under which name it epitomised the Russian Orthodox Church. The town was not given this name until 1930 when Stalin wanted to commemorate a young revolutionary who had been assassinated in 1919: Vladimir M. Zagorsky. It resumed its former name, Sergyev Possad, in September 1991.

Rail
from Yaroslavl
Station

As well as its function as the spiritual centre of the Russian Orthodox Church Sergyev Possad (pop. 115,000) is also an important centre of art and crafts and toy production (toy museum: Pr. Krasnoy Armii 123; near the pond a few hundred metres south of the monastery). Other important industries are electronics, furniture and knitwear production, agricultural machinery.

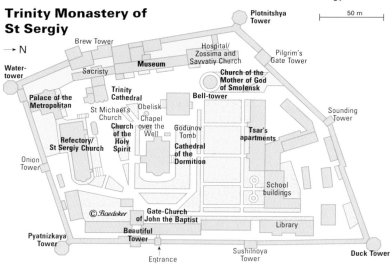

Trinity Monastery of St Sergiy

Trinity Monastery of St Sergiy

Plotnitshya Tower

50 m

→ N

Brew Tower

Water-tower

Sacristy

Museum

Hospital/ Zossima and Savvatiy Church

Pilgrim's Gate Tower

Church of the Mother of God of Smolensk

Palace of the Metropolitan

Trinity Cathedral

St Michael's Church

Obelisk Chapel

Bell-tower

Sounding Tower

Refectory/ St Sergiy Church

Church over the Holy Spirit

Church over the Well

Godunov Tomb

Tsar's apartments

Onion Tower

Cathedral of the Dormition

School buildings

© Baedeker

Gate-Church of John the Baptist

Library

Pyatnizkaya Tower

Beautiful Tower

Entrance

Sushilnoya Tower

Duck Tower

** Trinity Monastery of St Sergiy

The Trinity Monastery of St Sergiy is one of the most famous and for its time the largest monasteries with 150 monks, in Russia. Even during the existence of the Soviet Union it was a place of pilgrimage for Christians from all parts of Russia. The Patriarch of Moscow moved his seat to the Danilov Monastery in 1988 but the spiritual seminary and the academy are still located in Sergyev Possad (the four year training at the seminar is a prerequisite for acceptance to the academy).

General

The monastery was founded around 1340 by Sergiy of Radonezh (1314–92). From a boyar family Sergiy took the monks' vows in 1337 and in 1344 he was ordained as a priest and abbot. Before battle (1380) he blessed the troops of the Grand Prince Dmitri. The triumphal victory over the Mongols strengthened the position of the monastery community. In 1408 it was almost completely destroyed in a Mongol attack but was soon rebuilt under Abbot Nikon, the successor of Sergiy who was beatified in 1422. From 1608 to 1610 the monastery withstood a 16 month-long siege by 30,000 Polish troops. This event made it a symbol of national resistance. The rulers took revenge with rich gifts. In the 17th c. – its heyday – the Trinity Monastery of St Sergiy owned vast estates with about 120,000 serfs. During the Streltsy uprising the monks were on the "right" side: Peter the Great took refuge from the Streltsy in the monastery in 1682 and 1689.

History

In 1742 a theological seminary was opened in the monastery followed by a ecclesiastical academy in 1814. In 1744 the Trinity Monastery was given the rank of "lavra" instead of "monastyr" in Russian, which is an honorary title awarded to only three other monasteries besides the one in Sergiy Possad (Alexander Nevsky Monastery in St Petersburg, and monasteries in Kiev and Volhynia).

After the October Revolution the monastery was dissolved but returned to the church in 1943. As a result it became as seat of the patriarch (moved to Danilov Monastery in 1988) one of the most important religious centres in

◄. *Cathedral of the Dormition in Trinity Sergius Monastery*

Trinity Monastery: magnificence behind white walls

the country. In 1992 President Yeltsin decreed that all buildings on the site of the Trinity Monastery should be transferred to the Moscow Patriarchate Church. Only the Museum of Art and History remained temporarily under state jurisdiction.

Tour

The entrance to the monastery is on the east side. Permits to take photographs or film are on sale at the kiosk. The entrance tickets to the museum and to part of the western defensive walkway and the Pilgrim Gate-tower (only possible in summer, recommended for the view) are available from inside the grounds at any of the respective buildings.

Monastery walls

The monastery grounds are in the shape of an irregular parallelogram. The complex is surrounded by a 1400m/4600ft long and 15m/50ft high defensive wall. In its present form it dates from the 16th/17th c. Eleven towers reinforce the wall, one of the most attactive being the so-called Duck Tower which is crowned by a stone duck. Peter the Great is said to have shot wild ducks from here, hence the name. Within the monastery walls are the most magnificent buildings. The eight churches and chapels, the refectory and the Metropolitan Palace are a most impressive reflection of the Russian architectural styles of several centuries.

Gate-Church of John the Baptist

After passing the Beautiful Tower the visitor comes to the Gate-Church of John the Baptist. It was built by the Stroganov family in 1692–99. The decoration on the façade of this five-domed church is similar to that of the Refectory.

Cathedral of the Trinity

The Cathedral of the Trinity was built above the tomb of St Sergiy in 1422 as the first stone building of the monastery. It is a very simple limestone church on a pedestal base built to a cruciform plan. The interior painting took place between 1425 and 1427 and was by Andrey Rublyov and Daniel Chornyi (the frescoes were extensively overpainted in the 17th c.). The iconostasis by the same artists has been preserved. One of Rublyov's most famous works are the icons of the Trinity (original stored in the Tretyakov Gallery since 1929). The silver memorial slab to Sergyi vaulted by a balda-chin also made of silver was the work of 16th c. craftsmen from the Armoury. The Nikon Chapel with the tomb of the Abbot Nikon was built on to the south façade of the Trinity Cathedral in 1548.

The Metropolitan Palace (or Patriarch's Palace) dates originally from the 16th c. but was later rebuilt several times. The façade is in 18th c. style.

Metropolitan Palace

The Refectory with the Church of St Sergiy (1686–92) is among the finest examples of Russian Baroque: limestone pillars are twined around by vine leaves, the walls are completely coloured with geometric patterns. A gal-lery surrounds the magnificent rooms of the main floor. To the east the large hall without pillars is the Church of St Sergiy. The working quarters are in the basement.

Refectory/ Church of St Sergiy

The Church of the Holy Spirit was built in 1476 by craftsmen from Pskov. In contrast to the Trinity Cathedral it is built from brick on a limestone base. It was the first time in the history of Russian architecture that glass tiles were used to decorate the façades. It is also the oldest preserved Russian church in which the bell-tower is integrated. The oil paintings inside date from the second half of the 19th c.; the iconostasis from 1866.

Church of the Holy Spirit

The Cathedral of the Dormition (1559–85) was commissioned by Ivan the Terrible who personally laid the foundation stone. It is inspired by the Church of the Dormition in the Moscow Kremlin. The frescoes in the interior were painted in only 100 days in 1684. The iconostasis dates from the end of the 17th c. On its reverse side high up is the choir – the faithful were to believe that the singing was coming directly from heaven.

Cathedral of the Dormition

In a west porch of the cathedral Boris Godunov together with his wife and two children was buried one year after his death. The porch was dis-mantled in 1780 so that the vault now occupies the space in front of the cathedral.

Godunov Tomb

The chapel was built at the end of the 17th c. in Russian Baroque style over a spring discovered in 1644 (long since dried up).

Chapel over the Well

The obelisk in front of the Chapel over the Well was a gift from the Metro-politan Platon in 1792. The four tablets chronicle the most important events in the history of the monastery.

Obelisk

The 88m/289ft high bell-tower (1740–70) is one of the most attractive buildings of its kind, built according to plans by I. Mitshurin and D. Uktom-sky. It took a long time to build because of the lack of an original plan and later disputes between the craftsmen and the clerics.

Bell-tower

The Church of the Mother of God of Smolensk is more reminiscent of a park pavilion than a church. It was built between 1746 and 1748 to a round ground plan.

Church of the Mother of God of Smolensk

The Church of Zosima and Savvatiy is integrated in the building of the former hospital. It was the only tent-roofed church of the monastery com-plex between 1635 and 1638.

Hospital with Church of Zosima and Savvatiy

The former sacristy and administration buildings have been made into a museum which adjoins the hospital building. The museum contains icons from the 14th to 17th c., embroidery, tapestries, liturgical equipment, gold and silverwork and costumes.

Museum

The former Tsar's Palace from the end of the 17th c. has been the seat of the Academy since 1814. It has colourful decor which resembles that of the Refectory. It also originally had an open gallery.

Tsar's Palace

Shchusev Museum of Russian Architecture H 12

Russian

Музей Архитектуры Им. А. В. Щусева
Muzey Arkhitektury Im. A. W. Shchuseva

Location
Ulitsa
Vosdvishenka 5

Metro
Biblioteka Imeni
Lenina/Arbatskaya

Open
Tue.–Thur., Sat.,
Sun. 11am–7pm

The Shchusev Museum of Russian Architecture gives an excellent survey of Russian architecture from Kievan Russia (St Sophia Cathedral) to the tower blocks of the present day with the help of models, sketches, photographs, plans, etc.

The museum has been housed since 1945 in a building from 1787 which was rebuilt at the beginning of the 19th c. It is named after the great Soviet architect Aleksey Viktorovich Shchusev (1873–1949), who designed, among much else, the Kazan Station and the Lenin Mausoleum in Red Square (see entry), which show Shchusev's development from the Old Russian "fairy-tale" style to a restrained and sober monumental style. Shchusev also played an important part in the urban planning of modern Moscow.

There is a branch of the Shchusev Museum in the Don Monastery (see entry).

State Art Gallery H 9

Russian

Картинная Галерея
Kartinnaya Galereya

Location
Krymsky Val 10

Metro
Park Kultury

Open
Tue.–Sun.
10am–7pm

Situated by the Moskva on the edge of Gorki Park the State Art Gallery is often referred to as the New Tretyakov Gallery as paintings from the collection of the Tretyakov Gallery were on display here temporarily while it was being renovated. The Central House of the Artists is in the same building. Until a few years ago the 20th c. was represented here only by works of social realism. Now there are exhibitions of paintings by Russia's avant garde (including Malevich and Kandinsky) together with different strands of contemporary art.

Television Tower H 17

Russian

Телебашня
Telebashnya

Location
Ostankino,
Ulitsa Akademika
Korolyova

Metro
VDNKh

The Television Tower, to the north of Moscow in the district of Ostankino (see entry), is the second highest tower of its kind (537m/1762ft). Pencil-slim for most of its height, it swells at the foot into a conical base which rests on ten concrete supports. Fast lifts take visitors up to the various viewing platforms and the revolving restaurant at 330m/985ft. It is advisable to book a table (see Practical Information, Restaurants).

In a wind of any strength the tower sways quite perceptibly: the timid have been warned!

Tolstoy House F 10

Russian

Музей-Усадьба Л. Н. Толстого
Muzey-Usadba L. N. Tolstogo

Location
Ulitsa Lva
Tolstogo 21

When Lev Nikolayevich Tolstoy (1828–1910) acquired this villa in the district of Kamovniki in 1882 it was close to unsightly factories and weaving mills. "By a strange coincidence all three factories near my house only produce things that one wears to a ball" Tolstoy observed in his diary. He spent the winters from 1882 to 1901 with his family in this spacious wooden house surrounded by gardens (the summer months were spent on an estate about 200km/124 miles away, Yasnaya Polyana). The house has been a museum since 1921 – on the orders of Lenin.

It has been preserved in its original state. In the great hall on the first floor A. Rubinstein, N. Rimsky-Korsakov and S. Rachmaninov played, Shalyapin sang, plays and sketches were performed, Tolstoy read to his visitors, who often included the artists N. Gay and I. Repin, the writers A. Chekhov and M. Gorky, from his own and other works. In a room where Tolstoy pursued his daily morning exercise and in which he had installed a small cobbler's workshop, there is a bicycle upon which, at the age of 67, he learnt to cycle in just three days. For most visitors the writer's study is like a shrine: at this desk Tolstoy wrote the novel "Resurrection", the novella "Kreutzer Sonata" and the play "Power of Darkness". The last time he wrote here was to write his "Reply to the Synod" concerning his excommunication in 1901. Afterwards he left Moscow and only returned to the capital briefly in 1909.

Metro
Park Kultury

Open
Tue.–Sun.
10am–5pm

Tolstoy Museum

G 10

Музей Л. Н. Толстого
Muzey L. N. Tolstogo

Russian

The Tolstoy Museum in the Pretshistenka Ulitsa (opposite the Pushkin Museum, see entry) is not another residence of Lev Nikolayevich Tolstoy (1828–1910) but a Classical palace (built 1817–22) which since 1921 has housed exhibits which are connected with the life of the writer. It contains over a million manuscripts, the writer's library and various portraits painted during Tolstoy's lifetime (including Repin, Kramskoy, Nesterov and Gay). The museum also has a comprehensive collection of photographs (more than 17,000) and numerous personal items belonging to Tolstoy. A phonograph which was a gift from Edison to the writer plays Tolstoy's voice. The museum, in which all available material on Tolstoy was transferred in 1939, is also a research institute.

Location
Pretshistenka
Ulitsa 11

Metro
Kropotkinskaya

Open
Tue.–Sun.
11am–5.30pm
Closed last Fri. of
month

**Tretyakov Gallery

J 10

Третьяковская Галерея
Tretyakovskaya Galereya

Russian

The Tretyakov Gallery was closed in the middle of the 1980s for extensive renovation work and the addition of a new wing. Some rooms have since been reopened. Part of the collection is on temporary display in the State Art Gallery (see entry).

The Tretyakov Gallery is the largest museum of Russian painting and sculpture from the 11th c. to the present day. With over 60,000 works of painting, graphic art, sculpture and applied art the Tretyakov Gallery is also one of the most important museums in the world. Before it was closed the museum had around 4000 visitors each day.

The founder of the gallery was the Moscow businessman, collector and art patron Pavel Mikhailovich Tretyakov (1832–98), who presented to the city of Moscow in 1892 the collection of Russian art which he and his brother Sergey had systematically built up from 1856 onwards.

Initially Pavel Tretyakov exhibited the paintings he acquired in his own house in Lavrushinski Street. However, as the collection grew – at the time of his death there were 3500 works – further extensions to the house became necessary. The gallery's present main building was erected in 1901/02, on the site of the former Tretyakov mansion, to the design of the "fairy-tale" painter Viktor M. Vasnetsov (see Vasnetsov House). Vasnetsov

Location
Lavrushinski
Pereulok 10

Metro
Novokuznetskaya/
Tretyakovskaya

Open
Tue.–Sun.
10am–7pm

New building of the Tretyakov Gallery

was one of the group of artists who gathered under the aegis of the industrialist and art patron Savva I. Mamontov on his estate of Abramtsevo (see entry) and were largely instrumental in promoting the return to old Slav traditions which reached its full flowering in Russian realism and Art Nouveau. The building is in the Old Russian or "fairy-tale" style characteristic of the turn of the century, the Russian version of Art Nouveau. The gallery, originally known as the O. and I. Tretyakov Municipal Art Gallery, was taken into State ownership by a decree of the Soviet Government on 3rd July 1918.

The collection, enormously increased by the nationalisation of private property, the incorporation of private collections and new acquisitions, soon outgrew the capacity of the original building, and a new right wing was added by Aleksey V. Shchusev in 1927–35. Since then the problem of space has become still more acute with new rooms having to be added. When it reopens the museum will consist of several interconnected buildings equipped with the latest museum technology. An exhibition in 1991 by Valentin Serov in the first newly opened rooms, which can be altered at will by room dividers, provided an example of this.

Collection

Cassette players with cassettes describing the most important exhibits in different languages can be hired at the entrance to the museum.

In both the lower rooms important icons are exhibited to which the Russian Orthodox Church lay claim. The "Virgin of Vladimir" (early 12th c. Byzant.) was returned to the Church of the Dormition in October 1993. Other important icons include the famous "Trinity" by Andrey Rublyov (d. 1430) which was originally made for the Trinity Monastery in Sergiev Possad (see entry). The icon "Virgin of the Don" is regarded as wonder-working as it allegedly caused Russian troops to defeat opposing armies: Grand Prince Dmitri carried it with him into battle and Ivan IV also believed in the miraculous powers of the icon in his campaign against Kazan in 1552.

Icon room in the Tretyakov Gallery

The exhibition rooms on the top floor are dedicated to Russian artists of the 18th and 20th c. The Tretyakov collection includes works by Ivan Nikitin (around 1680–1742), who was court artist at St Petersburg from 1720, the historical painter Anton Lossenko (1737 to 1773), Karl Bryullov (1799–1852; "The Last Days of Pompeii"), Alexander Ivanov (1806–58; "Christ Appearing before the People"), Nikolay Gay (1831–94; "Peter I Interrogating the Tsarevich", Vasily Perov (1834–82; "Portrait of Dostoyevsky"), Ivan Kramskoy (1837–87; "Christ in the Wilderness"), Vasily Surikov (1848–1916; "Boyarins Morozova"), Valentin Serov, often compared with Renoir by Russian art historians (1865–1911; "Girl with Peaches"), Isaak Levitan (1860–1900; "Spring tide") and Viktor Vasnetsov (1848–1926), whose themes are taken from fairy-tales and legends. The greatest Russian painter of the 19th c. is Ilya Repin (see Famous People). Since the beginning of the Gorbachov era works by Russian avant-garde artists have been allowed to be shown. Paintings by Vassily Kandinsky (1866–1944) and Kasimir Malevich (1878–1935) are displayed in the Tretyakov Gallery.

Tsaritsyno

M 3

Царицыно
Tsaritsyno

Russian

South of the city centre, situated near Kolomenskoe, Tsaritsyno is an unfinished Imperial palace. The palace stands in a beautiful park with various pavilions and ruins which are undergoing restoration. In the middle of the 18th c. the estate belonged to the father of the well-known Russian satirist and poet A. Kantemir, but in 1775 Catherine the Great bought it. She wanted a summer residence "in order to live near Moscow like a simple estate-owner", as she expressed it. The architect V. Bashenov

Location
Radialnaya
Ulitsa 4

Metro
Orekovo/
Tsaritsyno

was given the project. He created a neo-Gothic palace but the Empress was not impressed. She had the almost finished building demolished in 1785 and M. Kasakov was brought in to build a new palace which took from 1787–93. In the mean time the Empress had lost all interest in Tsaritsyno. The main palace, which consists of two buildings joined together by a cross-building, remained uncompleted, as did many of the other buildings in Tsaritsyno (pavilions, working quarters, bridges, gateways). At the beginning of the 19th c. a few neo-Classical pavilions in the park were built, including the Temple of Ceres and the so-called Graceful Pavilion (both 1803).

Tverskaya Street   G 14–H 13

Russian	Тверская Улица Tverskaya Ulitsa
Location North-west of city centre **Metro** Ochotnyi Ryad/ Tverskaya/ Mayakovskaya	The origins of Tverskaya Street go back to the 15th c. It owes its name to the fact that it connected Moscow and Tver. It was the first street of the Russian capital to be paved. In the 18th c. the street, along which the Tsars drove from the new to the old capital, became a desirable residential area. During the 19th c. prestigious business houses were located here. Under Stalin the street, which was named after the writer Maxim Gorky in 1932 (it assumed its former name in 1932), was widened from 15m/50ft to 40m/130ft, with six lanes. This magnificent street, now climbing in an almost straight line from Prospekt Marksa to where it joins Leningradsky Prospekt, is some 7km/4½ miles long. Most of the old churches and houses were demolished during the building of the street and replaced by modern buildings. Comparisons with the Champs-Elysées in Paris and the Kurfürstendamm in Berlin may be somewhat far-fetched but it is worth taking a stroll down Tverskaya Street with its busy traffic; the visitor can study the shopping habits of the Muscovites and here and there sense some of the flair of days gone by.
Hotel National	The first impressive building in Tverskaya Street is the Hotel National on the corner of Manege Square (see entry). Behind it towers the less attractive block of the Hotel Intourist.
Yermolova Theatre	Built at the end of the 19th c. No. 5 houses the Yermolova Theatre which was founded in 1925 (seats 800). Modern plays by Russian and foreign dramatists are chiefly performed.
Artists' Theatre	In a side street off to the right (Kamergersky Pereulok 3) is the Moscow Artists' Theatre. Founded in 1898 by Stanislavsky and Nemirovich-Danchenko it moved into the building designed by Shekhtel in 1902. Several plays by Chekhov and Gorky were given their first perfomances here.
Savvin's Court	In the courtyard of No. 6 is the remarkable so-called Savvin's Court. It is an Art Nouveau style building dating from 1907 which was moved back 50m/164ft when the road was widened.
House No. 9	The granite slabs with which house No. 9 is covered originally had a different purpose: after the victory over the German army they were intended for a victory monument – a rather rash command.
Memorial to Yury Dolgoruky	The equestrian statue on Sovyetskaya Ploshchad, unveiled in 1954, is in memory of Yury Dolgoruky, the founder of Moscow.
Moscow State Soviet	Opposite the statue, on the other side of the street, stands the Moscow State Soviet (Mossovyet). The Classical building by the well-known architect Kasakov dates from 1782; it was set back by 13.5m/44ft when the street was widened, then raised by two-storeys and modernised.

Pushkin Monument in Pushkin Square

The Hotel Zentralnaya (No. 10), an Art Nouveau building from 1911, is the former Hotel Lux. After the Revolution famous members of the Communist International such as Walter Ulbricht, Ernst Thälmann, Herbert Wehner and Chou-en-Lai stayed here.

Hotel Zentralnaya

In building No. 14, around the turn of the century, the world famous delicatessen shop "Yeliseyev" was located. It was opened as a branch of the St Petersburg business. One could buy every kind of delicacy as long as one could afford it. This gourmet's paradise met its end before the revolution. The Yeliseyevs were forced to flee the country following a scandal. Today this building with its impressive Art Nouveau interior, its glittering crystal lustres, dark wood panelling, pillars and carved arabesques still houses a food shop.

Gastronome No. 1

Continuing along the Tverskaya Ulitsa to Pushkin Square, which is always busy, is the Pushkin Monument from 1880. Near several publishing houses on the square is one of the largest cinemas, the "Rossiya" (2500 seats). On the other side of the road the first branch of McDonald's was opened in 1989. At first there were very long queues to try western fast food but these have since subsided, although it is still very popular.

Pushkin Square

The Central Museum of the Revolution is located at No. 21. In the 19th c. the building housed the English Club, a centre of cultural life at that time, Tolstoy and Pushkin were often guests here. From 1924 the history of the Russian Revolution from 1905 to 1917 has been documented here (open: Tue., Thur., Sat. 10am–5.30pm, Wed., Fri. 10am–6.30pm, Sun. 10am–4.30pm).

Central Museum of the Revolution

Beyond the Triumfalnaya Ploshchad (named after the victory over the Swedes in the Nordic War, 1721) the street – now called Pervaya Tverskaya– leads to the White Russian Railway Station (Belorussky Vokzal). It

White Russian Railway Station

was built in 1909 in the Old Russian "fairy-tale" style and is the terminus for trains coming from western Europe.

Vasnetsov House   J 15

Russian

Дом-Музей В. М. Васнецова
Dom-Muzey Vasnetsova

Location
Vasnetsova
Pereulok 13

Metro
Prospekt
Mira

Open
Wed.–Sun.
10am–5pm

The house once occupied by the painter Viktor Mikhailovich Vasnetsov (1848–1926), noted particularly for his paintings of fairy-tales, is now a museum. Vasnetsov, architect of the Tretyakov Gallery (see entry), also designed his own house: built of logs in the Old Russian or "fairy-tale" style, it has the aspect of an enchanted castle lost amid the tower blocks which have sprung up all round it.

The interior of the house and the studio have been left exactly as they were during the thirty-two years Vasnetsov lived here. On the walls are sketches, pictures of scenes from fairy-tales and legends ("Prince Ivan on the Grey Wolf", "The Frog Queen", "Kashchey the Immortal", etc.), figures of witches and designs for stage sets.

Yaroslavl Station   L 15

Russian

Яарославский Вокзал
Yaroslavsky Vokzal

Location
Kalantshovskaya
Ploshchad

Metro
Komsomolskaya

The Yaroslavl Station is one of the sights of Moscow both by virtue of its striking architecture and on account of the mixture of peoples to be observed here. This is the station for Zagorsk and Yaroslavl; but its most important function is as the starting-point of the "Trans-sib", the Trans-Siberian Railway which links Moscow with Vladivostock 9300km/5800 miles away on the Sea of Japan.

The station, in the Old Russian style of the turn of the century, was built in 1902–04 to the design of Fyodor Shekhtel on the site of an earlier station of the mid 19th c. The majolica decoration on the façade was the work of a group of artists who worked on the estate of Ambramtsevo between the 1870s and 1890s, under the aegis of the wealthy industrialist and art patron Savva I. Mamontov, and who evolved the Russian version of Art Nouveau. Shekhtel (1859–1926) was a member of this group.

Kazon and
Leningrad
Stations

Also on the Kalantshovskaya (formerly Komsomolskaya) Ploshchad are the Kazon and Leningrad Stations (see Practical Information, Railway Stations).

The GUM store ▶

Practical Information

Accommodation

See Camping, Hotels

Advance Booking

See Theatre and Concerts

Airlines

Aeroflot
Leningradsky pro. 37; tel. 5 78 91 01
Departures information: 5 78 78 16
Arrivals information: 5 78 55 18

Airport

Sheremetyevo II

Moscow has five large airports (see map on p. 178) but the only one of importance for Western visitors is Sheremetyevo II, the international airport some 30km/19 miles north-west of the city centre. Taxis into the city are on standby 24 hours a day and take about half an hour. The journey by bus is just under an hour, leaving about once every two hours.

Arrival

On leaving the plane you first have to pass through passport control where you will have to present your visa as well as your passport so that the official can retain the counterfoil. Delays are only likely at this juncture if there is any problem with identification.
Once through passport control collect your luggage from the carousel and go to customs control where you must produce passport, visa and customs declaration. This should already have been completed on the plane if possible (see Customs Regulations). Only rarely is anyone asked to open up all their luggage for inspection.

Transfer to hotel

Couriers will be waiting beyond customs control to collect their groups. The situation can appear rather chaotic at times but if you cannot find your courier go to the information desk.
Lone travellers who are concerned about being overcharged or even mugged if they take a roving taxi can order one from the Intourist desk (payment in hard currency in advance).

Return flight

Before the return flight complete the customs declaration form which can be found in the clearance building. There is a large duty-free shop in the departure hall.

Banya

The banya is the Russian answer to the Finnish sauna and a national tradition of long standing. Records of these wooden cabins where Russians

went daily go as far back as the 11th c. and a session in one of these steam baths is still a popular pastime today. Temperatures are mostly between 60 and 80°C but the humidity is substantially higher than in the Finnish version. The ritualistic fashion with which the bathers rain down blows, however gently, on one another's sweaty bodies with the enormous bundles of birch twigs may come as quite a surprise to first-time visitors to a public banya, but all this is intended to stimulate the circulation. In other respects passage through the banya follows a similar process to a sauna. After showering and drying you go into the steam room then take a cold shower and rest for a while. This is repeated two or three times, with the final trip through the sauna followed once more by a thorough cleansing. Saunas are also available in the luxury hotels but the city's public banyas have much more local colour. One of the best, with separate sections for men and women, is near the Hotel Metropol:
Sandunovskiye, Uliza Neglinnaya 14; tel. 9 25 46 31
Metro: Kusnezky Most. Open: 8am–8pm daily.

Banks

See Currency

Business Hours

Shops open every day except Sundays and public holidays from 9 or 10am to about 8 or 9pm. Many of them close on Mondays and most shut for an hour for lunch between 1 and 2pm or 2 and 3pm.
The arrival of an increasing number of privately-run shops has brought greater flexibility of opening hours and many of the food shops which take hard currency now open all day on Sundays as well.

Shops

Department stores are open from 8am to 9pm Monday to Saturday.

Department stores

Opening times are given under the individual museums (see entries in the A–Z section and Museums in this part of the guide). Bear in mind that most museums are closed on either the first or last day of each month or on the first or last Monday or Tuesday of each month, as well as closing at least one day a week. The safest course is to check with Intourist or at the hotel information desk before setting out.

Museums

Post offices are open Mon.–Sat. 9am–8pm. The head post office is open Mon.–Sat. 8am–10pm.

Post offices

As a general rule restaurants are open between noon and 3pm then from 6 or 7pm to 11pm. Cafés are open from 9am to 3pm and 4 to 9pm.

Restaurants, Cafés

Cafés

''Kafe'', the Russian word for café, usually refers to a cafeteria-style stand-up snackbar rather than the Continental type of café which serves alcohol. There are several of these cafeterias on New Arbat (Café Ivushka at no. 28) and in Tverskaya Street (Café Moskowskoye at no. 6).

Cafeterias

Ice-cream parlours (kafe morozhenoe), which are very popular both in summer and winter, are often much more formal than their Western counterparts (doorman, cloakroom, etc.).

Ice-cream parlours

A few more Continental-style cafés are starting to appear. The Italian café at 10 Ulitsa Petrovka, for example, serves excellent espresso and capucchino coffee.

Cafés

Café in the Arbat

Otherwise anyone with a taste for cakes and pastries should seek them out in the pleasant setting of the cafés in major hotels such as the Olympic-Penta, Metropol or Savoy. The Hotel Rossia also serves ice-cream on the terrace in summer.

Camping

Intourist Travel Limited (see Information) organises camping trips in the European part of Russia between 1st June and 30th September for independent visitors travelling by car.
Campsites have washing, cooking and leisure facilities, restaurants and shops and make provision for vehicle maintenance.

Moscow
campsites

Moskayky
Moskayskoye Shosse 165 (16km/10 miles west of city centre)

Solnetchny
Varsshavskoye Shosse 21 (about 25km/15 miles from the city centre)

Car Rental

A number of the international car rental companies are starting to set up their own agencies in Moscow. Cars can also be rented in advance through Intourist (see Information) but they are very expensive.

Avis

Sheremetyevo II Airport; tel. 5 78 56 46 or 80 03 31 10 84

Europcar

Novaya Pl. 14; tel. 9 23 97 49 or 5 71 38 78

Car hire companies also have representatives in a number of hotels (Olympic Penta, Novotel, Mezhdunarodnaya and Pullman Iris; see Hotels).

Caviar

Caviar, the most expensive food in the world, is the roe of the sturgeon found in the Caspian Sea and lower reaches of the Volga. Of the 20 or so species of this saltwater fish which swims up rivers to spawn only three provide caviar – Beluga, Osyotr and Sevruga.

The most expensive caviar comes from the Beluga, which is also the largest, the female weighing up to 500 kilos and producing 15 to 20 kilos of large-grained caviar. The Osyotr, which is more common and whose caviar therefore costs less, weighs an average 25 to 40 kilos and produces 4 to 10 kilos of caviar. Which is the better of the two caviars is something gourmets fail to agree on but no-one disputes the fact that both are more highly prized in every way than Sevruga. Here the female weighs 9 to 10 kilos, giving about 2 kilos of fine-grained caviar.

Types of sturgeon

Be sure to buy caviar which is tinned rather than in glass jars. The best type is the slightly salted Malossol version – look out for the name on the tin. Sturgeon usually only produce black caviar (red caviar comes from the salmon) but occasionally it can be silver-grey, light brown or gold-brown, its rarity value making it more expensive. In the old days white caviar, mostly from albinos, was reserved for the Tsar.

Buying caviar

Caviar should not be eaten with lemon but with blini (buckwheat pancakes), potato fritters or pancakes, and connoisseurs scoop it out of the tin, chilled in ice, with a horn, mother of pearl or tortoiseshell spoon.

Eating caviar

Chemists

See Medical Assistance

Circus

The internationally famous Moscow Circus uses two different venues. The old circus building, re-opened in 1990 after its complete renovation, stages the traditional circus acts, while the emphasis in the new building is more on light entertainment and clowns and has animal acts in a watery setting.

Old Building
Zwetnoy Bulvar 13; tel. 2 00 06 68

New Building
Wernadskogo Prospekt 7; tel. 9 30 28 15

Concerts

See Theatre and Concerts

Clothing

Visitors to Moscow from Western Europe should take the summer clothes they would normally wear at home, but it is worth remembering that the temperature can quite often soar to over 30°C.

Summer

Crime

Winter In winter warm clothing is essential, especially warm footwear and outerwear and headgear which comes down over the ears.

Ankle-length coats are best avoided since even in December and January a sudden thaw can set in, bringing with it deep puddles. Make sure that boots have non-slip soles since there is usually a sheet of ice under the snow – in Moscow sand rather than salt is spread on the pavements.

Crime

The times are past when visitors could walk the streets of Moscow city centre at night and not worry about carrying valuables and a reasonable amount of cash. Crime has increased dramatically over the past few years, and for some the temptation to steal is very great in a country where the average wage is less than £12 a month. There is no undue cause for alarm, however – simply take the same precautions here as in most other European inner cities.

Currency

Unit of currency

The unit of currency in the CIS is the rouble. This is made up of 100 kopeks although hyperinflation has rendered these virtually meaningless. Since the reform of the rouble in July 1993 the only valid banknotes (here in denominations of 100, 200, 500, 1000, 5000, 10,000 and 50,000) are those issued since 1993 but regulations are changing so fast it is best to check on the spot.

Changing money

Cash and other forms of money can be changed into roubles at banks, in hotels (see Hotels) and at the exchange bureaux found everywhere throughout the city. The customs declaration has to be produced when changing money in banks but not in the private-enterprise exchange bureaux. The exchange rate in August 1993 was about 1000 roubles to the American dollar but galloping inflation means that this can alter almost daily.

Be advised against changing money on the black market. Not only is it unnecessary since Russian citizens are officially permitted to buy hard currency, the rate is actually only slightly more favourable and there is a big chance of falling prey to professional conmen.

Only change a small amount into roubles to start with since many things such as theatre tickets, taxi fares, foreign goods, etc. have to be paid for in Western currency. Many restaurants and bars will also only accept payment in hard currency. The wisest course if possible is to take plenty of coins and small banknotes in hard currencies such as the Dollar and the Deutsche Mark.

Currency import and export

The import and export of Russian currency is forbidden. There is no restriction on the import of freely convertible currency, paper securities or precious metals and their products (but not gold coins), but these must be declared. Keep the customs declaration with you throughout your stay in the CIS. Currency and valuables up to the amount declared on entry may be exported on departure. At the moment this is not being monitored very closely, but could soon change.

Eurocheques

Eurocheques have yet to gain wide acceptance in Russia. If necessary call at the Foreign Trade Bank (Serpuchovsky Val 8).

Credit cards

An increasing number of shops, hotels, restaurants, etc. will accept credit cards such as American Express, Diners Club, Eurocard and Visa.

Customs Regulations

The following may be imported into the Russian Federation without payment of duty: personal effects, two still cameras with accessories, a portable video recorder, a video camera, a transistor radio, a portable musical instrument, a tape recorder, a portable typewriter and two watches plus 6kg canned food for the journey, 250g coffee, 100g tea and for persons over sixteen 250 cigarettes or 250g of other forms of tobacco, and for persons over twenty-one 0.5 litre of spirits and 1 litre wine.
It is forbidden to import gold coins, Russian currency, weapons and ammunition or any kind of narcotics.
A customs declaration in duplicate must be completed before passing through customs. The forms are available in various languages. Take care to put "no" or "none" and not just a dash in all sections which do not apply. To avoid any problems on departure it is advisable to enter all valuables and not just legal tender and items in precious metals. Although customs inspection has become less rigorous than it used to be keep the copy of the customs declaration in a safe place so that it can be produced again on departure.

Entry

The export of roubles is prohibited. Antiques and objets d'art may be taken out only with a permit from the Ministry of Culture and on payment of a duty of 100% of the estimated value of the articles as shown in the export permit.
For cigarettes, tobacco and spirits the same limits apply as for imports; caviar, black or red, may only be exported if it has been bought in a hard currency store.
Another customs declaration has to be completed on departure before passing through customs and should be handed in together with the form filled in on arrival.

Exit

On returning to a member country of the European Union the duty-free allowances for persons over fifteen are 500g coffee or 200g powdered coffee and 100g tea or 40g teabags, 50g perfume and 0.25 litre toilet water, and for persons over seventeen 1 litre spirits with more than 22% alcohol or 2 litres spirits with less than 22% alcohol or 2 litres sparkling wine and 2 litres table wine and 200 cigarettes or 100 cigarillos or 50 cigars or 250g tobacco.

Re-entry to
EU countries

For countries outside the European Union the allowances are as follows: Australia 250 cigarettes or 50 cigars or 250g tobacco, 1 litre spirits or 1 litre wine; Canada 200 cigarettes and 50 cigars and 900g tobacco, 1.1 litre spirits or wine; New Zealand 200 cigarettes or 50 cigars or 250g tobacco, 1.1 litre spirits and 4.5 litres wine; South Africa 400 cigarettes and 50 cigars and 250g tobacco, 1 litre spirits and 2 litres wine; USA 200 cigarettes and 100 cigars and a reasonable quantity of tobacco, 1 litre spirits or 1 litre wine.

Re-entry to
non-EU countries

Diplomatic Representation (Embassies)

Starokonyushenny Pereulok 23; tel. 2 41 58 82	Canada
Grokholsky Pereulok 5; tel. 2 88 41 01	Eire
Naberezhnaya Morisa Toreza 14; tel. 2 31 85 11	United Kingdom
Novinskiy Bulvar 19/23; tel. 2 52 24 51 or 2 52 24 59	United States

Electricity

The standard voltage is 220 volts. Sockets require a continental-type plug or adaptor.

Emergency Services

Fire	01
Police	02
Ambulance	03

Events

In terms of cultural events there are two main highlights in the Moscow year.

"Moscow Stars"

The first is the Festival of the Moscow Stars held annually between 5th and 13th May. Performances by the country's leading theatre and dance ensembles, choirs, chamber orchestras and soloists are staged in the various theatres and concert halls of the capital. Talented young artists are also given their chance to perform before a wider public.

"Russian Winter"

The second main cultural event is the Russian Winter Festival which runs from 25th December to 5th January every year. This is when theatres put on top productions with a special emphasis on performances by choirs and folk-dance groups.

See also Public Holidays

Excursions

Abramtsevo

This mansion about 70km/44 miles north of Moscow (see A–Z, Abramtsevo) belonged to Savva Mamontov, an industrialist and patron of the arts, who established an artists' colony here between the 1870s and 1890s which made a decisive contribution to the development of Russian Art Nouveau.

Arkhangelskoe

Arkhangelskoe (see A–Z) is a village 23km/14 miles west of Moscow in a beautiful setting on the river Moskva with an 18th/19th c. estate (mansion, theatre, outbuildings, park).

Borodino

The village of Borodino on the Minsk road 124km/77 miles west of Moscow was where on 26th August 1812 the decisive battle took place between the Russian army and the forces of Napoleon, an event marked by fortifications, memorials and the Borodino War Museum (open Tue.–Sun. 10am–6pm).

Gorky Leninskiye

Gorky Leninskiye, 35km/22 miles south of Moscow, is the site of the house, now a museum, where Lenin stayed at times after 1918 until his death there on 21st January 1924. His rooms have been preserved as they were in his lifetime.

Klin

This is an old Russian town, founded in 1318, about 85km/52 miles north-west of Moscow on the banks of the River Sestra. Besides a 16th c. church and a monastery in Moscow Naryshkin Baroque style, the main attraction is the Tchaikovsky Museum in the house which was the composer's home until his death in 1893 (open Mon., Tue., Fri.–Sun. 10am–6pm).

New Jerusalem

The New Jerusalem monastery at Istra 35km/22 miles from Moscow was founded in 1656 by the Patriarch Nikon. It owes its name to the fact that the Patriarch modelled its great Church of the Resurrection on the Church of the Holy Sepulchre in Jerusalem. After its destruction by fire the church was rebuilt by Tsarina Elisabeth in Russian Baroque style. Besides the monastery and church buildings, which have been skilfully restored in recent decades, New Jerusalem has an impressive open-air museum of timber buildings.

Anyone wanting to see more of the countryside would do well to take the trip 20km/13 miles out of Moscow to visit the typical Russian writers' village of Peredelkino. Boris Pasternak died and was buried here in 1960.

Peredelkino

Russia's greatest monastery, founded by St Sergius in 1340, lies about 75km/46 miles from Moscow (see A–Z, Sergiyev Posad).

Sergiyev Posad

Food and Drink

The Russians eat relatively well. Breakfast usually includes something hot such as sausages, omelette, fried egg or blinis (buckwheat pancakes with sour cream) as well as bread, butter, jam, cheese and sausage. The midday and evening meal consists of three or four courses, ending with tea or coffee.
In hotels breakfast tends to be served between 8 and 10am and lunch between noon and 2pm. In restaurants the Russians like to take plenty of time over dinner, often with a musical accompaniment. Most restaurants are busy from 7pm onwards and it could prove difficult to order a meal in many places after 10pm.

For the Russian vocabulary for food and drink and eating out see the section on Language.

Food

Traditionally the Russian cuisine is one of good, rich food. Visitors should not expect too much, however, even although there has been a considerable improvement in what is on offer with the opening of many privately owned and joint Russian-foreign ventures in recent years. The catering in hotels, though, does not reflect the national shortages in many foodstuffs.

The main meals at midday and in the evening almost always begin with a starter (zakuski) which Russians wash down with a vodka.
Typical zakuski are Russian (i.e. vegetable) salad, smoked salmon or sturgeon, salmon roe, herring with onions and fish or meat in aspic. Bliny with caviar (see entry) is a particular delicacy. Pirogy, pasties with various fillings, are another favourite and sold from innumerable stands on the street.

Starters

The Russians are famous for their tasty soups. Best known of all is borscht, with beetroot its main ingredient, served with a swirl of sour cream. Oroshka is a cold soup of potatoes, radish, cucumber, chives, diced meat and a dash of "kvass". Solyanka comes in two versions, either with boiled or fried meat, plus cucumber, onions, tomato purée and olives, or with white fish and vegetables. Shchi is cabbage soup with carrots, tomato purée and sour cream.

Soup

The number of meat dishes is relatively limited, and often diners have to content themselves with a none too tender steak. Beef stroganoff when it appears on the menu is thin strips of beef braised with onions, mushrooms and sour cream. Various versions of meat rissoles are also quite popular.

Meat

Fish plays an important part in Russian cuisine, especially sturgeon in various guises. Salmon, trout and pike-perch also figure prominently on the menu. Srsy consists of fillets of fish with a filling of mushrooms, onions and parsley.

Fish

Choice of dessert is usually between ice-cream and various cakes and pastries.

Dessert

Drink

Soft drinks

The all-conquering invasion of Moscow by Coca Cola and other soft drinks from the West means there are fewer of the old-style vending machines selling such Russian beverages as kvass, the mildly alcoholic fermented brew of rye, buckwheat, malt, fruit and sugar which once used to be very popular. Russian lemonade tends to be very sweet and the mineral water tastes strongly of minerals. Imported Western soft drinks are now available almost everywhere.

Tea, coffee

Most meals end with tea or coffee. While visitors may not always find the coffee to their taste Russian tea is excellent. The customer takes this from a samovar; the cup or glass should be filled to about half full with the tea concentrate kept hot in the container over the samovar and then topped up with the samovar's boiling water.

Beer

Russian beer is very light and generally to be recommended. Foreign beer is also available for hard currency.

Wine

Russian wine may seem rather too sweet for some tastes but there are also dryer red and white wines from Moldavia and the Ukraine. Russian champagne is on offer in most restaurants but the dryer versions are more difficult to find.

Vodka

Tots of vodka, the national drink, are measured in grams rather than litres, as is the case with all alcoholic drinks in the CIS. When drinking in company the glass has to be downed in one go although the aftermath can be tempered by a chaser of mineral water.

Freedom of Movement

The tourist visa for a visit to Moscow (see Travel Documents) still only entitles the visitor to freedom of movement within 40km/25 miles of the Russian capital. In fact there is currently nothing to prevent the foreign visitor leaving the city on an excursion into the surrounding area. On organised sightseeing trips the tour operator is automatically responsible for attending to the formalities.

Galleries

Works for sale

Art Moderne Gallery
Ulitsa Bolshaya Ordynka 39; open: Tue.–Fri. 11am–8pm, Sat. 11am–6pm
Paintings and sculpture by contemporary Russian artists

Compromise
Ulitsa Gerzena 53; open: daily noon–7pm
Prints and paintings

Contemporary Art Centre
Ulitsa Dimitrova 6; open: Tue.–Sat. noon–7pm
Several galleries each with a different focus

The Art Gallery of Modern Art
Ulitsa Malaya Filevvskaya 32; open: Tue.–Sun. noon–8pm
Modern avant-garde Russian art

The Exhibition Hall of MOSKHA
Kuznetsky Most 11; open: Mon., Wed.–Sun. noon–7pm
Various exhibitions, mostly of a high standard

The Exhibition Hall of the Union of Artists
Tverkaya Ulitsa 25/9; open: Tue.–Sun. 1–6pm
Russian avant-garde from the Twenties to the Sixties

Solyanka
Ulitsa Solyanka 1/2; open: Wed.–Sun. 11am–6pm
Temporary exhibitions of sculpture, painting, photography, etc.

See Museums   Art collections

Getting to Moscow

The easiest way to get to Moscow is by air. There are direct flights daily by a   By air
number of international airlines to Sheremetyevo II international airport
from most of Europe's major cities including London (British Airways and
Aeroflot). The flight from London to Moscow takes about 3¾ hours. Aeroflot also operates regular weekly flights from New York with a flight-time of
about 11 hours.
The cheapest and most trouble-free way to travel is to take a package trip.
This still leaves group members free for sightseeing in Moscow on their
own if they wish (see Group Travel).

There are trains to Moscow from other major cities in Western and Central   By rail
Europe but it is a long and tedious journey and few visitors opt for this
mode of travel. The Paris to Moscow express runs daily, stopping at
Aachen, Cologne, Hanover and Berlin (see also Rail Stations).

Travel by private car can be undertaken in the CIS at any time but road   By road
journeys in Russia bear no comparison with elsewhere in Europe. The
wisest course is to leave Intourist (see Information) to make the
arrangements.
In view of the lack of facilities away from the main roads and the road
standards (see Motoring), although foreign visitors are no longer restricted
to specific routes, the best way to get to Moscow by car or motorcycle is still
via Warsaw and Minsk.

Group Travel

Package tours to Moscow are available from a number of international tour
operators as well as Intourist. Generally there is little to choose between
them in terms of price and what is on offer. They usually last for between
three and eight days and often combine a stay in Moscow with a short visit
to St Petersburg.
Group travel in a package of this kind is undoubtedly the cheapest way to
get to Moscow. The price includes reduced air fares and accommodation
costs (independent travellers tend to pay twice as much for hotels) and
visits to the theatre, ballet, museums, etc. Generally speaking group visitors also tend to get preferential treatment over independent travellers
when it comes to service in restaurants or admission to museums, yet
another reason, apart from the cost, for recommending a package tour of
this kind. Once in Moscow it is always possible to break away from the
group and only opt for programme highlights such as the sightseeing tour
of the city or museum visits – this avoids waiting in a long queue.

Hotels

Visitors to Moscow who are not part of a group must expect to pay between
£80 and £160 a night for a single room with breakfast; the price of a double

room is between £88 and £200. All rooms, even in the more modest hotels, have a bath or shower and toilet as well as a telephone, fridge and television. With group travel single people travelling alone will normally be expected to share, in which case the single-room supplement they have paid in advance will subsequently be refunded by the tour operator.

Passports and visas have to be handed in at the hotel on arrival and they should both be returned once the registration form has been filled in.

One special feature of Russian hotels is the card stating the room number and dates of arrival and departure. This may have to be shown from time to time on entering the hotel but must be produced when collecting the room key from reception.

Some of the older hotels still have a female attendant on each floor who is in charge of the keys for that floor. Besides presiding over a stock of drinks and medicines, she also arranges telephone calls and should deal with any problems that may arise.

Hotel stock

Moscow's hotel stock has become more diverse as several of the older establishments have been lavishly restored and new luxury hotels have been built, with yet more to come. However, although there are now enough hotel rooms at the top of the price range those which come up to Western standards further down the price scale continue to be in short supply.

All the hotels listed here have more than one restaurant. Some take roubles and hard currency, others take hard currency only, and Western imported spirits and alcohol can only be bought with hard currency. Every hotel has a hard currency shop, its own sub-post office, money-changing facilities, and a service desk with English-speaking staff who can organise excursions, arrange for car rental, make restaurant reservations, book theatre tickets, etc.

A selection of Moscow hotels

Aerostar
Leningradsky Prospekt 37; tel. 1 55 50 30
Metro: Aeroport
417 rooms; built in 1992, the hotel is part of a large complex. The rooms are quite modest but tastefully furnished.

*Baltschug Kempinski
Baltschug Ulitsa 1; tel. 2 30 95 00
Metro: Novokusnetskaya
235 rooms; this comfortable hotel was opened in October 1992 and is on the Moskva directly opposite Red Square. The façade is the only part retained from the Hotel Bucharest which used to stand on this site.

Belgrade
Smolenskaya Ploshchad 5; tel. 2 48 16 43
Metro: Smolenskaya
920 rooms; modernisation planned.

Budapest
Petrovskye Linii 2/18; tel. 2 94 88 20
Metro: Kuznetsky Most
214 rooms.

Cosmos
Prospekt Mira 150; tel. 2 17 07 85
Metro: VDNKh
1777 rooms; built for the 1980 Olympic Games and an old favourite with Western visitors. Its distance from the centre helps to keep down the room prices but there is a Metro station next door.

Hotel Baltshug-Kempinsky

Intourist
Tverskaya Ulitsa 3/5; tel. 2 03 15 65
Metro: Okhotny Ryad, Teatralnaya, Ploshchad Revolyutsii
450 rooms; a typical hotel of the Soviet era. Popular with tourists because of its central position and relatively low prices (restaurants, evening floor-show, casino).

Leningradskaya
Kalenchovskaya Ulitsa 21/40; tel. 9 75 30 32
Metro: Komsomolskaya
Built 1953; 513 rooms, casino.

＊Metropol
Teatralny Proesd 1/4; tel. 9 27 64 54
Metro: Teatralnaya, Okhotny Ryad, Ploshchad Revolyutsii
415 rooms; built in Art Nouveau style 1899–1903, and reopened in 1991 following extensive restoration. Fascinating interior with halls of marble columns and crystal chandeliers. Above the central restaurant there is a vast dome of honey-coloured Tiffany glass.

Mezhdunarodnaya I and II
Krasnopresnenskaya Nab. 12; tel. 2 53 13 92
Taxi recommended (nearest Metro: Krasnopresnenskaya)
1090 rooms; for a long time regarded as Moscow's only luxury hotel and mainly used by people travelling on business.

Minsk
Tverskaya Ulitsa 22; tel. 2 99 13 00
Metro: Pushkinskaya, Mayakovskaya
559 rooms; relatively cheap with fittings to match.

*Moscow Palace Hotel
Tverskaya Yamskaya Ulitsa 19; tel. 9 56 31 52
Metro: Mayakovskaya
228 rooms; opened in 1993, part of the Marco Polo Group.

Moskva
Okhotny Ryad 7; tel. 2 91 10 00
Metro: Okhotny Ryad, Teatralnaya, Ploshchad Revolyutsii
1580 rooms; Hotel Moskva was built as the first Soviet hotel by the architect
Alexei Shchussev in 1935. An American hotel group is now trying to bring it
up to western standards.

National
Mokhovaya Ulitsa 14/1
Metro: Okhotny Ryad, Teatralnaya, Ploshchad Revolyutsii
Built in 1903; many famous people have stayed here (see A–Z, Manege
Square). Due for reopening in 1994 as a luxury hotel.

*Novotel
At Sheremetyevo II Airport; tel. 2 20 66 11
Bus shuttle service to the centre or taxi recommended.
516 rooms.

*Olympic Penta Hotel
Olympyisky Prospekt 18/1; tel. 9 71 63 01
Metro: Prospekt Mira
500 rooms; opened in 1991 as another luxury hotel.

Peking
Ulitsa Bolshaya Sadovaya 1/5; tel. 2 09 24 42
Metro: Mayakovskaya
246 rooms; built 1946–50 in Old Russian style.

*Pullman Iris
Korovinskoya Shosse 10; tel. 4 88 80 00
Taxi recommended.
211 rooms; opened in 1991 as a Russian/French joint venture. 20km/
12 miles from the city centre.

Rossiya
Ulitsa Varvarka 6; tel. 2 98 54 00
Metro: Kitay-Gorod
Built in 1967 with 5360 rooms, this is Russia's largest hotel; some rooms
have breathtaking views of St Basil's Cathedral and the Kremlin.

*Savoy
Ulitsa Rozhdestvenka 3; tel. 9 28 85 00
Metro: Kuznetsky Most, Lubyanka
86 rooms; opened under Russian/Finnish management in 1989 in the
former Hotel Berlin (built 1912). Its exquisite old interior makes this one of
Moscow's finest hotels.

*Sovietskaya
Leningradsky Prospekt 32/2; tel. 2 50 72 53
Metro: Belorusskaya
60 rooms; now run as a Russian/French joint venture, this was formerly
reserved for official guests and visiting delegations

Sport
Leninsky Prospekt 90; tel. 1 31 11 91
700 rooms; originally chiefly reserved for sports visitors, quite basic but
very reasonably priced.

Hotel Rossiya

Ukraina
Kutusovsky Prospekt 2/1; tel 2 43 30 30
Metro: Kievskaya
1600 rooms; Gothic skyscraper built in 1956 and diagonally opposite the
White House.

Zentralnaya (former Hotel Lux)
Tverskaya Ulitsa 10; tel. 2 29 85 89
Metro: Pushkinskaya, Tverskaya
Following a failed takeover by the Hilton chain negotiations are now under
way on using foreign capital to renovate the building (see A–Z, Tverskaya
Ulitsa).

Information

Intourist, which used to be the state-run tour operator for all foreign visitors
to the Soviet Union, has been privatised and now has to compete in the
market with other tourist companies. There is no official tourist information
service in the CIS but all hotels have service desks which can deal with
enquiries, arrange excursions, city tours and theatre and concert tickets,
make restaurant reservations, book taxis, etc. These service points are
usually staffed by English-speaking personnel who are at their post from
9am to 9pm.

Intourist
Mochovaya Ulitsa 13; tel. 2 92 37 86 and 2 92 44 03

Information
in Moscow

Intourservice
Ulitsa Belinskogo 4; tel. 2 02 99 75 and 2 03 89 43

Insurance

in Canada	Intourist 1801 McGill College Avenue, Suite 630, Montreal, Quebec H3A 2N4; tel. 514 849 6394
in the United Kingdom	Intourist Travel Limited Intourist House, 219 Marsh Wall, London E14 9FJ; tel. 071 538 8600
in the United States	Intourist 630 Fifth Avenue, Suite 868, New York NY 10111; tel. 212 757 3884

Insurance

Visitors are strongly advised to ensure that they have adequate insurance including loss or damage to luggage, loss of currency and jewellery. Although British citizens are entitled to free medical services, short-term health cover is also essential and should include provision for air transport home in an emergency.

Motorists driving their own vehicles in Russia should take out a fully comprehensive insurance for the CIS since third party insurance there is not compulsory and the usual Green Card is not valid.

Language

It is not absolutely essential for visitors to Moscow to know Russian, since guides and group leaders speak English and it is usually possible in a hotel or restaurant to find someone who understands English; but in order to be able to understand the names of streets and Metro stations it is advisable to know at least the Russian (Cyrillic) alphabet.

The Alphabet

Cyrillic alphabet		Transliteration	Pronunciation
А	а	a	a
Б	б	b	b
В	в	v	v (f at end of syllable)
Г	г	g	g*
Д	д	d	d
Е	е	e	e (after consonant) ye (after vowel, and and at beginning of word)
Ё	ё	ë, o, yo	o (after , , and) yo (in all other cases)
Ж	ж	zh	zh (like s in "treasure")
З	з	z	z
И	и	i	yi (after) i (in all other cases)
Й	й	y	y (vocalic)
К	к	k	k
Л	л	l	l
М	м	m	m
Н	н	n	n
О	о	o	o
П	п	p	p
Р	р	r	r

Cyrillic alphabet		Transliteration	Pronunciation
С	с	s	s
		t	t
Т	т	u	u
У	у	f	f
Ф	ф	kh	ch (as in "loch")
Х	х	ts	ts
Ц	ц	ch	ch
Ч	ч	sh	sh
Ш	ш	shch	shch
Щ	щ		(hardens following vowel)
Ъ	ъ		
Ы	ы		y (vocalic)
Ь	ь		(softens following vowel)
Э	э	e	e
Ю	ю	yu	yu
Я	я	ya	ya

* Exceptionally, the *g* in the masculine genitive ending *ogo, ego* is pronounced *v*,

Useful Words

English	Pronunciation
Address	ádres
Airport	aeropórt
Bad	plókho
Bank	bank
Bar	bar
Bridge	most
Britain	velikobritániya
Bus	avtóbus
Canada	kanáda
Cash-desk	kássa
Caution!	vnimánie!
Chemist's	aptyéka
Closed	zakrýto
Day	dyen
England	ángliya
Entrance	vkhod
Excuse me!	izvinítye!
Exit	vykhod
Floor (storey)	etázh
Foodshop	gastronóm
Garden	sad
Good	khoroshó
Goodbye	do svidániya
Good day; how do you do?	zdrávstvuitye
Good evening	dóbry vécher
Here	zdyes
Hotel	gostínitsa
Ireland	irlándiya
Key	klyuch
"Key lady" (in hotel)	dezhúrnaya
Left (to the)	na lévo
Lift	lift
Market	rýnok
Menu	menyú

English	Pronunciation
Museum	muzéy
Newspaper	gazyéta
No	nyet
Open	otkrýto
Pedestrian crossing	perekhód
Please	pozhalsta
Post office	póchta
Railway station	voksál
Restaurant	restorán
Right (to the)	na právo
Room (in hotel)	nómer
Scotland	shotlándiya
Shop	magazín
Square	plóshchad
Stop	Stop
Street	úlitsa
Taxi	taksí
Telephone	telefón
Thank you	spasíbo
There	tam
Toilet	twalét
Train	póezd
Tram	tramváy
Underground (railway)	metró
United States	soedinyónye shtáty
Waiter	ofitsiánt
Waitress	dyévushka
Wales	wels
When?	kogdá?
Where?	gdye?
Yes	da
Your health!	na zdoróvye!

Numbers

English	Pronunciation
one	odín, odná, odnó
two	dva
three	tri
four	chetýrye
five	pyat
six	shest
seven	syem
eight	vósem
nine	dyévyat
ten	dyésyat

Days of the Week

Sunday	voskresénye
Monday	ponedyélnik
Tuesday	vtórnik
Wednesday	sredá
Thursday	chetvérg
Friday	pyátnitsa
Saturday	subbóta

Food and Drink

English	Pronunciation
Appetiser	zakúska
Beer	pívo
Bread	khlyeb
Butter	máslo
Caviare	ikrá
Chicken	kúritsa
Coffee	kófye
Egg	yaitsó
Fish	rýba
Ice(-cream)	morózhenoe
Meat	myáso
Milk	molokó
Pepper	pérets
Salmon	syómga
Salt	sol
Sausage	kolbasá
Soup	sup
Sugar	sákhar
Tea	chay
Water	vodá
Wine	vinó

Markets

The markets supplied by farmers and smallholders with produce from every part of the country show no signs of food shortages. There is a wide choice of fruit and vegetables and the meat and poultry are excellent. Flowers will also always find a buyer. However, compare the prices with the average Russian wage and it soon becomes obvious that the ordinary man or woman in the street can only afford to shop there in exceptional circumstances.

Farmers' markets

Farmers' markets are held daily from 9am to 5pm in every part of Moscow. They are a colourful part of the street scene and well worth a look even if you are not planning to buy anything.

Dorogomilovsky Rynok
Ulitsa Moschayski Val 16; Metro: Kiyevskaya

Leningradsky Rynok
Tchassovaya Ulitsa 11; Metro: Sokol

Cheryomushkinsky Rynok
Lomonossovsky Prospekt 1; Metro: University

Zentralny Rynok
Zvetnoy Bulvar 15; Metro: Zvetnoy Bulvar

Ismailovsky Park
Eastern edge of the city; Metro: Ismailovsky Park
Open: Sat., Sun. 9am–5pm

Flea market

The area of stalls in Ismailovsky Park is expanding all the time and getting to the stage where it is almost impossible to take in the whole array of Russian souvenirs on offer. These include some very fine handicrafts and imaginative wooden toys as well as the inevitable junk.

Flower market outside a Metro station

Bird market	Ulitsa Bolshaya Kalitnikovskaya 42
	Metro: Proletarkaya (or by taxi); open: Sat., Sun. 9am–5pm

Moscow's bird and animal market is one of the sights of the city, worth a visit just for the spectacle. Besides birds it sells pets of all kinds, from rabbits to fish, and all the paraphernalia that goes with them.

Medical Assistance

In a minor emergency requiring first aid or in a case of non-serious illness tell the hotel reception or information service desk and they will call a doctor. In more serious cases also consult the appropriate embassy (see Diplomatic Representation).

Medical centres

American Medical Center
Shmitovsky Proyesd 3 (near Hotel Mezhdunarodnaya);
tel. 2 56 82 12 and 2 56 83 78. 24-hour emergency service.

European Medical Centre
Grusinsky Pereulok 3;
tel. 2 53 07 03 (at night and weekends: tel. 2 40 99 99)
24-hour emergency service.

Medication

A limited range of medication is also obtainable from these medical centres and some Western brands are stocked by the chemists listed below. However, anyone taking medicines on prescription should ensure that they have a sufficient supply with them since there is no guarantee that these will be available in Moscow. Aspirin, razor blades, items of personal hygiene, etc. are also expensive or in short supply in Russia so it would be sensible to take supplies of these as well.

The famous bird market

Pharmacon, Ulitsa Tverskaya 2
The upper floor where payment is in hard currency has a broader range of products than the ground floor where payment is in roubles.

Chemists

Stary Arbat, Ulitsa Arbat 25
Payment in hard currency.

Medical treatment is free in the casualty departments of the State clinics but not in the private medical centres listed above. The wisest course is to take out short-term medical insurance. This should include cover for an emergency flight home.

Medical insurance

Motoring

The old system of restricting visiting foreign motorists to designated roads within the former Soviet Union has been abolished and there is freedom of movement throughout the country apart from closed military areas. However, given the nature of road travel in the CIS, which bears no resemblance to other parts of Europe, it is still advisable to get Intourist to make the arrangements (see Information).

Freedom of movement

The quality of the Russian roads is very variable. Minor roads, including those in and around Moscow, have deep potholes. Tram and trolley tracks often stand out well above the road surface while sewer covers are sunk well below. There are no road markings outside the towns and no hard verges.

State of the roads

Drive on the right and overtake on the left. Road signs and traffic rules are generally in line with those of the rest of Europe.

Roads signs and traffic rules

Speed limits	60kph/37mph in built-up areas; elsewhere 90kph/56mph for vehicles up to 3.5 tonnes, 70kph/43mph for vehicles over 3.5 tonnes. Anyone who has not held a driving licence for more than two years may not drive at speeds in excess of 70kph/43mph.
Right of way	Traffic on main roads has the right of way if the road has signs with a yellow square in a black and white surround. On other roads traffic from the right has priority at intersections and on roundabouts. Cars must give way to trams and buses at all times.
Seat belts, fire extinguishers	The wearing of seat belts is compulsory and there are heavy fines for non-compliance. Vehicles must carry a fire extinguisher.
Lights	Lights should be kept on low beam at night in places with street lighting.
Drinking and driving	The CIS has an absolute ban on driving after drinking even the very smallest amount of alcohol.
Fuel	The supply situation for petrol and diesel is very variable. The wisest course is to keep the tank topped up although the queues waiting at the pumps can be very long.
Insurance	There is no compulsory third party liability insurance in the CIS so it is advisable to take out fully comprehensive cover for the duration of the visit. The international insurance certificate, or Green Card, does not apply but most insurance companies will issue special certificates.
Accidents, repairs	A number of Western car makers now have their own repair services in Moscow but it still makes sense to carry major spare parts. Always notify the police in the event of an accident (ring 02 for police, 03 for ambulance). Any accident should also be reported to Ingosstrach, the national insurance company (Pyatnizkaya Ulitsa 12, 113 035 Moscow; tel. 2 33 20 70).
Vehicle papers	See Travel Documents
	See also Getting to Moscow

Museums

Many museums are closed on the first or last day of the month or on the first or last Monday or Tuesday in addition to the usual days during the week.

The cost of admission to most of them seems extremely cheap to foreigners but for the Russians themselves it is very high. Consequently long queues waiting to get in are becoming a thing of the past even for the major museums. Admission to some of them, such as the Tretyakov Gallery, has to be paid for by foreigners in hard currency at prices which largely correspond to those for similar Western European museums. Guided tours of museums organised by Intourist (see Information) and other tour operators also require payment in hard currency which makes them correspondingly expensive.

Historical museums	Borodino Panorama Kutuzovsky Prospekt 38; Metro: Kutuzovskaya Open: Mon.–Thu., Sat., Sun. 10am–6pm This museum is built around the enormous panorama (115m/377ft× 15m/49ft) by Franz Rubo (1856–1928) of the Battle of Borodino when the Russians defeated Napoleon's army on 26th August 1812 at the village of Borodino about 120km/75 miles west of Moscow (see Excursions).

Boyar's House
See A–Z, Kitay-Gorod

Historical Museum
See A–Z

Museum on the History and Reconstruction of Moscow
See A–Z

Central Lenin Museum. See A–Z

Central Museum of the Revolution
See A–Z, Tverskaya Street

Lenin Funeral Train Museum
Pavaletsky Station
Paveletskaya Ploshchad; Metro: Paveletskaya
Open: Mon., Wed.–Sun. 10am–6pm
Part of the train which brought Lenin's body back to Moscow on 23rd
January 1924 (see Rail Stations).

Lenin Museum in the Kremlin
See A–Z, Kremlin: Presidential Residence

Andrei Rublev Museum. See A–Z, Andronikov Monastery

Museums of
Fine Art

Central Exhibition Hall. See A–Z, Manege

Golubkina Museum
12 Ulitsa Shukina; Metro: Smolenskaya
Open: Mon.–Fri. noon–7pm; Sat., Sun. 10am–5pm
Apartment and studio of sculptress Anna Golubkina (1864–1927).

Museum of Applied and Folk Art. See A–Z

Buildings of the Central Lenin Museum

Museums

Museum of Ceramics
See A–Z, Kuskovo

Museum of Folk Art
Ulitsa Stanislavskogo 7; Metro: Arbatskaya
Open: Tue., Thu. noon–8pm; Wed., Fri.–Sun. 10am–5pm
Russian folk art from the 17th to 19th c. (lacquer painting, wood carving, textiles) and outstanding examples of modern craftwork.

Museum of Oriental Art
See A–Z, Boulevard Ring

Museum of Serf Art
See A–Z, Ostankino Castle

Pushkin Museum of Fine Art
See A–Z

Shchusev Museum of Russian Architecture
See A–Z

State Armoury
See A–Z, Kremlin

State Art Gallery (New Tretyakov Gallery)
See A–Z

Tretyakov Gallery
See A–Z

Tropinin Museum
Shchetininsky Pereulok 10; Metro: Novokusnetskaya
Open: Mon., Thu., Fri. noon–6.30pm; Sat., Sun. 10am–4.30pm
This museum is devoted to the work of painter Vassily Tropinin and some of his contemporaries, and exhibits mainly portraits of personalities who played a role in the cultural life of Moscow in the 18th and early 19th c.

Vasnetsov Museum
See A–Z

Museums of
literature

Bulgakov Apartment
Although not strictly a museum, the former home, or rather its stairwell, of Michail Bulgakov (1891–1940; see Quotations) is of interest to devotees of Russian literature. The plaque in the passageway to the rear courtyard commemorates the writer whose work first gained recognition in the USSR in the 1960s. The stairwell is the other side of the courtyard and its walls have been decorated by Bulgakov's admirers with drawings and quotations from his work. Flowers are often placed outside the door of his apartment (No. 50 on the 4th floor).

Chekhov House
Sadovaya-Kudrinskaya Ulitsa 6
Metro: Krasnopresnenskaya, Barrikadnaya
Open: Tue., Thu., Sat., Sun. 11am–5pm; Wed., Fri. 1–7pm
Anton Chekhov, writer, dramatist and doctor (1860–1904), lived in this house, which he himself likened to a cupboard, with his mother and brothers and sisters from 1886 to 1890. Visitors can see the room where he held his surgery from noon to 3pm every day and where he wrote short stories and his first plays.

Dostoevsky House
Ulitsa Dostoevskogo 2; Metro: Tsvetnoy Bulvar
Open: Wed., Fri. 2–7pm; Thu., Sat., Sun. 11am–6pm. Closed last day of month.
The apartment in which Dostoevsky (1821–81) spent his childhood is in a wing of the former paupers' hospital where his father worked as a doctor. It is still furnished as it was in Dostoevsky's day and has many of his personal belongings.

Gorky Literary Museum
Ulitsa Povarskaya 25a; Metro: Arbatskaya
Open: Wed., Fri. noon–7pm; Mon., Tue., Thu. 10am–5pm. Closed last Thu. in month.
This museum, opened in 1937, brings together first editions of Maxim Gorky's works, his manuscripts and many other documents.

Gorky Museum (in the Shekhtel House)
See A–Z

Herzen Museum
Pereulok Sivtsev Vrazhek 27
Metro: Kropotskinskaya, Arbatskaya
Open: Tue., Thu., Sat., Sun. 11am–6pm; Wed., Fri. 2–8pm
The author and journalist Alexander Herzen (1812–70) lived in this house from 1843 to 1846. The illegitimate son of a German mother and a wealthy Russian landowner, as a young man Herzen advocated the abolition of serfdom and these revolutionary ideas led to his arrest and banishment. He left for Western Europe in 1847. The museum contains many of his personal belongings and various pictures and books; the furniture is in period but not the original.

Herzen Museum

Mayakovsky Museum
Proesd Serova 3/6; Metro: Kusnetsky Most, Lubyanka
Open: Mon. noon–6pm; Tue., Fri., Sat., Sun. 10am–6pm; Thu. 1–9pm
Although this museum is in the house where the writer Vladimir Mayakovsky (1893–1930) lived from 1919 to the end of his life, its redesign in the
1980s makes it quite different from most of the other museums in the
homes of famous Russian artists. The exhibits present a total work of art, a
powerful collage into which the viewer feels himself irresistibly drawn.
Also on display are pieces from an exhibition of "Twenty Years' Work"
which Mayakovsky had assembled in 1930 a few weeks before he shot
himself in his workroom.

Pasternak House. See A–Z, Peredelkino

Pushkin House. See A–Z, Arbat

Pushkin Museum. See A–Z

Tolstoy House. See A–Z

Tolstoy Museum. See A–Z

Yermolova Museum. See A–Z, Boulevard Ring

Museums of
Science

Darwin Museum
Closed at present and due to be rehoused.

Geographical Museum
Lomonosov University
Lomonosovsky Prospekt; Metro: University

Metro Museum
In Sportivnaya Metro Station
Open: Mon.–Fri. 9am–4pm
An insight into the history of the Moscow Underground.

Mineralogical Museum
18 Leninsky Prospekt
Metro: Schabolovskaya, Leninsky Prospekt
Open: Tue.–Sat. 10am–6pm

Museum of Palaeontology
Leninsky Prospekt 16
Metro: Shabolovskaya, Leninsky Prospect

Museum of Sport and Physical Culture
See A–Z, Luzhniki Sports Complex

Museum of Space Travel
See A–Z, All-Russia Exhibition Centre

Planetarium
Sadovaya Kudrinskaya Ulitsa 5
Metro: Barrikadnaya, Krasnopresnenskaya
Open: Mon., Wed.–Sat. 1–6pm, Sun. 10am–6pm

Polytechnic Museum. See A–Z

Timiryazev Museum of Biology
Malaya Grusinskaya Ulitsa 15
Metro: Ulitsa 1905 Goda, Krasnopresnenskaya, Barrikadnaya
Open: Tue., Thu., Sat., Sun. 10am–6pm; Wed., Fri. noon–8pm

Zoological Museum
Ulitsa Gertsena 6
Metro: Okhotny Ryad, Teatralnaya, Ploshchad Revolyutsii
Open: Tue., Sat., Sun. 10am–5pm, Wed., Fri. noon–8pm

Bakhrushin Theatre Museum
Ulitsa Bakrushina 31/12; Metro: Paveletskaya
Open: Mon., Thu., Sat., Sun. noon–7pm; Wed., Fri. 2–9pm
The theatre museum began as the private collection of patron of the arts
Alexander Bakhrushin (1865–1929) and now has over a million exhibits.

Glinka Museum of Musical Culture
Ulitsa Fadeyeva 4; Metro: Novoslobodskaya
Open: Tue., Thu. 2–7pm; Wed., Fri.–Sun. 11am–7pm
Innumerable sound records, manuscripts, letters, etc. connected with
major Russian and foreign composers and musicians are kept here and
used for research. The collection of musical instruments alone comprises
over 2000 items.

Nemirovich-Danchenko Museum
Ulitsa Nemirovich Danchenko 5
Metro: Tverskaya/Pushkinskaya
Open: Wed.–Sun. 11am–6pm
Director, writer and dramatist Vladimir Nemirovich-Danchenko (1835–
1943), one of the founders of the Moscow Actors' Studio, lived here during
the last five years of his life.

Shalyapin House
Ulitsa Tchaikovskogo 25; Metro: Smolenskaya
This museum commemorating the great Russian opera singer Fyodor
Shalyapin (1873–1938) was first opened in 1989.

Skryabin Museum
Ulitsa Vakhtangova 11
Metro: Smolenskaya, Arbatskaya
Composer and pianist Alexander Skryabin (1872–1915) lived here in the
Ulitsa Vakhtangova from 1912 until his death.

Stanislavsky Museum
Ulitsa Stanlislavskogo 6
Metro: Tverskaya, Pushkinskaya
Open: Wed., Fri. 2–9pm; Thu., Sat., Sun. 11am–6pm
This small museum is devoted to Konstantin Stanislavsky, director, actor
and co-founder of the Actors' Studio, who died in 1938.

(margin note) Theatrical and musical museums

Newspapers and Periodicals

Newspapers and periodicals from the West are on sale in the larger hotels
while Moscow News, the English-language daily, provides the local news
on political happenings and also has entertainment and restaurant listings.

Night Life

Although Moscow still has relatively little night life compared with most
major Western cities this too is changing with the times.

The hotels (see entry) all have a number of bars selling wine, beer and
spirits from the West for hard currency. Foreign visitors virtually have these

(margin note) Bars

bars to themselves, usually without any accompanying programme of light entertainment. The Sadko Arcade (Expocenter, Krasnogvardeysky Proyesd 1) also has several bars and pubs.

Nightclubs and floor shows	**Russkaya Troika** Hotel Oryonok, Ulitsa Kossygin 15 Floor show (Thu.–Sun. only) with dancing after the two-hour show.

Night Flight
Ulitsa Tverskaya 17; 9pm–5am daily (restaurant until 4am).
Swedish-run nightclub. Hard currency charge for admission.

Metropol Hotel Night Show
Dancing after 11pm with floor show.

Intourist Hotel Floor Show
Starts at 10.30pm, followed by a disco.

Many restaurants (see entry) also have floor shows and orchestras for dancing.

Casinos

Casino Royale
In the Hippodrome, Begovaya Ulitsa 22; daily 8pm–5am.
Blackjack, roulette, poker, etc. in elegant surroundings.

Alexander Blok
(on board the ship of the same name)
Krasnopresnenskaya Nabereshnaya 12; daily 8pm–3am.

A number of hotels (see entry) such as the Savoy, Intourist and Leningradkaya also have casinos.

Jazz

Sinyaya Ptiza (Blue Bird)
Ulitsa Chechova 23; guest appearances by Russian and internationally famous jazz groups and musicians.

Arkadia Jazz Club
Teatralny Proyesd 3; restaurant from 7pm, jazz after midnight.

Opening Times

See Business Hours

Parks and Gardens

Moscow's parks and gardens play an important role in a city not over-endowed with leisure facilities and provide popular meeting places and a whole range of opportunities for entertainment.

Botanic Garden of the Academy of Sciences
Botanicheskaya Ulitsa 3 Metro: Botanichesky Sad

Fili Recreation Park
Novozavodskaya Ulitsa; Metro: Filyovsky Park

Gorky Park. See A–Z

Izmailovsky Culture and Recreation Park
Narodny Prospekt 17; Metro: Izmailovsky Park

The largest park in the east of the city where numerous walks, extensive streams and lakes, sports facilities and swings and roundabouts provide peace and quiet as well as all the fun of the fair. A further attraction is the weekend flea market on the edge of the park (see Markets).

Silver Grove (Serebryany Bor)
Metro: Poleshayevskaya (then 20, 21 or 65 bus)
Silver Grove is a recreational area in the west of the city with a beach on the Moskva. It is particularly popular at the weekends, when many Muscovites come here to relax in their dachas.

Zoological Garden
Ulitsa Kranaya Presnya; Metro: Barrikadnaya/Krasnopresnenskaya
Open: daily from 9am to 8pm in summer, 6pm in spring and autumn, 5pm in winter. (The ticket gives admission to both parts of the complex.).

Photography and Film

There is still a ban on filming or photographing military and industrial installations, airports, train stations, bridges and radio transmitters. Although photography from the air, which used to include pictures taken from tall buildings, is still forbidden this has been eased in so far as a panoramic view of the city from a high vantage point is now permitted. Photography is allowed in most museums apart from the Tretyakov Gallery but a small fee is charged in some of them. Filming is not permitted in the Kremlin Cathedral or in many of the other churches.

When and when not to photograph

Although foreign film can now be bought in various shops and hard currency stores it is usually much more expensive than in the West and particular brands can be hard to find. The best course is to make sure to take an adequate supply of film, batteries, etc.

Film

Souvenir slides of Moscow are on sale in hard currency stores and many similar places but they are not always top quality.

Souvenir slides

Post

Letter boxes for mail to destinations outside Moscow are blue. The occasional red ones are for mail within the city to speed delivery.
Letters, parcels and telegrams can also be sent from the postal kiosks in nearly every hotel of any size. Like post offices and newsagents they also sell stamps, but galloping inflation has meant that these are becoming an increasingly rare commodity except in hard currency stores at high prices.

Main post office: Myasnizkaya Ulitsa 26a

International post office: Varshavskoe Shosse 37

A Russian post-box

Post offices

Public Holidays

Following the transformation of the Soviet Union into the Commonwealth of Independent States a number of political public holidays such as

May Day and the Anniversary of the October Revolution have been discontinued and religious ones such as the Russian Orthodox Christmas reinstated.

1st January	New Year: there is an exchange of presents, and fir trees are put up in people's homes and public squares. The festive meal on New Year's Eve is followed by the popping of champagne corks at midnight and fireworks to usher in the New Year.
7th January	Christmas: since 1991 church services have again marked the Orthodox Russian Christmas but the way people celebrate this in their homes still varies since hitherto New Year's Day has enjoyed many of the trappings of Christmas.
8th March	International Women's Day: women receive a little gift from their menfolk.
9th May	Victory Day: the celebration of the ending of the Second World War in Europe is primarily a day for war veterans who hold rallies at various points in the city.
12th June	Independence Day: the anniversary of Russia's declaration of independence in 1991.

Public Transport

Metro, buses, trams, trolleys

For public transport Moscow has its famous Underground, the Metro, as well as buses, trams and suburban trolleys. The fastest and most convenient way of getting around is the Metro (see plan on page 168/69) which has over 140 stations – indicated by a red "M" which is lit up at night – throughout the city and more are being planned as the network expands. Several of the stations are worth seeing in their own right even for non-passengers (see Baedeker Special pp. 104/5).

Public transport runs every day from 6am until 1am, with the morning and evening rush hours coming at between 7 and 9am and 4 and 6pm. At peak times there are trains every 40 seconds as compared with the usual 1½ to 2 minutes. Digital clocks on every platform show the time and how long has elapsed since the last train. Trams and buses are less frequent with waits of up to ten minutes in some cases.

Fares

There are no conductors on Moscow's public transport. Buses, trams and trolleys all have the same tickets. These can be bought in strips from kiosks, in hotels or at a slightly higher price from the driver. Passengers then have to punch their own tickets in the automats when they board. A different system operates for the Metro. Here tokens are purchased at the station and inserted into the slot at the barrier. The actual fare is constantly changing with currency devaluation – as of summer 1993 the cost of a token was 10 roubles.

Finding the way

When using public transport in Moscow it helps to be able to read the names in Cyrillic script (see plan of the Metro on page 168/69, also Language, Cyrillic alphabet). The colours correspond to those of the lines as displayed on the plans in the Metro stations, but otherwise there is no colour coding of the directions inside the stations or on the platforms. These simply give the names in Cyrillic script of the stations on that line. Trams and buses have boards on their sides giving the names of the main places they stop at.
Although the names of the stops are always announced knowing when to get off at the right bus or tram stop can still be something of a problem. It is easier in the Metro where the plans in every carriage make it easier to follow the journey.

Nevertheless, changing from one line to another can still prove quite difficult. If for example you are travelling on the red line to Ochotny Ryad and want to change onto the green line to get to Tretyakovskaya you have to walk for some distance through the subway to Teatralnaya station and then board the train for Tretyakovskaya. To complicate matters further some stations can have two or even three different names.

In summer there is a river bus service on the Moskva. Boarding stages include those at Gorky Park and close by the Kremlin.

River buses

Rail Stations

Moscow has nine main-line stations with eleven electrified lines from abroad as well as from other states in the CIS and all parts of Russia which terminate here. Local trains also provide a relatively cheap way of getting quickly to places worth seeing in the vicinity of the city (see Excursions). Travelling by train can be quite an adventure for anyone unable to speak Russian since usually it is only by asking that you find out which platform the train actually leaves from. However a visit to the station is an experience in itself even for non-travellers because of the colourful mix of passengers such as those waiting to catch the Trans-Siberian express at Yaroslavsky Station.

All the stations lie between the Garden Ring and the outer ring road. Most of them are close to the Garden Ring and all are easy to get to by Metro. Some date from the 19th c. but for a large part they are in the Old Russian style of the turn of the century.

Belorussky Voksal
See A–Z, Tverskaya Street

Belorussian
Station

Kasansky Voksal
Kalantshovksya Ploshchad; Metro: Komsomolskaya
Trains to Kasan, the Urals and Central Asia
The building dates from 1926 and was the work of Shchusev.

Kazan Station

Kievsky Voksal
Kievskogo Voksala Ploshchad; Metro: Kievskaya
Trains to Prague, Bucharest, Belgrade, Budapest, Kiev
The neo-classical building is the work of J. Rerberg and was built between 1914 and 1917.

Kiev Station

Kursky Voksal
Kurskogo Voksala Ploshchad; Metro: Kurskaya
Trains to the Crimea and the Caucusus
Built in 1896 and extended in the 1970s.

Kursk Station

Leningradky Voksal
Kalantshovskaya Ploshchad 3; Metro: Komsomolskaya
Trains to St Petersburg, Murmansk and Finland
As yet not renamed, Leningrad Station is Moscow's oldest and was built in 1851 by the architect Konstantin Thon for the first railway line between Moscow and St Petersburg. The same architect was also responsible for a station similar in every detail in St Petersburg.

Leningrad
Station

Pavaletsky Voksal
Pavaletskaya Ploshchad; Metro: Pavelezkaya
Trains to Kursk, Charkov, Simferopol, Erevan and Baku
Pavelesky Station, built in 1900, was where the train arrived in January 1924 bringing Lenin's body back to Moscow. This is commemorated in the Lenin Funeral Train Museum (see Museums).

Pavaletsky
Station

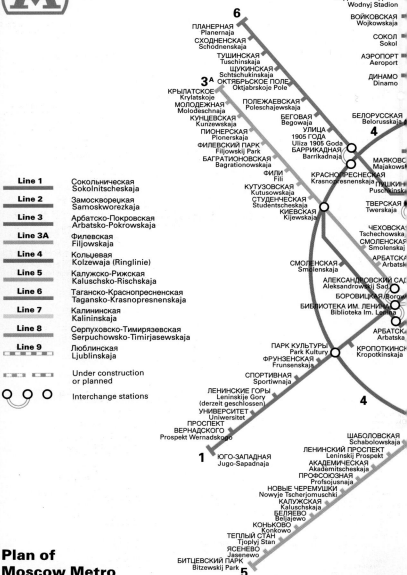

РЕЧНОЙ ВОКЗАЛ
Retschnoj Woksal

ВОДНЫЙ СТАДИОН
Wodnyj Stadion

ВОЙКОВСКАЯ
Wojkowskaja

СОКОЛ
Sokol

АЭРОПОРТ
Aeroport

ДИНАМО
Dinamo

6

ПЛАНЕРНАЯ
Planernaja
СХОДНЕНСКАЯ
Schodnenskaja
ТУШИНСКАЯ
Tuschinskaja
ЩУКИНСКАЯ
Schtschukinskaja
3ᴬ ОКТЯБРЬСКОЕ ПОЛЕ
Oktjabrskoje Pole

КРЫЛАТСКОЕ
Krylatskoje
МОЛОДЕЖНАЯ
Molodeschnaja
КУНЦЕВСКАЯ
Kunzewskaja
ПИОНЕРСКАЯ
Pionerskaja
ФИЛЕВСКИЙ ПАРК
Filjowskij Park
БАГРАТИОНОВСКАЯ
Bagrationowskaja
ФИЛИ
Fili
КУТУЗОВСКАЯ
Kutusowskaja
СТУДЕНЧЕСКАЯ
Studentscheskaja
КИЕВСКАЯ
Kijewskaja

ПОЛЕЖАЕВСКАЯ
Poleschajewskaja
БЕГОВАЯ
Begowaja
УЛИЦА
1905 ГОДА
Uliza 1905 Goda
БАРРИКАДНАЯ
Barrikadnaja

КРАСНОПРЕСНЕНСКАЯ
Krasnopresnenskaja

БЕЛОРУССКАЯ
Belorusskaja
4

МАЯКОВС
Majakows

ПУШКИН
Puschkinsk

ТВЕРСКАЯ
Twerskaja

ЧЕХОВСКА
Tschechowska
СМОЛЕНСКАЯ
Smolenskaja
АРБАТСКА
Arbatsk

СМОЛЕНСКАЯ
Smolenskaja

АЛЕКСАНДРОВСКИЙ САД
Aleksandrowskij Sad
БОРОВИЦКАЯ/Borow
БИБЛИОТЕКА ИМ. ЛЕНИНА
Biblioteka Im. Lenina

АРБАТСКА
Arbatska

ПАРК КУЛЬТУРЫ
Park Kultury
ФРУНЗЕНСКАЯ
Frunsenskaja

КРОПОТКИНС
Kropotkinskaja

СПОРТИВНАЯ
Sportiwnaja
ЛЕНИНСКИЕ ГОРЫ
Leninskije Gory
(derzeit geschlossen)
УНИВЕРСИТЕТ
Uniwersitet
ПРОСПЕКТ
ВЕРНАДСКОГО
Prospekt Wernadskogo

4

1 ЮГО-ЗАПАДНАЯ
Jugo-Sapadnaja

ШАБОЛОВСКАЯ
Schabolowskaja
ЛЕНИНСКИЙ ПРОСПЕКТ
Leninskij Prospekt
АКАДЕМИЧЕСКАЯ
Akademitscheskaja
ПРОФСОЮЗНАЯ
Profsojusnaja
НОВЫЕ ЧЕРЕМУШКИ
Nowyje Tscherjomuschki
КАЛУЖСКАЯ
Kaluschskaja
БЕЛЯЕВО
Beljajewo
КОНЬКОВО
Konkowo
ТЕПЛЫЙ СТАН
Tjoplyj Stan
ЯСЕНЕВО
Jasenewo
БИТЦЕВСКИЙ ПАРК
Bitzewskij Park
5

Line 1	Сокольническая
	Sokolnitscheskaja
Line 2	Замоскворецкая
	Samoskworezkaja
Line 3	Арбатско-Покровская
	Arbatsko-Pokrowskaja
Line 3A	Филевская
	Filjowskaja
Line 4	Кольцевая
	Kolzewaja (Ringlinie)
Line 5	Калужско-Рижская
	Kaluschsko-Rischskaja
Line 6	Таганско-Краснопресненская
	Tagansko-Krasnopresnenskaja
Line 7	Калининская
	Kalininskaja
Line 8	Серпуховско-Тимирязевская
	Serpuchowsko-Timirjasewskaja
Line 9	Люблинская
	Ljublinskaja

Under construction
or planned

○○○ Interchange stations

Plan of Moscow Metro

difference whether payment is in roubles or hard currency, they will simply apply the current exchange rate.

Most restaurants open throughout the week for lunch and then from 6pm until they close at around 11pm.

Opening times

Arlecchino (credit cards)
Ulitsa Drushynovskaya 15; tel. 2 05 70 88
Average Italian food at excessive prices.

Top category
restaurants

Boyarsky (hard currency and credit cards)
In the Hotel Metropol (see Hotels)
Probably the most appealing of the Metropol's four restaurants, a former Russian tearoom under a vast glass dome with atmosphere and live music. Buffet service only.

Glazour (credit cards)
Smolensky Bulvar 12 (first floor); tel. 2 48 44 38
Luxurious joint venture serving lovingly prepared Russian food. The starters are a work of art in themselves (background music folk at lunchtime, occasionally jazz at night).

Imperial (hard currency)
Ryleyeva Ulitsa 9; tel. 2 91 60 63
Privately-owned with good Russian food in elegant surroundings.

Kropotkinskaya 36 (hard currency)
Ulitsa Prechistenka 36; tel. 2 01 75 00
Quality in the first co-operative restaurant in Moscow may vary but the ambience is invariably pleasing. On two floors of what was Count Trubetskoy's stately home, there are two dining rooms, one in the more formal surroundings of the ground-floor salon, the other in the cosier setting of the vaulted basement. Recommended specialities include the soups – borscht and shchi – and blini and Siberian pelmeni (meat pasties). Wines from France, Georgia and California feature on the wine-list.

Potel & Chabot (hard currency)
Bolshaya Kommunisticheskaya 2A; tel. 2 71 07 07
Exceptionally fine French cuisine and a good selection of wines (light business menu at lunchtimes).

Savoy (hard currency and credit cards)
In the Hotel Savoy (see Hotels)
Dining in elegant Art Nouveau splendour, complete with potted palms and tinkling piano, although the food is not always up to the standard of the decor.

Swiss Chalet (hard currency)
Korobeynikov Pereulok 1/2; tel. 2 02 01 06
Swiss dishes in a sophisticated setting with an outstanding wine-list.

Writers' Union (hard currency)
Ulitsa Vorovskogo 52; tel. 2 91 21 69
The Writers' Union, previously only open to members and their guests, has been opened up to the public relatively recently and is worth a visit if only to see its grand panelled interior.

Yevropeysky Sal (European Hall; hard currency and credit cards)
In the Hotel Metropol (see Hotels)
The Hotel Metropol's second magnificent restaurant, with its dining "à la carte" and the kind of service and cuisine to be expected from such a richly traditional establishment.

Restaurants

Middle category

Aragvi (roubles)
Ulitsa Tverskaya 6; tel. 2 29 37 62
The Aragvi, in its lovely vaulted cellars, used to enjoy an excellent reputation with its typically Georgian dishes but this has become somewhat tarnished of late. Specialities include chicken in hazelnut sauce, spicy brown beans, shashlik and above all the hot round flat bread.

Arbat (roubles). Ulitsa Novy Arbat 29; tel. 2 91 14 45
Moscow's largest restaurant with seating for around 1000 and a favourite with big Russian family parties (stage show, dancing).

Atrium (roubles and hard currency)
Leninsky Prospekt 44; tel. 1 37 30 08
Delicious food in a Roman setting amid enormous marble columns.

Delhi (roubles/hard currency)
Ulitsa Krasnaya Presnya 23b; tel. 2 52 17 66 (rouble restaurant),
tel. 2 55 04 92 (hard currency)
Excellent Indian food with two separate dining rooms, one with payment in roubles, the other, with a rather higher standard of food, decor and entertainment, hard currency only.

Italia (hard currency). Ulitsa Arbat 49; tel. 2 41 43 42
A little Italian restaurant where customers can sit outside in summer and watch the world go by on the Arbat, but do not expect too much of the food – or the service.

Pirosmani (roubles and hard currency)
Novodyevichy Proezd 4; tel. 2 47 19 26
Delicious Georgian food in a delightful setting (see Sightseeing Programme).

Prague (roubles and hard currency)
Ulitsa Arbat 2; tel. 2 90 61 71
The grand decor makes up for the usually rather indifferent food (live music for dancing).

Russkaya Isba (roubles)
In the village of Ilyinskoya 40km/25 miles outside Moscow; tel. 5 61 42 44
Typical Russian hospitality in a two-storey timbered building on the banks of the Moskva. It often gets very lively with the music on the ground floor, but upstairs is quieter.

Sedmoya Nebo (Seventh Heaven; roubles)
On the Ostankino TV tower; tel. 2 82 22 93
See A–Z, Television tower
Ordinary Russian fare, but with a fantastic view. Seating tickets are issued from the kiosk at the entrance; passports have to be shown on entering the lift as a security measure.

Slavyansky Bazaar (roubles and hard currency)
Ulitsa Nikolskaya 13; tel. 9 21 18 72
This restaurant made history in 1897 when Stanislavsky and Nemirovich-Danchenko spent 18 hours over a meal here deciding to set up the Moscow Actors' Studio. Other famous diners have included Chekhov and Tchaikovsky, and its illustrious past makes this vast restaurant a favourite spot with tourist groups and large Russian family parties, although the fare and live music are only average.

Taganka Bar (roubles for food, hard currency for alcohol)
Ulitsa Radishchevskaya 15; tel. 2 72 43 51
Usually packed, this cramped and noisy cellar bar has excellent sakuski; gypsy music.

Zolotoy Drakon (Golden Dragon; roubles and hard currency)
Ulitsa Plushchika 64; tel. 2 41 22 99
Many consider this by far the best Chinese restaurant in the city.

Cafe Union (roubles)
Bernikov Pereulok 2/6; tel. 2 27 28 05

Fast food and more basic surroundings

Coffeehouse (roubles)
Sadko Arcade, Krasnogvardeysky Proesd 1; tel. 9 40 40 71

McDonald's (roubles)
Ulitsa Bolshaya Bronnaya 29 (on Pushkin Square); tel. 2 00 16 55

Pizza Hut (roubles)
Ulitsa Tverskaya 12; tel. 2 29 20 13
Kutosovsky Prospekt 17; tel. 2 43 17 27

Shopping

Although Moscow is still far from a shopper's paradise the standard has improved considerably owing to the growing number of joint ventures with foreign retailers.

The typical Russian shop calls for a certain amount of patience on the part of the buyer. Once you decide on a purchase you have to find out the price, pay at the cash desk and then produce the receipt before you can finally collect the desired article from the sales counter.

Russian shops

The state-owned "beryozkas" ("little birches" in Russian) which once sold souvenirs for hard currency have been replaced by private enterprise stores which only take credit cards or dollars and other hard currencies. There are now many well-stocked food shops exclusively selling Western brands, as well as countless boutiques, camera shops, perfumeries, etc. which deal in hard currency only. Prices are roughly on a par with those of the West or in many cases somewhat higher, and can vary considerably from shop to shop.
All hotels catering for foreign visitors also have their own hard currency shops with a limited range of drinks, sweets, cigarettes, books, souvenirs, etc.

Hard currency stores

Most shops are open daily except Sundays and public holidays from 9 or 10am until around 8 or 9 pm, usually closing for an hour at lunch time. Many are also closed on Mondays. The advent of private enterprise has brought greater flexibility in opening hours and many of the hard currency food stores now open on Sundays as well.

Opening times

For GUM see A–Z.
Even GUM now has a number of in-store hard currency Western boutiques.

Department stores

Moskovsky Univermag
Kalantshevskaya Ploshchad 6
Although Moskovsky Univermag covers a larger floor area than GUM it cannot match it for the range of goods.

Petrovsky Passage
Ulitsa Petrovka 10
An upmarket sister shop to GUM selling men's and women's fashions, foreign designer wear, cameras, leather goods, etc. for hard currency or payment by credit card, with an Italian café.

Zum
Ulitsa Petrovka 2 (near the Bolshoi Theatre)
Traditional Russian department store.

Petrovsky Passash: here can be found . . .

. . . the most elegant boutiques

Yantar
Ulitsa Grusinsky Val 14
Relatively cheap amber for roubles.

Kommissiony
Ulitsa Tverskaya Yamskaya 16
Large selection of crystal and porcelain.

Unisat
Ulitsa Vachtangova 5
Fine porcelain and 19th c. arts and crafts, silver, samovars and pictures.

Other antique shops tend to be concentrated around the Arbat. Remember that the export of antiques from Russia is forbidden and that this general ban extends to paintings, drawings, sculpture, carpets, icons, church and domestic objects, weapons, furniture, clothing, books, musical instruments and costly items made before 1945.

Dom Knigi
Ulitsa Novy Arbat 26
The range of books available from what was Moscow's largest bookshop is currently very limited. To make up for the lack of books, antiques and even shoes are now sold here.

Inostrannaya Kniga
Ulitsa Kachalova 16
Foreign literature, art books.

Zwemmer
Kusnezky Most 18
English bookshop; hard currency.

Books, including art books and reference books, are also sold at stalls all over the city. The price tends to be negotiable and may not necessarily work out less than in the shops.

See Medical Assistance

Ulitsa Myasnizkaya 4
Modern Russian china and glass at low prices; roubles.

Andy's Fashion
Vernadskogo Prospekt 9/10
Upmarket men's and women's fashions; hard currency.

Benetton
Ulitsa Arbat 13
Men's, women's and children's clothing; hard currency.

Karstadt
Boutique in the GUM department store on Red Square; hard currency.

Stockmann
Leninsky Prospekt 73
Wide range of Western clothing; hard currency.

Petrovsky Arcade (Ulitsa Petrovka 10) is another source of upmarket men's and women's fashions.

Cosmetics can be bought in many of the stores in the foodstuffs section as well as in GUM and the Petrovsky Arcade.

Fuji Film Centre
Ulitsa Novy Arbat 25; hard currency.

Shopping

	Kodak GUM, ground floor Petrovsky Arcade, Ulitsa Petrovka 10; hard currency.
Foodstuffs	Danone Shop Ulitsa Tverskaya 4 Dairy products; hard currency.
	Garden Ring Supermarket Bolshaya Sadovaya (not far from Hotel Peking) Large range of foreign foods and spirits; hard currency.
	Irish House Supermarket Ulitsa Novy Arbat 19 Irish-made cheese, biscuits and snacks as well as clothing, toys, etc.; hard currency.
	Julius Meinl Leninsky Prospekt 146 Austrian products; hard currency.
	Sadko Ulitsa Boshaya Dorogomilovskaya 16 Swiss-run supermarket; hard currency.
	Gastronome No. 1/Yeliseyev Ulitsa Tverskaya 14 Moscow's most famous shop (see A–Z, Tverskaya Street) sells a limited range of foodstuffs; roubles.
	Gastronome No. 20 Ulitsa Bolshaya Lubyanka 14 Typical Russian foodshop; roubles.
Galleries	See entry
Gifts	Russky Souvenir Kutusovsky Prospekt 9 Jewellery and a broad range of high quality souvenirs at prices to match; roubles.
	There are many other shops selling typical Russian souvenirs (see entry) on the Arbat.
Maps, atlases	Atlas Kusnesky Most 10
Markets	See entry
Records	Melodya Ulitsa Novy Arbat 40; roubles.
Shoes	Salamander In GUM, Red Square; hard currency.
Sports goods	Top Sport Sadko Arcade, Expocenter, Krasnogvardeysky Proyesd 1 Hard currency
Toys	Detsky Mir Teatralny Prospekt 2 Once the world's largest store for toys and children's clothes, this shop

now sells many other items (cars included) but is still the best place in town for toys.

Sightseeing Programme

This sightseeing programme is aimed at the independent traveller who has only a limited time in Moscow and wants to make the most of it. Places printed in **bold** are covered in the A–Z section under that heading.

Because of the distances between sights anyone with just one day in Moscow should spend the morning taking one of the guided tours of the city. These can be arranged through the hotel service desk.

Day One

This then allows time in the afternoon to take a closer look at the buildings around Red Square and to see inside the Kremlin. The first place to visit on **Red Square** is undoubtedly **St Basil's Cathedral** with opposite it at the northern end of the square the **Historical Museum**. One Moscow attraction that is missing since autumn 1993 is the guard of honour outside Lenin's tomb (**Red Square**). The **GUM** department store on the north-east side of the square is also worth a visit, if only for some window-shopping.

Passing through the **Alexander Garden** you come to the Kutafiya Tower, the main visitor's entrance into the **Kremlin** where tickets are sold for the precincts of the Kremlin and entry into its cathedrals. Allow sufficient time to look around the magnificent cathedral interiors and see something of the State apartments and the Palace of the Patriarchs.

An evening outing to one of Moscow's great cultural events is a highlight of the visit – a performance at the **Bolshoi Theatre** perhaps, or a trip to the internationally renowned Moscow Circus (see Circus).

One way of starting a second day in Moscow could be a visit to the **Pushkin Museum of Fine Art** which has an outstanding collection of European Great Masters.

Day Two

This could be combined with a walk around the western part of the city centre which borders on the Pushkin Museum. Stroll down Volchonka Ulitsa, passing the enormous open-air Moscow Swimming Pool, onto the **Boulevard Ring** then head north to get to Arbatskaya Square. Here turn into **Arbat Street**, now a busy pedestrian precinct with its pastel-coloured stucco façades recalling the Moscow of times past. Walk down Arbat Street to where it enters the Garden Ring by the Ministry for Foreign Affairs, turn right onto the Ring then right again into **Novy Arbat**, where the modern buildings of this "new" Arbat are a stark contrast to those of the "old" Arbat. Returning along Novy Arbat to Arbatskaya Square continue this tour of the city along the **Boulevard Ring** where the most interesting buildings are on the Tverskoy Boulevard section. Leave the Ring at Pushkin Square and follow **Tverskaya Street** past Moscow City Hall and towards the centre as far as **Manege Square** from where it is but a short distance, walking north-east, to the **Bolshoi Theatre**. Here a good place for a well-deserved rest would be one of the cafés or restaurants in the luxurious Metropol Hotel (see Hotels). The Metro stations near the Bolshoi Theatre provide easy access to other parts of the city.

Sightseeing in the afternoon could include the **Novodevichy Convent**, one of the most famous in Russia and worth a visit as much for its New Cemetery, where many of the famous are buried, as for its magnificent buildings.

If the visit to the convent seems likely to last until early evening it is a good idea to round off the day with a meal at the "Pirosmani", the Georgian restaurant opposite (see Restaurants), but it is necessary to book in advance.

Although not all of the rooms in the newly restored and expanded **Tretyakov Gallery** are open to the public as yet, a visit to its unmatched collection of Russian art is highly recommended. Cassettes with interesting insights

Day Three

Sightseeing Programme

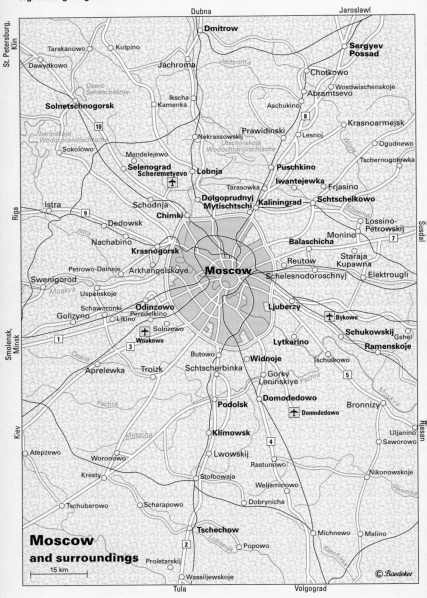

St. Petersburg, Klin

Dubna

Jaroslawl

Dmitrow

Tarakanowo Kulpino

Dawydkowo

Jachroma

Jachroma

Sergyev Possad

Chotkowo

Wosdwischenskoje

Osero Seneschskoje

Abramtsevo

Ikscha
Kamenka

Aschukino

8

Krasnoarmejsk

Solnetschnogorsk

10

Prawidinski

Lesnoj

Ogudnewo

Istrinskoje Wodochranilischtschje

Sokolowo

Nekrassowskij

Utschinskoje Wodochranilischtschje

Tschernogolowka

Mendelejewo

Selenograd
Scheremetyevo

Lobnja

Puschkino

Iwantejewka

Frjasino

Riga

Istra

Tarasowka

Dolgoprudnyj
Mytischtschi

Kaliningrad

Schtschelkowo

Kljasma

9

Schodnja

Chimki

Lossino-Petrowskij

Istra

Dedowsk

Monino

7

Nachabino

Krasnogorsk

Balaschicha

Susdal

Petrowo-Dalneje

Arkhangelskoye

Moscow

Reutow

Staraja Kupawna

Swenigorod

Moskwa

Uspenskoje

Schelesnodoroschnyj

Elektrougli

Schaworonki

Odinzowo

Ljuberzy

Golizyno

Likino

Peredelkino

1

Solnzewo

Bykowo

Schukowskij

Gshel

Smolensk, Minsk

3

Wnukowo

Lytkarino

Ramenskoje

Butowo

Widnoje

Tschulkowo

Aprelewka

Troizk

Schtscherbinka

5

Desna

Gorky
Leninskiye

Pachra

Bronnizy

Podolsk

Domodedowo

Kiev

Pachra

Motscha

Domodedowo

Moskva

Uljanino

Saworowo

Atepzewo

Woronowo

Klimowsk

4

Nikonowskoje

Kresty

Lwowskij

Rastunowo

Sewerka

Stolbowaja

Weljaminowo

Rjasan

Tschubarowo

Scharapowo

Dobrynicha

Moscow
and surroundings

Tschechow

Michnewo

Malino

2

Popowo

Lopasnja

Kaschirka

Proletarskij

Wassiljewskoje

Tula

Volgograd

© *Baedeker*

15 km

into the major works are available for the foreign visitor. Options for the afternoon include an excursion to somewhere further afield. **Kolomenskoe**, the former summer residence of the Tsars, is still within the city limits and can be reached by Metro. Anyone with enough time to spare should make the trip to **Sergiyev Possad** for such treasures of Russian art and architecture as the Trinity Monastery of St Sergius.

For evening entertainment tickets are nearly always available to visitors – at a price – for concerts by famous soloists and orchestras. And the nightly floor shows and variety acts in several hotels and restaurants are often remarkably good (eg Hotel Intourist, see Night Life in this section).

Souvenirs

Hand-crafted items make particularly good souvenirs from Russia and the rest of the CIS. The best known are the Matryoshkas, painted sets of as many as six or more plump little wooden dolls one inside the other. These date back to late 19th c. Moscow and came to be made mostly in Serjiyev Possad where they are still fashioned from limewood which has been seasoned for two to three years before being turned, painted and varnished. They are all roughly the same colour and design but the details vary because they are hand-painted. The craft has since spread to other parts of Russia but not always with the skills to match. They still make a highly original souvenir however, especially the more recent political version starting with Yeltsin and ending with a tiny Lenin or Tsar Nicholas.

Matryoshkas

Other fine pieces of handicraft include miniatures and lacquered boxes from Palekh, brightly painted brooches, trays and caskets from Fedoskino using fairy-tale themes, the traditional black, red and gold bowls, jugs and

Handicrafts

Portrait painters on Pushkin Square

179

	spoons from Khokhloma, as well as artistic filigree and enamel work, embroidery, pottery and carpets. Amber jewellery is also a favourite with visitors.
Sketches, water-colours	For something different it is well worth considering the water-colours, oils and sketches offered for sale by the many artists at work on the Arbat and around Pushkin Square and other points in the city centre or who sell through the various private galleries (see Galleries).
	Another idea is to have your portrait painted by one of the street artists who tend to concentrate around Arbat and Pushkin Square. The quality will vary but so can the price and it is quite in order to haggle.
Books, videos	Coffee-table books, records and stamps – there are some truly wonderful ones – also make good souvenirs, as do videos of Moscow and of opera, ballet and circus performances.
Caviar	For visitors who wish to take back some caviar the prices in the hard currency shops are likely to be similar to those at home. If it is offered on the street remember that there is no guarantee of the quality (it could turn out to be boot polish!) and customs require a receipt.
Shops	The main area for souvenir shops is in and around the Arbat. For specialist shops see Shopping.

Sport

Golf	Even golf-courses can be found in Moscow: Tumba Golf Course, Ulitsa Dovshenko 1; tel. 1 47 83 30 Moscow Country Golf Club; tel. 5 61 29 73
Horse-riding	Horse-riding sessions can be arranged in the Hippodrome. This is also the venue for horse-racing and trotting on Wednesday and Saturday evenings and Sunday afternoons.
Swimming	There are good-sized pools in the Mezhdunarodnaya and Cosmos Hotels which are open to non-residents on payment of a hard currency admission fee.
	Courageous visitors may care to venture into the city's enormous open-air pool, the Moskva (see A–Z, Boulevard Ring).
Tennis	Places with tennis courts include the Chaika Sports Complex (Kropotkinskaya Nabershnaya 3/5; tel. 2 02 04 74) and the Luzhniki Sports Complex (see A–Z, Luzhniki Sport Complex; tel. 2 01 16 55).
Sauna	See Banya

Taxis

	Moscow's official taxis, most of which are yellow, have a narrow chequered band round the sides or on the roof and a green light behind the windscreen to show they are free.
	Taxi ranks are marked by a sign with the letter T, but finding a taxi there or hailing one on the street is becoming increasingly difficult. This is because the shortage of fuel makes it less worthwhile to take passengers paying in roubles. On the other hand there are usually several taxis stationed opposite foreigners' hotels or in the city centre which will take passengers paying in hard currency. The fare, which can be well above elsewhere in Europe, needs to be negotiated in advance. Never run the risk of a mugging by getting into a car or taxi which already has someone else inside.

The wisest course is to order a taxi or chauffeur-driven car from the service desk in the hotel. Even though this may involve waiting it does mean that the fare – usually in hard currency – has already been settled.

Telephone

Local calls from telephones in hotel rooms are free. In recent years it has become much less complicated to make calls abroad, and many hotels have their own satellite booths which take credit cards or phone cards. However, making a call on a private line still involves long waiting times and can be very frustrating.

Telephone directories are virtually impossible to find. The number for directory enquiries is 09 but the operators only speak Russian. For information in other languages call 2 71 91 03.

To Moscow: the international code followed by 70 for Russia then 95 for Moscow.

International dialling codes

From Moscow: 8 followed by the code of the country and telephone number required (Australia 61, Canada 1, Eire 353, New Zealand 64, South Africa 27, United Kingdom 44, United States 1).

Telegrams can be sent using the hotel postal service. Otherwise the main telegram office is at 7 Ulitsa Tverskaya and is open 24 hours a day. Faxes and telexes can also be sent from the business centres in the big hotels.

Telegrams

Theatre and Concerts

Moscow's theatre season is from late September to mid-June.

Theatre season

The easiest way to order tickets is through the hotel service desks. Since a certain quota is always reserved for foreigners, by booking in good time you can usually get tickets for a chosen performance. These have to be paid for in hard currency.

Tickets

It is also possible to try to get a ticket direct from the theatre and pay for it in roubles. Although considerably cheaper the chances of managing to do so are usually virtually nil.

All performances in Moscow theatres start about 7pm; concerts and circus shows usually begin about 7.30pm.

Starting time of performances

Bolshoi Theatre
Teatralnaya Ploshchad; tel. 2 92 00 50
See A–Z, Bolshoi Theatre

Opera, ballet

Musical Studio Theatre
Leningradsky Prospekt 71; tel. 1 98 72 04
The 60-piece repertoire includes operas by Mozart, Rossini and Stravinsky and contemporary composers. Most are staged by Boris Pokrovsky, former chief director of the Bolshoi Theatre.

Stanislavsky/Nemirovich-Danichenko Musical Theatre
Pushkinskaya Ulitsa 17; tel. 2 29 04 05

Operetta Theatre
Pushkinskaya Ulitsa 6; tel. 2 92 04 05
Musicals and comedies as well as light opera.

Light opera

Maly (Little) Theatre
Teatralnaya Ploshchad 1/6; tel. 9 23 26 21
Founded in 1824, the theatre mainly puts on Russian classics.

Drama

Theatre and Concerts

Mayakovsky Theatre
Ulitsa Gerzena 19; tel. 2 90 46 58
Russian, Soviet and international drama.

Moscow Actors' Studio
Many works which were later to become world famous were first performed in the Actors' Studio founded by Stanislavsky and Nemirovich-
Denichenko. The company split up in 1987 since when there have been
both the Chekov and the Gorky Actors' Studio.

Chekov Actors' Studio
Kamergersky Pereulok 3; tel. 2 29 87 60

Gorky Actors' Studio
Tverskoy Bulvar 22; tel. 2 03 89 71

Pushkin Playhouse
Tverskoy Bulvar 23; tel. 2 03 42 21
Modern and classical drama.

Romen Theatre
Leningradsky Prospekt 32; tel. 2 12 03 33
Moscow's gypsy theatre.

Sovremenik Theatre
Tchistoprudny Bulvar 19a; tel. 9 21 66 29
Experimental drama, contemporary plays.

Taganka Theatre
Taganskaya Ploshchad; tel. 2 72 63 00
For a long time this was Moscow's only even mildly critical theatre.

Theatre for Young Audiences
Sadovsky Pereulok 10; tel. 2 99 87 06
This theatre first became famous for its classical plays adapted for children
and young people but more recently its progressive works have increasingly been aimed at an adult audience.

Theatre on the Malaya Bronnaya
Ulitsa Malaya Bronnaya 4; tel. 2 90 40 93
Famous for its outstanding productions of classical and modern plays.

Theatre of Satire
Ploshchad Triumfalnaya 2; tel. 2 99 63 05
Comedies, light entertainment.

Vakhtangov Theatre
Ulitsa Arbat 26; tel. 2 41 07 28
See A–Z, Arbat

Yermolova Theatre
Ulitsa Tverskaya 5; tel. 2 03 72 87
Critical works by modern authors
See A–Z, Tverskaya Street

Children's
theatre

Children's Musical Theatre
Prospekt Veradskogo 5; tel. 9 30 70 21
Fairy tales but also productions of, for example, Madam Butterfly adapted
for children.

Obraztsov Puppet Theatre
Sadovaya Samotetchnaya Ulitsa 3; tel. 2 99 33 10
Sergei Obraztsov's puppet theatre is famous far beyond the confines of Moscow, delighting adults and children alike.

Theatre of Animals
Ulitsa Durova 4; tel. 2 81 67 96
Animal acts.

Conservatorium
Ulitsa Gerzena 13; tel. 2 29 81 83   *Concerts*

Hall of Columns
In the Trade Union building
Pushkinskaya Ulitsa 1; tel. 2 82 48 64

Palace of Congresses
See A–Z, Kremlin

Tchaikovsky Concert Hall
Ploshchad Triumfalnaya 20; tel. 2 99 34 87

See entry   *Circus*

Time

Moscow time is 3 hours ahead of Greenwich Mean Time and 8 hours ahead of New York time. In summer (1st April to 30th December) the clocks are put forward one hour.

Tipping

Although a service charge is usually included in hotels and restaurants you will still be expected to leave a tip of about 5 to 10% of the bill. Cloakrooms in theatres and restaurants are free but a small tip is unlikely to go amiss. Hotel maids will also be pleased to get some kind of gift such as coffee, tights, cosmetics, chocolate, etc., preferably from the West.

Travel Documents

Visitors to Russia need a full passport – a British Visitor's Passport is not enough – and a visa. This is usually obtained by the travel agent but must be applied for at least two weeks before departure, although it is possible to speed up the process for a higher fee. The application has to be accompanied by a passport (valid at least until the end of the tour) or a copy, the visa application form, duly completed, and three identical photographs as well as the fee. There are tourist visas (independent travellers need confirmation of accommodation bookings), business visas, which should be accompanied by an invitation from a business partner in the CIS, and transit visas.   *Passports, and visas*

Drivers should carry an international driving licence or their national licence with a Russian translation (this can be bought at the frontier) and their vehicle registration papers.
The Green Card international insurance certificate is not valid in Russia (see Motoring). Vehicles must display the oval sticker of their country of registration.   *Vehicle papers*

Anyone planning to bring pets into the CIS needs to have with them a veterinary health certificate which is no more than ten days old.   *Pets*

When to Go

Climatic Table

Month	Air temperature in °C		Sunshine hours per day	Days of Rain	Rainfall in mm
	Average maximum	Average minimum			
January	−6.4	−14.2	1.0	17	31
February	−3.7	−15.7	1.9	15	28
March	0.5	−10.5	3.7	14	33
April	8.8	−1.4	5.2	13	35
May	18.4	5.0	7.8	12	52
June	22.1	8.7	8.3	15	67
July	23.7	11.9	8.4	16	74
August	22.1	9.3	7.1	16	74
September	17.0	3.8	4.4	17	58
October	10.0	−1.8	2.4	16	51
November	1.4	−6.0	1.0	17	36
December	−4.5	−11.5	0.6	19	36
Year	9.1	−1.9	4.4/1597	187	575

The best time for a visit to Moscow is in summer during June, July and August. Although these are the rainiest months this is when there is the greatest chance of seeing the city basking in sunshine rather than under depressingly grey skies. On the other hand it can be oppressively hot with possible temperatures of well over 30°C.

The other extreme is the long cold winter; spring and autumn are very brief, and the ice and snow of winter often set in as early as October. From November to February on average 20 out of the 30 days in the month are gloomy and overcast, although any traveller who has the good fortune to be out of doors on a crisp cold day in a snow-covered Moscow under a clear blue sky will find it an exhilarating experience.

Index

Notes

Notes

Notes